THE BIBLE IN THE PUBLIC SQUARE

Society of Biblical Literature

Biblical Scholarship in North America

Number 27

THE BIBLE IN THE PUBLIC SQUARE

ITS ENDURING INFLUENCE IN AMERICAN LIFE

Edited by
Mark A. Chancey, Carol Meyers, and Eric M. Meyers

SBL Press
Atlanta

Copyright © 2014 by SBL Press

All rights reserved. No part of this work may be reproduced or transmitted in any form or by any means, electronic or mechanical, including photocopying and recording, or by means of any information storage or retrieval system, except as may be expressly permitted by the 1976 Copyright Act or in writing from the publisher. Requests for permission should be addressed in writing to the Rights and Permissions Office, SBL Press, 825 Houston Mill Road, Atlanta, GA 30329 USA.

Library of Congress Cataloging-in-Publication Data

The Bible in the public square : its enduring influence in American life / edited by Mark A. Chancey, Carol Meyers, and Eric M. Meyers.
    p. cm. — (Society of Biblical Literature biblical scholarship in North America ; umber 27)
Includes bibliographical references and index.
ISBN 978-1-58983-981-6 (paper binding : alk. paper) — ISBN 978-1-58983-983-0 (electronic format) — ISBN 978-1-58983-982-3 (hardcover binding : alk. paper)
  1. United States—Church history. 2. Bible—Influence—United States. 3. Bible—United States—History. 4. Christianity and politics—Biblical teaching. I. Chancey, Mark A., editor of compilation.
  BR515.B547 2014
  220.0973—dc23   2014012148

Printed on acid-free, recycled paper conforming to
ANSI/NISO Z39.48-1992 (R1997) and ISO 9706:1994
standards for paper permanence.

Contents

Introduction
    Mark A. Chancey, Carol Meyers, and Eric M. Meyers 1

Part 1: The Bible and Politics

The Bible in the Presidential Elections of 2012, 2008, 2004, and the Collapse of American Secularism
    Jacques Berlinerblau 15

Biblical Imagery, the End Times, and Political Action: The Roots of Christian Support for Zionism and Israel
    Yaakov Ariel 37

Part 2: The Bible, America's Founding Era, and American Identity

Does America Have a Biblical Heritage?
    John Fea 65

"God's New Israel": American Identification with Israel Ancient and Modern
    Shalom Goldman 81

The Image of the Protestant Bible in America
    David Morgan 93

Part 3: The Bible and Popular Culture

Holy Words in Hollywood: DeMille's *The Ten Commandments* (1956) and American Identity
    Adele Reinhartz 123

History, Memory, and Forgetting in Psalm 137
    David W. Stowe 137

Comic Book Bibles: Translation and the Politics of Interpretation
    Rubén Dupertuis 159

Part 4: The Bible and Public Schools

Battling over the Bible in Public Schools: Is Common
Ground Possible?
    Charles C. Haynes 181

Public School Bible Courses in Historical Perspective:
North Carolina as a Case Study
    Mark A. Chancey 193

Contributors 215

Subject Index 219

Introduction

Mark A. Chancey, Carol Meyers, and Eric M. Meyers

"The morality that helped build our country is based on the values that are found in the Bible.... And in my little small way, I want to encourage people to get back into those values." So explained Tom Hayden, mayor of Flower Mound, Texas, when he announced that 2014 would be the city's "Year of the Bible."[1] Hayden directed citizens to a website maintained by a local nondenominational church, Calvary Chapel, which divided the Protestant Bible into 365 sections to help readers work through all sixty-six books in a year.

Hayden's action predictably drew a mixture of effusive support and angry backlash from various constituents and other observers. He argued that twenty-five area churches enthusiastically backed the measure.[2] For Hayden and his supporters, the (Protestant) Bible was a source for ethics, civic values, and even American identity. As the Calvary Chapel's website described it, the mayor's "desire was to bring our town back to a Biblical foundation which our country was founded and built upon."[3] One resident unswayed by such arguments was a local candidate for the state legislature, who suggested that "by declaring this year the 'Year of the Bible,' Mayor Hayden is essentially saying that anyone who is a Muslim, Hindu, Zoroastrian, atheist, or not even his particular brand of Christianity that they are not welcome in this town, which is a value that does not belong in

---

1. "Mayor Declares 2014 the 'Year of the Bible,'" FoxNews.com, January 2, 2014. Online: http://www.foxnews.com/us/2014/01/02/mayor-declares-2014-year-bible-in-texas-city/.

2. Terry Evans, "Flower Mound Mayor's Bible Proclamation Draws Mixed Reaction," *Fort Worth Star-Telegram*, January 3, 2014. Online: http://www.star-telegram.com/2014/01/03/5458068/flower-mound-mayors-religious.html.

3. "Year of the Bible: Flower Mound, Texas." Online: thebible2014.com/welcome/.

any public office anywhere in Texas."[4] For this citizen, the mayor's official affirmation of the Bible smacked of religious privilege that ignored the diversity of his constituents.

Hayden's proclamation was directly inspired by a precedent that had likewise generated diverse reactions: President Ronald Reagan's designation of 1983 as the "Year of the Bible." Reagan, too, characterized the Bible as one of the primary sources for American identity. According to him, "of the many influences that have shaped the United States of America into a distinctive Nation and people, none may be said to be more fundamental and enduring than the Bible." For him, the Bible offered "resources of spirit" more precious than those of "technology, education, and armaments," resources needed by America as it faced "a decade of enormous challenge" and the prospect of being "tested as we have seldom, if ever, been tested before."[5]

The Flower Mound mayor's office is not the only government unit to try to follow Reagan's 1983 example. Pennsylvania made 2012 "The Year of the Bible" to the praise of some and the chagrin of others.[6] A Georgia legislator urged President Barack Obama to make 2010 the "Year of the Bible," crafting a resolution claiming that the "priceless, timeless message of the Holy Scripture … has unified, healed and strengthened its [e.g., America's] people."[7] Cities where similar declarations have been introduced or debated include Miamisburg, Ohio in 1997 and Truth or Consequences, New Mexico in 1998.[8] Municipalities seeking a smaller scale observance

---

4. Eric Nicholson, "The Mayor of Flower Mound has Declared 2014 the 'Year of the Bible,'" *Dallas Observer*, January 2, 2014. Online: http://blogs.dallasobserver.com/unfairpark/2014/01/its_officially_the_year_of_the.php.

5. Ronald Reagan, "Proclamation 5018: Year of the Bible, 1983," February 3, 1983. Online: http://www.reagan.utexas.edu/archives/speeches/1983/20383b.htm; Curtis J. Sitomer, "Does 'Year of the Bible' Cross the Church/ State Line?" *The Christian Science Monitor*, May 2, 1983. Online: http://www.csmonitor.com/1983/0502/050235.html/(page)/3.

6. "Pennsylvania House Names 2012 'Year of the Bible,'" *Church & State* 65 (2012): 22.

7. Associated Press, "Georgia Republican Wants Obama to Make 2010 Year of the Bible," FoxNews.com, May 22, 2009. Online: http://www.foxnews.com/politics/2009/05/22/georgia-republican-wants-obama-make-year-bible/.

8. Jeremy Leaming, "Ohio Mayor Rescinds Bible Year Proclamation After State ACLU Objects," First Amendment News, Jan. 5, 1999. Online: http://www.firstamendmentcenter.org/ohio-mayor-rescinds-bible-year-proclamation-after-state-aclu-

than a whole year might opt instead for a "Bible Week," as Gilbert, Arizona did in 1997.[9]

Such efforts and the controversies they generate reflect old and ongoing tensions in American society regarding the Bible and its role in public life. Most Americans in the Founding Era were Protestants, but they did not explicitly and formally incorporate bibliocentric Protestant theology into their new national governmental framework. Instead, they adopted the First Amendment, with its prohibition of any congressional law "respecting an establishment of religion" or "prohibiting the free exercise thereof." Although such provisions initially applied only to the federal government, they would later come to apply to states and cities as well. But Americans have never agreed entirely on what "an establishment" or "free exercise" of religion means, with the result that proponents of measures such as a "Year of the Bible" can cite the Free Exercise Clause for support while opponents can appeal to the Establishment Clause.

Jews and Roman Catholics may have been small in number in the colonial era, but immigration in the following century expanded the sizes of both groups as well as that of Eastern Orthodox Christians. The resulting religious diversity complicated the notion of what the Bible is, since each of those traditions has its own canon. Clashes over the role of the Bible in public life even escalated to violence on occasion, as happened in Philadelphia in 1844 when Protestants and Roman Catholics battled over the reading of the King James Bible in local schools.[10]

Yet the religious diversity of that era does not begin to compare to that of the present. Subsequent immigration, particularly following the Immigration Act of 1965, has resulted in the presence of so many different religious traditions from around the globe that Diana L. Eck's already classic book, *A New Religious America*, is subtitled *How a "Christian Country" Has Become the World's Most Religiously Diverse Nation*.[11] Jews, Protestants, Catholics, and Eastern Orthodox Christians may have differed over

---

objects; Sue Anne Pressley, "Year of the Bible Brouhaha: Church-State Debate Comes to Truth or Consequences, N.M.," *Washington Post*, March 8, 1998.

9. *Arizona Civil Liberties Union v. Cynthia L. Dunham*, 88 F. Supp. 2d 1066 (1999).

10. Joan DelFattore, *The Fourth R: Conflicts over Religion in American Public Schools* (New Haven: Yale University Press, 2004), 32–46.

11. Diana L. Eck, *A New Religious America: How a "Christian Country" Has Become the World's Most Religiously Diverse Nation* (San Francisco: HarperSanFrancisco, 2001).

the form, translation, and interpretation of the Bible; but adherents of most other traditions reject its authority altogether.

The 1960s brought another significant shift regarding the place of the Bible in American society: the Supreme Court's prohibition of public-school-sponsored Bible reading in *Abington v. Schempp*.[12] Coupled with the court's related decision on school prayer the preceding year,[13] *Schempp* signaled the increasing secularization of public education and of other spheres of American culture as well. At the same time, however, it affirmed the worthiness of the study of religion in public schools as long as it is conducted from an objective and secular perspective.

Opposition to increased secularization and unease with changing religious demographics are no doubt partly responsible for "Year of the Bible" measures. Yet such measures are indisputably accurate in their general characterization of the Bible as enormously influential in American culture. For better or for worse, changing demographics and legal landscape or not, the Bible in its various forms is still a source of artistic, literary, ideological, philosophical, and, needless to say, religious inspiration today. The essays in this volume explore some of the roles in the public square that the Bible has played in the past and continues to play. They employ a range of methodological perspectives (American history, the history of ideas, film studies, visual studies, cultural studies, education, church-state studies) to explore four themes: the Bible and politics, the relationship between the Bible and notions of American identity, the Bible and popular culture, and the treatment of the Bible in public education. This collection of essays is aimed at a broad audience consisting not only of biblical scholars but also of those in other academic disciplines as well as educators, students, and the general public.

This volume is based on a conference held at Duke University in 2012. Recognizing that the Bible was, is, and probably will continue to be an important part of American life, the conference was organized in order to highlight the diverse ways the Bible appears in various aspects of national culture. The papers presented over the course of two days were then posted on the Duke University website.[14] But the conveners felt that the conference videos were not sufficient to convey the rich scholarship and

---

12. *Abington School District v. Schempp*, 374 U.S. 203 (1963).
13. *Engel v. Vitale*, 370 U.S. 421 (1962).
14. "The Bible in the Public Square Conference Videos: Session 1, The Bible in Presidential Politics," Duke University Center for Jewish Studies, September 9–10,

provocative ideas that characterized the presentations. They thus decided to have the papers prepared for publication so that readers would have access to the expanded—and also refined, as the result of the discussions built into the conference program—versions along with documentation. The four sections of this book cover the themes that were explored in the conference.

The first theme, "The Bible and Politics," appears in part 1. Because 2012 was an election year, the issue of the Bible and presidential politics was addressed in the opening lecture of the conference and now is the lead article of this volume. Jacques Berlinerblau documents the increasing use of "God talk" and scriptural references in the last three presidential elections, elements of religiosity that reflect a backlash against secularism in the public arena. He traces the reemergence of the Bible as a rhetorical resource in American presidential campaigns. This trend, retriggered by the candidacy and subsequent presidency of George W. Bush, presents unique challenges to exegetes. Among these is the strange fact that much of the specialized training that marks the great achievement of professional biblical scholarship is of relatively little use in clarifying the markedly flat, at times anti-intellectual, and seemingly politically motivated way in which both Democrats and Republicans invoke Scripture. After identifying basic ground rules and conceptual tools for scholars to use when trying to make sense of campaign "God Talk," this paper compares the use of the Good Book in political oratory in recent campaigns. In so doing, it identifies new rhetorical developments and explores their significance for America's understandings of the relationship between church and state.

The second paper in part 1 explores the intersection of the Bible and politics in relation to foreign policy. Yaakov Ariel examines this intersection as it appears in the Middle Eastern policy of the United States. He shows how politics concerning the land of the Bible have been influenced by evangelical Christianity, which often supports the Zionist endeavor, frequently to the exclusion of support for Arab causes; his article also identifies the shortcomings of such reasoning. Ariel provides vivid details about the way biblical imagery has played a decisive role in shaping conservative Protestant understanding of history as well as its hopes for the future and the details of its eschatological scenarios, all of which have

---

2012. Online: http://jewishstudies.duke.edu/the-bible-in-the-public-square/conference-videos.

a bearing on their understanding of the purpose of the State of Israel. Because evangelical Christians often view the Bible as containing "God's plans and purposes in the ages," they tend to read the Bible more literally than liberal Christians, and many of them have adopted a premillennialist faith. Many consider the Jewish people to be heirs and continuers of biblical Israel and as a people destined to fulfill an important role in the events of the end times. Likewise, such Christians typically view Palestine as ground zero of the apocalyptic events prophesied in the Bible. Because they have expected the return of the Jews to Palestine and the building of a Jewish commonwealth as essential stages that precede the second coming of Christ, they welcomed the rise of the Zionist movement, despite its secular character, and were likewise supportive of the State of Israel. Since 1967, conservative Protestant theological and physical involvement with Israel has increased considerably. The evangelical Christian millennialist faith has played a growing role in determining the political stand of this segment of American Christianity towards the Arab-Israeli conflict and the developments in the Middle East in general.

The three essays in part 2, "The Bible, America's Founding Era, and American Identity," which explore the relationship between the Bible and notions of national identity in the United States, complement the two papers in part 1. In the first, "Does America Have a Biblical Heritage?" John Fea explores how the Bible was used by public intellectuals in the eighteenth century and then explains how both the Left and the Right have co-opted the country's religious history, albeit in different ways, in the current "culture wars." He makes it clear that any serious student of American history must take into account the powerful role that the Bible has played in the collective life of the nation, but he also insists that we should also be wary about approaching that history with a celebratory mindset informed by what he calls "the heritage crusade." His essay explores the role the Bible played in the founding of the United States. He has argued in another publication that it is difficult to make the case that the United States was founded as a Christian nation.[15] Here he asks if it was founded as a biblical nation. What role did the Bible play in the founding era—the years leading up to the American Revolution, the Revolution itself, and the Revolution's immediate aftermath? He cuts through

---

15. John Fea, *Was America Founded as a Christian Nation? A Historical Introduction* (Louisville: Westminster John Knox, 2011).

the political rhetoric of the Christian heritage crusaders and tries to make some historical sense of the complicated ways in which eighteenth-century patriots, founders, and loyalists utilized the Bible in the midst of the imperial crisis with England.

The second paper in part 2, "'God's New Israel': American Identification with Israel Ancient and Modern," echoes many of the ideas presented in Ariel's paper in its consideration of the favored position of Israel in current Middle Eastern policy. Within the framework of two disciplines—the history of ideas and the history of religion—Shalom Goldman examines three related phenomena in Protestant American culture: Christian Hebraism, the idea of the promised land, and evangelical Christian Zionism. Drawing on case studies that represent both "high" and "low" cultural productions, he traces the sequential development of these phenomena in the history and culture of the United States and concludes with informed speculation on the future of the "special relationship" between the State of Israel and the United States.

The third essay in part 2, "The Image of the Protestant Bible in America," provides a segue to part 3. David Morgan considers American identity in the colonial period by focusing on the Bible's place in visual expressions of authority, where it held a central place until it was later supplanted by the American flag. Whatever the Bible may be as a text or collection of texts, it also has a career as an image in the history of representations in American culture, a history that consists of the circulation of images in many arenas, including advertisement and commerce, entertainment, religious instruction, devotional literature, and proselytism. Morgan traces the visuality of the Bible in popular illustrations from the late eighteenth century to the present. He shows how the image of the book was put to use in popular piety from the private home to the public square. The Bible as object and image became one of the most widely recognized and readily evoked symbols of authority throughout late colonial period and in early national American life. Eventually it was eclipsed by the American flag, which underwent intense sacralization in the last decades of the nineteenth century and the early twentieth to become the nation's preeminent icon within the rising civil religion. Yet the image of the Bible remains primary in nationalistic iconography and is often closely associated with the flag by those who champion the idea of America as a Christian nation.

The three essays in part 3, "The Bible and Popular Culture," provide further examination of the place of the Bible in several widely disseminated cultural productions.[16] The first essay, "Holy Words in Hollywood: DeMille's *The Ten Commandments* (1956) and American Identity," uses an iconic film, *The Ten Commandments*, as an exemplar of how Hollywood, no less than the Puritans of an earlier era, drew on biblical themes to express cultural values. Adele Reinhartz shows how DeMille's classic film projected an image of America as a savior in the international community. *The Ten Commandments* served as a Cold War manifesto that refashions Moses as a Jesus-like redeemer figure who symbolizes the American struggle against the Red Menace. The paper contrasts DeMille's triumphalist view by concluding with reflections on films made after the Vietnam War. The biblical imagery in those films are much more critical of America's role in foreign affairs, as illustrated by the 2007 film *In the Valley of Elah*, which concerns the American army in the era of the Iraq war.

The role of the Bible in psalms and hymns is examined in the second essay in part 3, "History, Memory, and Forgetting in Psalm 137." David Stowe approaches this topic by tracing the role of the text of Ps 137, which begins with the words "by the rivers of Babylon," in song and hymn in the United States from revolutionary times to the present. "By the Rivers of Babylon" has served as America's longest-running protest song, lending support to anticolonial movements since the American Revolution. Its most prominent use in the United States has been in antiracist movements. Psalm 137 has also been used to express alienation and marginalization of a more private, existential variety. Stowe show how the three distinct sections (vv. 1–4; vv. 5–6; vv. 7–9) of the psalm speak to different situations and have been put to different uses. The first four verses conjure up communal memories of better times remembered in moments of dislocation and humiliation. The two middle verses, which take the form of an oath calling for paralysis of tongue and hand if the psalmist forgets Jerusalem, have been of particular interest to political movements that invoke collective memory to mobilize collective action. The last three verses call for vengeance and have usually been excised in the North American contexts. In whole or in part, Ps 137 has been widely adopted in Christian contexts, and recent popular culture shows increasing Jewish use of the text.

---

16. An earlier publication of the Society of Biblical Literature focused on the Bible in music and in literature; see Philip Culbertson and Elaine M. Wainwright, *The Bible in/and Popular Culture: A Creative Encounter* (Semeia Studies 65; Atlanta: Society of Biblical Literature, 2010).

The third essay in part 3, "Comic Book Bibles: Translation and the Politics of Interpretation," provides an analysis of comic books, specifically, comic book Bibles, as a medium of popular culture. Rubén Dupertuis shows how biblical materials are translated into a format that merges the printed word with pictorial illustrations, and he explores the often problematic meanings or values transmitted in this medium. He explains in this essay that all translations involve the process of replacing one set of cultural signifiers in a source text with a different set of signifiers that can be understood by readers of the target language text. This cultural transaction is inherently messy and imprecise, requiring translators to choose between foregrounding the cultural distance to the source-language text or privileging the values and cultural assumptions of the target-language reader. He argues that comic book Bibles, which should be understood as translations of the Bible into the comics medium, provide a useful arena in which to explore contemporary battles over the meaning and value of Bible.

The fourth theme, the treatment of the Bible in public education, is addressed in the two essays of part 4, "The Bible and Public Schools." The first essay, "Battling over the Bible in Public Schools: Is Common Ground Possible?" is concerned with the role of the First Amendment and related legal issues in determining the way Bible courses enter the curricula of public schools. Well aware that there is more religion in public schools in the United States now than at any time in the past century, Charles Haynes focuses on recent conflicts over Bible electives in public schools. He considers whether the consensus guidelines on the Bible in schools, published by the First Amendment Center in 2000, helped educators resolve disputes and create constitutionally sound Bible courses. He also assesses the impact of "Bible bills" passed in six state legislatures on local school districts in those states and lays out the challenge for educators to "get it right" in the curricula of public schools.

The second essay in part 3, "Public School Bible Courses in Historical Perspective: North Carolina as a Case Study," is a fitting sequel to Haynes's contribution. Mark Chancey traces the place of the Bible in education, using practices in North Carolina as an example. He has chosen that state for his case study because it has unusually rich source materials for some historical aspects of its Bible courses. At the same time, what has happened in North Carolina probably illuminates national trends. Chancey examines public school Bible courses in their larger historical context. He first considers their relation to the older practice of Bible reading and then the creation of Bible courses as a part of early twentieth-century religious education programs. He also discusses another important factor, the impact of the 1963 United States Supreme Court decision *Abington Township School District v. Schempp* and subsequent related lower court rulings. He concludes by describing efforts to define the characteristics of constitutionally permissible courses and by noting the basic contours of the present situation.

A third paper on this topic, "Rightly Dividing the First Amendment? An Evaluation of Recent Decisions regarding the Bible and Public Schools," was presented at the conference. The paper's author, Melissa Rogers, was at that time the Director of the Center for Religion and Public Affairs of the Divinity School of Wake Forest University. She was subsequently appointed by President Obama as Special Assistant to the President and Director of the White House Office on Faith-Based and Neighborhood Partnerships. The demands of her new position meant she was unable to prepare her conference paper for publication. Her paper considered the role of the First Amendment in court cases across the country regarding the Bible and public education, focusing particularly on the issues of Bible distribution (as done by Gideons International, for example) and students' right to free expression (such as student selection of the Bible as the subject of her oral presentation on her favorite book). With her training as a lawyer, Rogers was able to assess the extent to which those lower court rulings correspond to Supreme Court precedents. She also outlined practical paths for students, parents, schools, and other parties to follow when faced with new controversies. A video of Rogers's presentation can be accessed at the conference's website.[17]

The authors would like to conclude by acknowledging the generous support of Duke University's Center for Jewish Studies, the primary sponsor of the conference in which the papers in this volume were presented. Additional support was provided by Southern Methodist University's Jewish Studies Program Fund and, at Duke University, the Religion Department (recently renamed the Religious Studies Department) and the Office of the Dean. Professor Shalom Goldman of Duke's Religious Studies Department, along with the editors of this book, was an organizer of

---

17. "The Bible in the Public Square Conference Videos: Session 5, The Bible and Public Schools," Duke University Center for Jewish Studies, September 9–10, 2012. Online: http://jewishstudies.duke.edu/the-bible-in-the-public-square/conference-videos/session-5-the-bible-and-public-schools.

the conference; and the editors are grateful to Professor Goldman for his wisdom in selecting topics and speakers. We are also thankful to have had the cheerful and expert assistance of Serena Bazemore, Program Coordinator of the Duke Center for Jewish Studies, who skillfully handled the myriad details involved in organizing the conference. Finally, we want to extend our appreciation to the Publications Staff of the Society of Biblical Literature for accepting our proposal to publish the conference papers and then expertly shepherding the manuscript through the publication process.

Part 1
The Bible and Politics

The Bible in the Presidential Elections of 2012, 2008, 2004, and the Collapse of American Secularism*

Jacques Berlinerblau

Biblical scholars who study the way the Scriptures are used in American politics are confronted with a unique and humbling dilemma. For the truth of the matter is that our vast erudition, specialized training, and broad linguistic competencies often fail to illuminate the subject matter that we explore. In a strange way, knowing as much as we do about the Bible is often a distinct intellectual handicap in the study of public affairs. To put it in colloquial terms, *our knowledge's no good here*!

This is because of the yawning abyss between what we study and what we know. There is a huge difference between the Bible of the public square on the one hand, and the Bible of university religious studies departments, seminaries, and divinity schools on the other. For all intents and purposes, they are *completely different Bibles*. Public and professorial users approach their Scriptures with vastly incompatible lenses, assumptions, and hoped-for outcomes.

Let me explain the disconnect in as pithy a manner as possible, going so far as to sloganize my insight. When a professional biblical scholar reads a verse, she sees a question. When a politician reads a verse, she sees an answer. For nonscholars, the Good Book is a fairly unproblematic document. It has a known and stable history. It has a clear message. It has an undeniable truth. Too, it has shovel-ready policy implications.[1]

---

* A somewhat different version of this essay, which was originally delivered as a lecture at Duke University on 11 September 2012, has been published in "The Bible in the Presidential Elections of 2012, 2008, 2004, and the Collapse of American Secularism," in *Interested Readers: Essays on the Hebrew Bible in Honor of David J. A. Clines*

These assumptions rarely carry the day among professional biblical scholars, and this accounts for the whopping incongruity between these two interpretive cultures. When we in the Guild are *good*, we traffic in complex and deep understandings of the Holy Scriptures. We master long-lost ancient languages, cognate to the original Hebrew and Greek. We control the often two-millennia-plus history of scriptural interpretation. We deploy sophisticated theoretical models culled from other academic disciplines. We do all of this in an earnest and honorable quest to make sense of the witnesses' beguiling and cryptic words (I forgo a discussion of what happens when we are *bad*).[2]

I have nothing but praise for the skill and dedication of my exegetical colleagues. But to paraphrase Kurt Vonnegut, bringing this academic arsenal to the study of American politics is like attacking a hot fudge sundae in a suit of armor. Quite simply, the manner in which political figures and their constituents use the Scriptures is singularly unamenable to analysis by the aforementioned scholarly precision tools.

The following examples should illustrate this point vividly. Of what use is hard-fought mastery of Aramaic in making sense of a phenomenon like former Arkansas governor Mike Huckabee? In 2008 he averred that "I believe it's a lot easier to change the Constitution than it would be to change the word of the living God, and that's what we need to do is to amend the Constitution so it's in God's standards rather than try to change God's standards."[3] Where does Aramaic come into that?

How does one's expertise in narratology help us make sense of Pastor Rick Warren's subdiscursive grunt to a perplexed Barack Obama at the Saddleback Civil Forum on the Presidency that same year: "At what point," queried Warren, "does a baby get human rights, in your view?"[4]

(ed. James Aitken, Jeremy M. S. Clines, and Christl M. Maier; Atlanta: Society of Biblical Literature, 2013).

1. These insights are explored in my *Thumpin' It: The Use and Abuse of the Bible in Today's Presidential Politics* (Louisville: Westminster John Knox, 2008).

2. The professional drama of the biblical scholar is discussed in my *The Secular Bible: Why Nonbelievers Must Take Religion Seriously* (New York: Cambridge University Press, 2005), 70–84.

3. Adam Aigner-Treworgy, "Huck, the Constitution, and 'God's Standards,'" NBC News. Online: http://firstread.nbcnews.com/_news/2008/01/15/4431338-huck-the-constitution-and-gods-standards?lite.

4. Lynn Sweet, "Transcript of Obama, McCain at Saddleback Civil Forum with

How could we make sense of John Edwards back in 2008—when he was apparently not right with God—invoking Matt 25:45 as his "favorite Bible verse"?[5] Matthew 25 in fact has become something like the official Blue Scripture. A full blown Democratic religious consulting company goes by the name of the Matthew 25 Network.[6] President Obama used that same verse in declaiming, "It's also about the biblical call to care for the least of these—for the poor; for those at the margins of our society. To answer the responsibility we're given in Proverbs to 'Speak up for those who cannot speak for themselves, for the rights of all who are destitute.'"[7] At the 2012 Democratic National Convention, senatorial candidate Elizabeth Warren interpreted that scripture in accord with what I have called the Democrats' "Theology of Togetherness": "The passage teaches about God in each of us, that we are bound to each other and called to act. Not to sit, not to wait, but to act—all of us together."[8]

A professional biblical scholar would have been hard pressed to parse Rick Santorum's Chanukah greeting card in December of 2011. That seasonal affirmation, some noted with bewilderment, contained a verse from John 8:12: "I am the light of the world. He who follows me will not walk in the darkness, but will have the light of life" (NASB).[9] Was this is a Hanukkah card for Jews or Messianic Jews?

Pastor Rich Warren," Chicago Sun-Times.com. Online: http://blogs.suntimes.com/sweet/2008/08/transcript_of_obama_mccain_at.html.

5. Katharine Q. Seelye, "Edwards Charged with Election Finance Fraud," *New York Times*, June 3, 2011. Online: http://www.nytimes.com/2011/06/04/us/politics/04edwards.html; H. Jeff Zeleny, "The Democrats Quote Scripture," *New York Times*, September 27, 2007. Online: http://thecaucus.blogs.nytimes.com/2007/09/27/the-democrats-quote-scripture/.

6. Michael Luo, "New PAC Seeks to Court Christians for Obama," *New York Times*, June 10, 2008. Online: http://thecaucus.blogs.nytimes.com/2008/06/10/new-pac-seeks-to-court-christians-for-obama/.

7. The White House Office of the Press Secretary, "Remarks by the President at the National Prayer Breakfast," The White House. Online: http://www.whitehouse.gov/the-press-office/2012/02/02/remarks-president-national-prayer-breakfast.

8. Politico, "Elizabeth Warren DNC speech," Politicio.com. Online: http://www.politico.com/news/stories/0912/80802.html. Jacques Berlinerblau, "Democrats' Theology of Togetherness," *Washington Post*, September 6, 2012. Online: http://www.washingtonpost.com/blogs/guest-voices/post/democrats-theology-of-togetherness/2012/09/06/1877df16-f7e0-11e1-8398-0327ab83ab91_blog.html.

9. David Weigel, "Happy Hanukkah from Rick Santorum," Slate.com. Online:

During the 2012 GOP presidential primaries, we heard Herman Cain compare his call to run with the call Moses received from God.[10] Similarly, think of Texas governor Rick Perry's own scripturally sourced justification for his candidacy. Invoking Isa 6:8, "Whom shall I send? And who will go for us?" (NASB), Perry exclaimed, "Here I am. Send me."[11] Would a scholar of Deutero-Isaiah be more helpful in illuminating such instances? Or a psychologist specializing in delusional narcissism?

Stateside, we are familiar with the expression "attack ad." This is a form of publicity in which one candidate enfilades another. The most recent presidential election inaugurated a new tradition: attack Scriptures. How our training equips us to deal with this is not entirely clear to me. Here is ordained Methodist minister and former Democratic governor of Ohio, Ted Strickland:

> Mitt Romney has so little economic patriotism that even his money needs a passport. It summers on the beaches of the Cayman Islands and winters on the slopes of the Swiss Alps. In Matthew, chapter 6, verse 21, the scriptures teach us that where your treasure is, there will your heart be also. My friends, any man who aspires to be our president should keep both his treasure and his heart in the United States of America. And it's well past time for Mitt Romney to come clean with the American people.[12]

Is any expertise in anthropological gift theory required to unpuzzle conservative Republican Congressman Paul Ryan's recent refusal to accept a Bible that was offered to him? He might have refused it because he is a devotee of Ayn Rand. More likely, he spurned the offering because the liberal advocacy group Catholics United was forcing it upon him. Moreover,

---

http://www.slate.com/blogs/weigel/2012/02/08/happy_hanukkah_from_rick_santorum.html.

10. Alana Horowitz, "Herman Cain: 'I Felt Like Moses.'" *Huffington Post*, October, 9, 2011. Online: http://www.huffingtonpost.com/2011/10/09/herman-cain-moses_n_1002744.html.

11. Christy Hoppe, "Perry Touts Values, Staying Power in Final Iowa Push," *Dallas Morning News*, January 2, 2012. Online: http://www.dallasnews.com/news/politics/perry-watch/headlines/20120102-perry-touts-values-staying-power-in-final-iowa-push.ece.

12. Politico, "Ted Strickland DNC speech," Politico.com. Online: http://www.politico.com/news/stories/0912/80699.html.

they had helpfully annotated the Witness with passages stressing Catholic social teachings on the poor.[13]

Our knowledge of the Bible's complex history might have alerted us to some strange goings-on back in a 2008 Republican debate. An audience questioner via video feed dangled a King James Version (KJV) of the Bible directly in front of the camera and stated:

> I am Joseph. I am from Dallas, Texas, and how you answer this question will tell us everything we need to know about you. Do you believe every word of this book [he places the cover that reads "Holy Bible" in front of the camera]? And I mean specifically, this book that I am holding in my hand [turning the spine of the text to the camera indicating that it is the King James Version]. Do you believe this book?[14]

Many Americans were not only baffled but also creeped out by Joseph from Dallas. He was probably posing what is referred to stateside as a "gotcha" question. Mormons, like Mitt Romney, to whom the prompt was likely addressed, revere the KJV as their standard translation. However, there is also the Joseph Smith Translation (JST), in which "hundreds of changes and additions" to the KJV were made by the religion's founder.[15] Was Joseph goading Romney to comment on the canonical difference between Latter-day Saints scriptures and evangelical scriptures? We may never know. True, one had to know something about the Latter-day Saints' canon to surmise Joseph's motivations, but one need not have spent seven years in graduate school to acquire that wisdom.

My point is this: Much of the training that we possess as scholars of the Bible and religion is regrettably tangential to the manner in which the text is cited in American politics. Actually, the text is not only cited but *physically brandished*—as it was by Catholics United, as it was by Joseph

---

13. Sarah Posner, "Paul Ryan's Bible, Jim Wallis', or None of the Above?" *Religion Dispatches* (June 2011). Online: http://www.religiondispatches.org/dispatches/sarah-posner/4708/.

14. Jacques Berlinerblau, "Is Mike Huckabee a Catholic?" Faithstreet.com. Online: http://www.faithstreet.com/onfaith/2007/11/30/at-wednesday-nights-republican/1555; Jacques Berlinerblau, "Postscript to the Republican Debate," Faithstreet.com. Online: http://www.faithstreet.com/onfaith/2007/12/02/postscript-to-the-republican-d/1777.

15. David Bitton and Thomas G. Alexander, *Historical Dictionary of Mormonism* (3rd ed.; Lanham, Md.: Scarecrow, 2008), 18.

from Dallas. Martin Marty, in a memorable contribution, spoke of "America's iconic book."[16] He meant that for many in this country the Bible elicited visceral—as opposed to intellectual—adoration and was revered as a holy object. We scholars scrutinize its words. We do not really think much about the physicality of the text, the simple albeit massively freighted significance its tangible presence has for its readers.

It emerges from this that, to understand our subject matter, we cannot bring it to us, but we must confront it on terms more conducive to the way American politicians and voters construe the text. Such was the argument I made in my *Thumpin' It: The Use and Abuse of the Bible in Today's Presidential Politics* in 2008. My comments above about methodology interface with a second concern I have about the plight of American secularism, advanced in my most recent study, *How to Be Secular: A Call to Arms for Religious Freedom*.[17] Namely, what does all of this Scripture bombing tell us about the plight of church-state relations in the United States? Would not an American political observer circa 1965 be flummoxed by the Scripture-heavy political rhetoric of America's current leadership class?

Prior to going further, we need to lay out one default ground rule for us to bear in mind when we hear politicians cite Scripture: Whether they are Democrat or Republican, liberal or conservative, Jew or Gentile, we must *never* make the mistake of assuming that their invocation is *not* motivated by political expediency. To assume that politicians cite the Bible spontaneously, hearts overflowing with God love, is to make a catastrophic category error. It is to confuse a pastor with a politician, a seminarian with a stumper, a devotee with a demagogue.[18]

With that said, permit me to elucidate four key issues that need to be taken into consideration when we study today's faith and values politicking. Most of these, as we shall see, are not necessarily illuminated by the methods and theories that those of us in the Guild devote our lives to mastering.

---

16. Martin Marty, "America's Iconic Book," in *Humanizing America's Iconic Book: Society of Biblical Literature Centennial Addresses, 1980* (ed. Gene Tucker and Douglas Knight; Chico, Calif.: Scholars Press, 1982), 1–23.

17. *How to Be Secular: A Call to Arms for Religious Freedom* (Boston: Houghton-Mifflin Harcourt, 2012). Also, see above nn. 2 and 3.

18. See Mark Noll, "The Politician's Bible," *Christianity Today*, October 26, 1992, 16–17.

Rhetoric or Policy?

Is the use of Scripture by American politicians merely rhetoric, or does it drive actual policy decisions? This crucial distinction, I regret to say, is often lost upon many journalists and even academics. It is one thing for a politician to quote chapter and verse; it is entirely another for him or her to predicate domestic and foreign policy on that line from the Good Book. This is tantamount to the difference between theory and practice.

In *Thumpin' It*, I came to a very clear conclusion—and bear in mind that the monograph went to bed in July of 2007 during George W. Bush's second term. At that time, those on the left exulted in tarring Bush as a loony fundamentalist, who took his marching orders from the Scofield Reference Bible. Think of a work like Kevin Phillips' *American Theocracy: The Peril and Politics of Radical Religion, Oil, and Borrowed Money in the 21st Century*.[19] The author had convinced himself of a one-to-one correlation between Bush's public scriptural effusions and his Middle Eastern national security program. Phillips speaks of "White House implementation of domestic and international policy agendas that seem to be driven by religious motivations and biblical worldviews."[20]

Now let there be no doubt, our forty-third president was a very religious man. This is a truism made prominent in his biography, *A Charge to Keep*.[21] That being said, I was hard-pressed to find any "smoking gun" or direct link between the president's well-known admiration for what is sometimes called "biblical worldview" and the policies he espoused.[22] For instance, I found no warrant for the oft-made claim that Bush's Middle Eastern foreign policy was predicated on premillennial dispensationalist schemes.[23] Such schemes, according to many reports, allegedly were

---

19. Kevin Phillips, *American Theocracy: The Peril and Politics of Radical Religion, Oil, and Borrowed Money in the 21st Century* (New York: Viking, 2006). Also see Richard Shweder, "George W. Bush and the Missionary Position," *Daedalus* 133 (2004): 26–36.

20. Phillips, *American Theocracy*, viii.

21. George W. Bush, *A Charge to Keep: My Journey to the White House* (New York: William Morrow, 2001).

22. Jeffrey Siker, "President Bush, Biblical Faith, and the Politics of Religion," *SBL Forum*. Online: http://www.sbl-site.org/Article.aspx?ArticleId=151; Dana Stevens, "Oh God," Slate.com. Online: http://www.slate.com/id/2099698/; "Bush on God," *St. Petersburg Times*, January 16, 2005.

23. Berlinerblau, *Thumpin' It*, 60–74.

dear to the hearts of evangelicals. But, as the scholar Timothy Weber has pointed out, only a small minority of evangelicals have actually subscribed to these views, and I did not reckon Bush as being among them.[24] Speaking to former Bush officials, some of whom were Jewish neoconservatives, corroborated my view that this was an inaccurate surmise, that this was simply not the way foreign policy is crafted in this country.

I did, however, see a clear connection between Bush's pro-life rhetoric and one famous executive decision he made. As is well known, in 2006 Bush vetoed H.R. 810, The Stem Cell Research Enhancement Act, also known as the Castle-DeGette Bill. It was Bush's first veto in six years of holding office.[25] That move, I gather, was a sop to the evangelical base and even something of an apology. After all, the Executive Branch did nothing to move the needle on repealing *Roe v. Wade* (the controversial 1973 decision legalizing abortion). That was undoubtedly something the "Values Voters" who put Bush into office in 2004 had hoped for.[26] By disallowing *federally* funded stem cell research, the president would seem to have been making amends. Here, we can get a faint glimpse of a policy that rides on the wings of a religious impulse, and I will have more to say about this below.

As for Obama, here as well there seems to be a disconnect between his biblical oratory and his policies.[27] For instance, Obama may make a lot of noise about the "least of these," he may refer over and again to Cain's demurral in Gen 4:9 (strangely, Cain there insinuates that he is *not* his brother's keeper), yet his critics on the Left feel that he has not lived up to the high standards interpreters assume these verses call us to obey.[28]

---

24. Timothy Weber, "How Evangelicals Became Israel's Best Friend," *Christianity Today*, October 5, 1998, 49.

25. Berlinerblau, *Thumpin' It*, 46–47. H.R. 810, 109th Cong. (2005).

26. John C. Green, Mark J. Rozell, and Clyde Wilcox, eds., *The Values Campaign? The Christian Right and the 2004 Elections* (Washington, D.C.: Georgetown University Press, 2006).

27. "Faith in America: Interviews with President Barack Obama and Governor Mitt Romney," *Cathedral Age*, Midsummer 2012, 21–25. Online: http://www.nationalcathedral.org/age/CAA-66319-MM000A.shtml#.U0cx8leJuIA.

28. Barack Obama, "A More Perfect Union," Politico.com. Online: http://www.politico.com/news/stories/0308/9100.html; "National Prayer Breakfast: President Obama's speech transcript," *Washington Post*, February 2, 2012. Online: http://www.washingtonpost.com/politics/national-prayer-breakfast-president-obamas-speech-transcript/2012/02/02/gIQAx7jWkQ_story_1.html.

Has President Obama punished the Wall Street 1 percent who pulverized the economy? Was he willing in the 2011 deficit battle to go to the wall against Congress and safeguard many government programs that protect the poor?[29] Did he, until the ghastly stimulus of the Newtown school massacre, ever take on the gun lobby whose activism was not indirectly correlated to disproportional murder rates in inner-city neighborhoods?[30] The scholar Cornel West dubbed Obama a "black mascot of Wall Street oligarchs and a black puppet of corporate plutocrats."[31] In West's view, not only has the president not lived up to Scripture's exigencies, he has also forsaken the prophetic vision.

I am reminded of the Texasism, "all hat, no cattle." In the main, Bible-thumpin' politicians are all rhetoric, no policy. There are, on the fringes, a few exceptions to this rule. And I concede that these exceptions have grown more normative in the gap since 2008, especially on the state level. Still, biblical scholars who study American politics are advised to assume as a default position that "biblical worldview" does not (yet) majorly or directly influence the federal government's domestic and foreign policy formation.

Biblical Influence or Religious Influence?

Enfolded within this distinction between rhetoric and policy is yet another subdistinction, and a confusing one at that. To wit, it is the difference between leaning on the Bible and leaning on the *interpretive tradition* spawned by the Bible. Here, I *do* think we scholars can be of some use.

---

29. Mark Landler and Michael D. Shear, "Obama's Debt Plan Sets Stage for Long Battle over Spending," *New York Times*, April 13, 2011. Online: http://www.nytimes.com/2011/04/14/us/politics/14obama.html; Jonathan Chait, "What the Left Doesn't Understand about Obama," *New York Times*, September 2, 2011. Online: http://www.nytimes.com/2011/09/04/magazine/what-the-left-doesnt-understand-about-obama.html.

30. James Barron, "Nation Reels After Gunman Massacres 20 Children at School in Connecticut," *New York Times*, December 15, 2012. Online: http://www.nytimes.com/2012/12/15/nyregion/shooting-reported-at-connecticut-elementary-school.html?ref=nyregion.

31. Glen Johnson, "West: Obama 'a Black Mascot' and 'Black Puppet.'" Boston.com. Online: http://www.boston.com/news/politics/politicalintelligence/2011/05/west_obama_a_bl.html.

In fact, I have often argued that the role of biblical scholars in public discourse is to clarify for the public complex matters such as this one.[32]

Many are the believers who thoughtlessly assume that their faith is based on the Bible. Many are the scholars who seek to disabuse them of that misconception. Jews, for example, tend to severely overestimate how much of their halakic worldview comes from the Tanak. They tend to underestimate the degree to which the Pharisaic Judaism to which they adhere is a product of the rabbinic corpus colloquially known as the Talmud.[33] In the opinion of many scholars, Judaism is *rabbinic* to the core, not biblical. In the opinion of many lay Jews, the distinction is nonexistent.

In Catholicism as well, the argument could be made that Catholics live more by the teachings of the church fathers and the interpretations of Holy Mother Church than they do by the Old and New Testaments. It was the Jesuit scholar Daniel Harrington who recalled a quip from his mother circa 1950: "We're Catholics. We don't read the Bible."[34]

Which brings us to evangelicalism, unique among the faiths mentioned because of its absolute insistence that it scrupulously lives in accord with biblical worldview. As Roger Olson notes, "Evangelicals revere the Bible as God's uniquely inspired and authoritative book; for them it is the supreme source and norm for Christian *faith* and practice."[35]

What must be stressed is that *professional biblical scholars*, not lay believers, tend to draw the distinctions just noted. Religious folks typically fail to grasp the difference between their primary Scriptures and the millennia of hermeneutical interpretation that—in my opinion, at least—often drowns out the originals.[36] This means that the thoughtful analyst must discern if a political initiative rests on a biblical or a postbiblical foundation (or neither). As an aside, I would note that the study of the significance of hermeneutics has often been assumed to be a "postmodern thing." Indeed, postmodern biblical scholars have done much to bring

---

32. Jacques Berlinerblau, "What's Wrong with the Society for Biblical Literature?" *Chronicle Review*, November 10, 2006. Online: http://chronicle.com/article/Whats-Wrong-With-the-Socie/12369/.

33. Berlinerblau, *Secular Bible*, 87–100.

34. Daniel Harrington, *How do Catholics Read the Bible?* (Lanham, Md.: Rowman & Littlefield, 1989), xi.

35. Roger E. Olson, *The Westminster Handbook for Evangelical Theology* (Louisville: Westminster John Knox, 2004), 154.

36. Berlinerblau, *Secular Bible*, 57–69.

the importance of scrutinizing this factor to our attention.[37] However, the examination of the interpretive history of the Bible is of such importance that one wonders whether all biblical scholars—postmodern or not—should be trained in understanding how the Bible's meanings are in flux across sociological time and space.

In any case, let's take the case of homosexuality as our first example of how actors can be influenced by the words of the Bible. The place of gay people within the church has been among the most divisive issues in the recent history of American Christendom.[38] Those who argue that homosexuals are not "affirmed in Christ" have what they believe to be very precise scriptural injunctions to this effect. There is, for example, Lev 18:22, translated by the New King James Version (NKJV) as follows: "You shall not lie with a male as with a woman. It is an abomination." Romans 1:27 rails against men "leaving the natural use of the woman" as a form of "sexual immorality" (1:29, NKJV).

In an earlier book, I pointed out that these verses are chockfull of linguistic ambiguities.[39] I personally, and professionally, would not translate or interpret either of these verses as an unambiguous repudiation of same-sex eroticism. What I will concede is that the *translations* referenced above do seem to offer believers fairly definite biblical condemnations of homosexuality. I repeat, I think those translations are misleading. I can see, however, how the verse clearly informs the policy initiatives of conservative Christians and the pressure groups that represent their interests. In other words, I understand the link between the Bible and the believer's reading of the Bible.

In other instances, it is harder to see this causal connection. Let us think of an issue that surfaced in the 2012 election cycle. I refer to the so-called "personhood amendments." Pro-life advocates on the far right have placed these on ballots in Mississippi, Colorado, Louisiana, Virginia,

---

37. E.g., Yvonne Sherwood, *A Biblical Text and Its Afterlives: The Survival of Jonah in Western Culture* (Cambridge: Cambridge University Press, 2000); George Aichele et al. (Bible and Culture Collective), *The Postmodern Bible* (New Haven: Yale University Press, 1997); David Clines, *What Does Eve Do to Help? And Other Readerly Questions to the Old Testament* (Sheffield: Sheffield Academic Press, 1990).

38. P. Deryn Guest, "Battling for the Bible: Academy, Church, and the Gay Agenda," *Theology and Sexuality* 15 (2001): 66–93.

39. Berlinerblau, *Secular Bible*, 101–15.

among other places.[40] In essence, this type of legislation tries to endow a zygote with full-blown human status protected by the Constitution. We need not detain ourselves with a discussion of how these amendments have fared across the nation. For our purposes, we should realize that it is exceedingly difficult to draw a clear connection between this type of activism and *anything* in the Scriptures. Insofar as the biblical authors could not have possibly known what a zygote was, insofar as the ancients were operating with the scantiest and most primitive medical knowledge about reproductive biology, to what degree can we say that the Scriptures have *any* viewpoint on the issue of human life at the cellular level? As John Rogerson points out, "The biblical writers knew nothing about fertilization."[41]

One final example about the complex interface between Scripture and political activism: For years, those on the Christian Right have been making theologically tinged antigovernment arguments. Paul Ryan, in his vice-presidential announcement speech, sloganized the sentiment as follows: "Our rights come from nature and God, not government."[42] All well and good, but this would seem to *directly contradict actual biblical verses well known to Christians*. For what, if any, meaning does "rendering unto Caesar" have if not to acknowledge that a Christian, at the very least, respects government?[43] What is Rom 13:1 talking about when it advises, "Let every person be subject to the governing authorities" (NRSV)? And what about 1 Pet 2:13–14 and 1 Tim 2:1?

---

40. Kate Sheppard, "Personhood Amendments: Coming to a Ballot Near You?" *Mother Jones*. Online: http://www.motherjones.com/mojo/2011/11/personhood-amendments-state-map.

41. John Rogerson, *Theory and Practice in Old Testament Ethics* (London: T&T Clark, 2004), 88. Also see Andreas Lindemann, "'Do Not Let a Woman Destroy the Unborn Babe in Her Belly': Abortion and Ancient Judaism and Christianity," *Studia Theologica* 49 (1995): 253–71.

42. Kenneth W. Smith Jr., "Full Text of Paul Ryan's V.P. Announcement Speech," *Washington Post*, August, 11, 2012. Online: http://www.washingtonpost.com/blogs/post-politics/post/paul-ryans-announcement-speech-we-wont-duck-the-tough-issues/2012/08/11/f5ed0548-e3b2-11e1-ae7f-d2a13e249eb2_blog.html.

43. A variety of interesting articles on this verse are found in Ernst Bammel and C. F. D. Moule, eds., *Jesus and the Politics of His Day* (Cambridge: Cambridge University Press, 1984). They include Gerhard Schneider, "The Political Charge against Jesus (Luke 23:2)," 403–14; H. St. J. Hart, "The Coin of 'Render unto Caesar...' (A Note on Some Aspects of Mark 12:13–17; Matt 22:15–22; Luke 20:20–26)," 241–48; and F. F. Bruce, "Render to Caesar," 249–63.

So-called "Teavangelicals" might believe that drowning the federal government in a bathtub is a Christ-sanctified idea, but there is significant evidence to the contrary.[44] Paul, after all, makes unambiguous reference to *delivering* taxes to whom they are due (Rom 13:7). How this squares with the antitax, antigovernment effusions of Tea Party enthusiasts, many of whom are conservative Christians, defies rational explanation.[45]

What I am saying, then, is that politicians and politically engaged citizens often assume that they are merely obeying the mandates of the Scriptures. In some cases, it is more precise to say they are obeying the mandates of a particular interpretation of the Scriptures. And in other cases, there is a whopping disparity between what the Scriptures seem to say and how the faithful construe their political advocacy.

Technical Usage

So far we've explored a series of hopefully helpful analytical dichotomies for scholars to take into consideration when studying the deployment of the Bible in the public square. The first was rhetoric versus policy, the second postbiblical versus biblical influence. Our third area of interest focuses on only one prong of another well-known binary: content versus form. Here, I urge analysts to look less at the messaging involved in Scripture citation and more at the technical way the message is conveyed. The danger of focusing on content alone is that exegetes tend to assume levels of subtlety and interpretive sophistication that are simply nonexistent among politicians and their constituencies. Often biblical scholars forget how one dimensional Bible reading can be. After all, most readers of Scriptures do not seek to revel in the glorious multivalence of its many possible interpretations. On the contrary, they engage the text to find *the* message, *the* truth, and so forth.

My investigation of biblical citations in public oratory in 2004 and 2008 yielded a fairly consistent conclusion. Scriptural allusions were almost always the essence of brevity. That is, to say the overwhelming majority of

---

44. David Brody, *The Teavangelicals: The Inside Story of How the Evangelicals and the Tea Party are Taking Back America* (Grand Rapids: Zondervan, 2012).

45. Public Religion Research Institute, "Fact Sheet: 'Teavangelicals': Alignment and Tensions between the Tea Party and White Evangelical Protestants," Public Religion Research Institute. Online: http://publicreligion.org/research/2011/11/fact-sheet-alignment-of-evangelical-and-tea-party-values/.

Bible talk by politicians goes by in a flash. Politicians don't linger. They don't exegete. They don't need footnotes. I called this technique "cite and run," that is, the use of breezy, shallow, and fast invocations. Its motto: "*Make the damn reference and get on with it!*"[46]

A few examples: Newt Gingrich, speaking at Judson University in March 2012, used the book of Proverbs to justify his candidacy, stating, "I believe what we need desperately in America today is captured in a simple Bible phrase: 'Without vision the people perish' [Prov 29:18, KJV]."[47] And consider this scene: Mitt Romney, at the memorial for the victims of the Aurora, Colorado shooting, cited the New Testament, when he said, "And we can mourn with those who mourn in Colorado" (see Rom. 12:15).[48]

At the Republican National Convention, Marco Rubio of Florida invoked Luke 12:48:"We're special because we've always understood the scriptural admonition, that for everyone to whom much is given, from him much will be required"—and left it at that. Notice that in all cases the reference is unadorned, as if its meaning were clear, uncontested, and most importantly, perfectly in sync with the politician's worldview.

In fact, sometimes the citation is not even explicitly articulated. Instead, it is smuggled into the oratory as a sort of high-pitch dog whistle audible only to certain constituencies. George W. Bush, I once noted, was the unparalleled master of sneaking snippets of Scripture into his speeches. In doing so, he executed a near perfect wink-and-nod to the evangelical base, while secularists remained oblivious to the signal that he has just relayed.

For instance, at the end of his 2001 State of the Union, Bush slipped in this praise for his fellow citizens: "We can make Americans proud of their government. Together we can share in the credit of making our country more prosperous and generous and just, and earn from our conscience and from our fellow citizens the highest possible praise: Well done, good and faithful servants." How many Americans actually noticed that he had

---

46. Berlinerblau, *Thumpin' It*, 44.

47. Alana Semuels, "Newt Gingrich Courts Churchgoers in South Carolina," *Los Angeles Times*, January 15, 2012. Online: http://articles.latimes.com/2012/jan/15/news/la-pn-newt-gingrich-courts-churchgoers-in-south-carolina-20120115.

48. Eric Marrapodi and Halimah Abdullah, "Romney Strikes Rare Notes of Faith in Aurora Speech," CNN Politics. Online: http://www.cnn.com/2012/07/20/politics/romney-religion-speech/index.html.

rustled in a little scripture from Matt 25:21?[49] I am fairly certain that Mitt Romney meant to do just this when at the Republican National Convention he invoked Amos 3:3 and declared: "Tonight I am asking you to join me to *walk together* to a better future."[50]

However, in 2012, we did see some notable and relevant innovations. In a more secular age, one used to hurry through or even conceal one's faith-based pandering. That was the logic animating the examples I just gave. But America is changing. Public expressions of religion are becoming more explicit, bolder, and lengthier. In a recent study, I have referred to this explosion of faith in the public square as the "revival" of American religion.[51] The revivalists seem hell-bent on saturating American discourse with sectarian religious imagery and creedal statements.

Most intriguing in this regards is Rick Perry's August 6, 2011 oration at an event he called "The Response." For those of you who have forgotten the details, Perry, freshly announced as a candidate for the GOP nomination, held court in front of thirty thousand prayerful people at Reliant Stadium in Houston. Writing in *The Washington Post*, I made this observation about the proceedings: "What Governor Perry did Saturday is unusual in the history of presidential campaigns, at least recent ones. He engaged in extended citation of passages from Joel, Isaiah, and Ephesians. He would reel off immense chunks of Scripture–without any interpretation whatsoever, as if the verses were self-explanatory."[52]

In other words, Governor Perry delivered a sermon. Any other politician in any other decade of the twentieth century would have used the occasion to articulate his policy prescriptions to the American people. Perry reversed that logic in accordance with the antisecular sentiment of the age: The piety *was* the policy. Those who observed the twenty Republican debates throughout 2011 and 2012 rarely lost sight of how important

---

49. C-SPAN, "Address of the President to the Joint Session of Congress," C-SPAN.org. Online: http://legacy.c-span.org/Transcripts/SOTU-2001-0227.aspx.

50. "Transcript: Mitt Romney's Acceptance Speech," NPR. Online: http://www.npr.org/2012/08/30/160357612/transcript-mitt-romneys-acceptance-speech.

51. Berlinerblau, *How to Be Secular*.

52. Jacques Berlinerblau, "Piety is the Policy at Rick Perry's Prayer Rally," *Washington Post*, August 8, 2011. Online: http://www.washingtonpost.com/blogs/georgetown-on-faith/post/piety-is-the-policy-at-rick-perrys-prayer-rally/2011/08/08/gIQAtpz52I_blog.html.

it was for the candidates to stress their religious bona fides in as explicit a manner as possible.[53]

My sense is, then, that the old cite-and-run techniques of 2008 *may* increasingly yield, at least among Republicans, to the longer-form interventions of Perry. On the Republican side of the aisle, anyhow, where traditionalist Protestants, Catholics, and Mormons have become a mainstay of the base, it makes perfect sense that their oratory would amplify previously muted strains of religious politicking. Whether the governor of Texas was an innovator or an outlier in this regard remains to be seen.

Effective Usage

One last category to be mindful of concerns the actual effectiveness of using scripture in political rhetoric. Did the cited verse have the desired outcome of swaying an audience, pulverizing an opponent, unloosening checkbooks at fundraisers, or garnering votes?

It is a tricky question and almost impossible to measure accurately. That's because a campaign's success or failure does not only hinge on a candidate's scripture references. The United States, after all, has not regressed to the point where voters only care about the religious character of their elected officials. Some not only don't care about such matters, but resent politicians who make such gestures. Data from the 2012 election suggests that the so-called "nones," or religiously unaffiliated, voted against the conservative-Christian-dominated agenda of the GOP with especial aplomb. That is to say, 70 percent of a constituency, that is reckoned to be one-fifth of the American people, voted for Barack Obama.[54] In any case, it is important to recall that elections are never won by Scripture alone. Countless other policies, ads, political positions, and backroom compromises seal a politician's electoral fate. Thus it is hard to discern metrics for gauging effective and ineffective biblical citation.

---

53. Jacques Berlinerblau, "Romney Takes Care of Business at Liberty University," *Chronicle of Higher Education*. Online: https://chronicle.com/blogs/brainstorm/romney-takes-care-of-business-at-liberty-university/46823.

54. Pew Forum on Religion and Public Life, " 'Nones' on the Rise: One-in-Five Adults Have No Religious Affiliation" (October 9, 2012). Pew Research Center. Online: http://www.pewforum.org/uploadedFiles/Topics/Religious_Affiliation/Unaffiliated/NonesOnTheRise-full.pdf.

Put in the most reductive terms possible, politicians who effectively cite Scripture *win* their respective contests. The case study here would have to be George W. Bush's 2004 victory over John Kerry.[55] The storyline there concerns a flailing incumbent, mired in an unpopular war, presiding over a sluggish economy, yet somehow still carrying the day because of the ballot of the so-called "values voters."

There does seem warrant for the claim that Bush's use of scriptural messaging was helpful. It is undeniable that what the journalist Dan Gilgoff termed "the Jesus machine" played a huge role in bringing out the vote for Bush, especially in Ohio.[56] Some scholars have pointed out that Bush prevailed, because he was able to woo a small percentage of African American conservatives to the red side of the ledger in that state.[57] One statistic that bears repeating is that Karl Rove's national operation had thousands of faith-based ground troops. Kerry's team, apparently, had *one* dedicated operative in charge of religious outreach.[58]

Broadly speaking, faith and values politicking is at its very best when employed for purposes of what I call "base-whip-up." In other words, there are large, organized voting blocs—particularly on the Christian Right—who are amenable to skillful biblical citation. I refer to evangelical and fundamentalist Protestants, traditionalist Catholics, and Mormons.

These religious conservatives expect to hear their candidates invoke the Bible, talk about their personal faith, and engage in the requisite culture war provocations on issues such as abortion and gay rights. A skilled politician—and let's be clear, this is usually going to be a Republican—knows just how to reach out to these constituencies using the Good Book. Perhaps no politician embodied these virtues more than former Pennsylvania Senator Rick Santorum. His epic 2012 run for the presidency was punctuated on an almost daily basis by assaults on secularists, laments

---

55. James Guth et al., "Religious Influences in the 2004 Presidential Election," *Presidential Studies Quarterly* 36 (2006): 223–42; Robert Denton, Jr., "Religion and the 2004 Presidential Campaign," *American Behavioral Scientist* 49 (2005): 11–31.

56. Dan Gilgoff, *The Jesus Machine: How James Dobson, Focus on the Family, and Evangelical America Are Winning the Culture War* (New York: St. Martin's, 2007).

57. Bob Wineburg, *Faith-Based Inefficiency: The Follies of Bush's Initiatives* (Westport, Conn.: Praeger, 2007), 88.

58. Gilgoff, *The Jesus Machine*, 242–67. Also see Berlinerblau, *How to Be Secular*, 120–36.

about the absence of prayer in American society, denunciations of "phony theology," and scathing reflections on gay lifestyles.[59]

Of course, sometimes one plays the Bible and religion cards too loudly or too insultingly. The case of interest here is that of Todd "Legitimate Rape" Akin. Representative Akin was the Republican nominee for Senate in Missouri, who in an interview remarked, "If it's a legitimate rape, the female body has ways to try to shut that whole thing down."[60] The ensuing uproar handed the election to his Democratic opponent, Claire McCaskill.[61] He was joined on this "rape slate" by another Republican, Richard Mourdock, who a few weeks later argued that "even when life begins in that horrible situation of rape, that it is something that God intended to happen."[62] The views of both of these men on abortion, medicine, and science were clearly informed by what they believed to be in the Bible.[63] And it is equally clear that their invocation of so-called biblical principles doomed their campaigns.

What the failed bids of these candidates demonstrate is that the use of biblical and religious themes in political oratory is not so much a double-edge sword as a double-edge nuke. Things can go hellaciously wrong

---

59. Jacques Berlinerblau, "The Death of American Secularism," *The New Humanist*, (May/June 2012). Online: http://newhumanist.org.uk/2788/the-death-of-american-secularism; Rosalind S. Helderman, "Rick Santorum's 'Phony Theology' Criticism of Obama Follows a Familiar Theme," *Washington Post*, February 22, 2012. Online: http://articles.washingtonpost.com/2012-02-22/politics/35442340_1_phony-theology-hogan-gidley-rick-santorum; Shushannah Walshe, "Rick Santorum Has Tense Exchange on Gay Rights and Health Care in Iowa," ABC News. Online: http://abcnews.go.com/blogs/politics/2011/12/rick-santorum-has-tense-exchange-on-gay-rights-and-health-care-in-iowa/.

60. William Saletan, "Todd Akin's Rape Fiasco," Slate.com. Online: http://www.slate.com/articles/news_and_politics/frame_game/2012/08/todd_akin_s_legitimate_rape_gaffe_shows_how_abortion_can_be_a_crime_issue_.html.

61. Diana Reese, "Claire McCaskill Legitimately Shuts Down Todd Akin in Missouri Senate Race," *Washington Post*, November 7, 2012. Online: http://www.washingtonpost.com/blogs/she-the-people/wp/2012/11/07/claire-mccaskill-legitimately-shuts-down-todd-akin-in-missouri-senate-race/.

62. Kim Geiger, "Joe Donnelly Triumphs over Richard Mourdock in Indiana Senate Race," *Los Angeles Times*, November 6, 2012. Online: http://articles.latimes.com/2012/nov/06/news/la-pn-indiana-senate-result-20121106.

63. On Akin's background, see Eliza Wood, "Todd Akin, the Bible, and Rape," *Huffington Post*, August 22, 2012. Online: http://www.huffingtonpost.com/eliza-wood/todd-akin-the-bible-and-r_b_1819333.html.

for a politician, terribly fast, when they fecklessly invoke religion. Think of presidential candidate John McCain's two pastors, Rod Parsley and John Hagee, and the uproar they created in 2008.[64] Think of the Reverend Jeremiah Wright and Obama's ill-advised jab at conservative religious Americans who "cling to guns or religion or antipathy to people who aren't like them."[65] What I mean to say is that faith and values politicking is an extraordinarily complicated business and, unless politicians have the skill of a George W. Bush or a Bill Clinton in invoking religious themes, they run the risk of sinking their own campaigns.

Conclusion: The Collapse of American Secularism

With this survey rendered, it is important to step back and place what we have just discussed in the context of broader patterns in recent American history. For, in the second half of the twentieth century, the Bible has never surfaced in political rhetoric as much as it has now.

Was it invoked as frequently by Eisenhower and Stevenson in 1952 and 1956? Kennedy and Nixon in 1960? Goldwater and Johnson in 1964? Nixon and Humphrey in 1968? Or Nixon and McGovern in 1972? The question for secular people, believers and nonbelievers alike is this: What does it mean when the Scriptures have been cited more frequently by presidential aspirants in these past four years alone than they have been across five decades of American history? Whatever happened to the old secular status quo, where God was publicly acknowledged and graciously venerated, albeit in restrained and vague terms?

When did this change occur, and why? That is the question I address at length in my recent book. The answer is quite complex, but let me, in closing, identify two interrelated factors that explain, in large part, the phenomenon we have been tracking here.[66] One reason for the increas-

---

64. "McCain Rejects Endorsements from Hagee, Parsley," *Huffington Post*, May 22, 2008. Online: http://www.huffingtonpost.com/2008/05/22/mccain-rejects-hagee-endo_n_103143.html.

65. Jeff Zeleny and Adam Nagourney, "An Angry Obama Renounces Ties to His Ex-Pastor," *New York Times*, April 30, 2008. Online: http://www.nytimes.com/2008/04/30/us/politics/30obama.html; Katharine Q. Seelye and Jeff Zeleny, "On the Defensive, Obama Calls His Words Ill-Chosen," *New York Times*, April 13, 2008. Online: http://www.nytimes.com/2008/04/13/us/politics/13campaign.html.

66. For a more detailed discussion, see my *How to Be Secular*.

ing salience of the Bible in American public life is the nearly half-century rise of the Christian Right. Awoken from its slumber by the anything-goes 1960s, conservative Christians reestablished their political footing in the 1970s. At first, it was Democratic presidential candidate Jimmy Carter who roused the sleeping giant that was evangelical America.[67] When conservative Christian leaders like Jerry Falwell lost faith in him, his followers pivoted to the candidacy of Ronald Reagan in 1980.[68] And with that began the dismantling of the old New Deal coalition of Franklin Delano Roosevelt. It is often forgotten that evangelicals were generally solid *Democratic* voters prior to the Reagan revolution of 1980.

We should never underestimate what Reverend Falwell accomplished. He executed, in the words of one commentator, the "biggest voter realignment" in the twentieth century.[69] He also perfectly identified the enemy, the "them," opposed to a pious, God-fearing "us." As Albert Menendez observed, Jerry Falwell's Moral Majority "made every effort to portray Reagan as a defender of traditional Judeo-Christian values, while the Democrats were depicted as agents of 'secular humanism,' the sinister cabal supposedly ruining America."[70] The dividend of Falwell's activism is this: the Religious Right is a mainstay of the GOP and in some estimations its true base. If the base wants the Bible, the base gets the Bible—and this in large part explains our scripture-saturated politics of the last decade or so.

That story is well known. Less well known is the complete unraveling of the secular status quo that took place in the second half of the twentieth century. American secularism has fallen upon hard times. As I have noted elsewhere, "Conservative religious leaders rampage against it, demagogues denounce it on the campaign trail, all three branches of government give it the cold shoulder, and among the general public it suffers from a distressing lack of popular appeal."[71]

---

67. Andrew Flint and Joy Porter, "Jimmy Carter: The Re-Emergence of Faith-Based Politics and the Abortion Rights Issue," *Presidential Studies Quarterly* 35 (2005): 28–47.

68. For a revealing glimpse of Falwell's political worldview, see Jerry Falwell, *Strength for the Journey: An Autobiography* (New York: Simon & Schuster, 1987).

69. Jeffrey Bell, "What Falwell Wrought: Just the biggest realignment in modern history," *Weekly Standard* 12 (2007): 13–14.

70. Albert Menendez, *Evangelicals at the Ballot Box* (Amherst: Prometheus, 1996), 145.

71. Berlinerblau, *How to Be Secular,* xv.

In 1960, a presidential candidate like Senator John F. Kennedy could deliver a speech in which he boasted that he "believe[d] in an America where the separation of church and state is absolute."[72] This was also an America in which the United States Supreme Court increasingly pushed religion out of public schools and public spaces.[73] As both the cause and effect of these developments, minorities—be they religious, ethnic, or sexual—were finding a voice in challenging the white, Anglo-Saxon, Protestant status quo.

Yet, in the intervening decades, all of that changed. In the judicial branch, the accomplishments of what is known as separationism have been undermined steadily at least since Justice William Rehnquist's dissent in the 1985 *Wallace v Jaffree* case. No fewer than four justices on today's court would seem to concur with Rehnquist's demurral that the wall of separation "is a metaphor based on bad history" and "should be frankly and explicitly abandoned."[74] For some contemporary court watchers, it's not a question of if the wall collapses, but when.

The legislative chamber, for its part, is teeming with conservative evangelicals who speak openly about America being a "Christian nation" and who seem intent on dismantling the wall brick by brick.[75] As for the executive branch, a *Democratic* President has presided over the supersizing of George W. Bush's Office of Faith-based and Community Initiatives. President Barack Obama recently called for national days of prayer on 9/7–9/9 (in advance of the commemoration of 9/11).[76] Although comparatively restrained, Obama invokes Christ in his rhetoric in ways that would have made John F. Kennedy and mid-century separationists despair.[77]

---

72. "Transcript: JFK's Speech on His Religion," NPR. Online: http://www.npr.org/templates/story/story.php?storyId=16920600.

73. Berlinerblau, *How to Be Secular*, 32.

74. *Wallace v. Jaffree*, 472 U.S. 38 (1985), 107.

75. Berlinerblau, *How to Be Secular*, 137–52.

76. The White House Office of the Press Secretary, "Presidential Proclamation—National Days of Prayer and Remembrance, 2012," The White House. Online: http://www.whitehouse.gov/the-press-office/2012/09/07/presidential-proclamation-national-days-prayer-and-remembrance-2012.

77. Jacques Berlinerblau, "Obama at the National Prayer Breakfast (2011)," *Chronicle of Higher Education*. Online: http://chronicle.com/blogs/brainstorm/obama-at-the-national-prayer-breakfast-raging-christ-fest-secular-wake/31816; Jacques Berlinerblau, "Obama at the National Prayer Breakfast (2012)," *Chronicle*

The point is that the Bible-thumpin' we examined above is a metric of secularism's own despair. Either it rethinks itself, retools, reevaluates or the long-form sermonizing of Governor Rick Perry becomes the norm, at least in Republican circles. Finally, either biblical scholarship ventures forth from the cloistered sanctity of specialization or its obsolescence in these matters of public concern will continue to be the norm.

---

of Higher Education. Online: http://chronicle.com/blogs/brainstorm/tag/national-prayer-breakfast.

Biblical Imagery, the End Times, and Political Action: The Roots of Christian Support for Zionism and Israel

Yaakov Ariel

In 1840 the leader of the evangelical movement in Britain, Lord Ashley Cooper, advocated that Britain take diplomatic initiatives toward the establishment of a Jewish state in Palestine.[1] Fifty-one years later an American evangelist, William Blackstone, organized a petition to the president of the United States urging him to convene an international conference that would decide to grant Palestine to the Jews. Shaftesbury and Blackstone, whose attempts to create a Jewish state in Palestine antedated the rise of political Zionism, were among the more well-known of these proto-Zionists. Motivated by a biblical messianic faith and the belief that a Jewish commonwealth in the land of Israel is a necessary stage in the preparation of the way for the return of Jesus of Nazareth to earth, a number of Protestant clergymen, writers, businessmen, and politicians supported, and at times labored actively for, the restoration of the Jews to Palestine and the establishment of a Jewish commonwealth there.

Christian Zionists have, at times, been more enthusiastic than Jews over the prospect of a Jewish political entity in Palestine. When Jews launched their Zionist movement at the turn of the twentieth century, Christian protagonists offered support. Christian political backing accompanied the birth of the State of Israel, gaining more momentum after the Arab-Israeli war in June 1967. In order to understand what has motivated

---

1. On Ashley Cooper, the seventh Earl of Shaftesbury, and his proto-Zionist efforts, see Barbara Tuchman, *Bible and Sword* (London: Macmillan, 1983), 175–207; Donald Lewis, *The Origins of Christian Zionism: Lord Shaftesbury and Evangelical Support for a Jewish Homeland* (Cambridge: Cambridge University Press, 2010).

Pietist and evangelical Christians to support the idea of a Jewish national restoration and a Jewish commonwealth in Palestine, one needs to explore the manner such Christians read and understand prophetic passages of the Old Testament, or the Hebrew Bible, and, at times, chapters and verses in the New Testament as well, and how they have related them to the Jewish people of recent generations and to Palestine, or Israel, the Holy Land.

Biblical Prophecies, the Jews, and the Holy Land

The messianic hope, which has served as the incentive for the rise of Christian Zionism, draws on a long tradition.[2] In its early generations, Christianity was messianically-inclined, its followers expecting the imminent return of Jesus to establish the kingdom of God on earth.[3] After Christianity became the dominant religion in the Mediterranean world in the fourth and fifth centuries, the Christian messianic beliefs became a-millennial, expecting the return of Jesus in a remote future, or interpreting biblical passages with messianic overtones as allegorical. According to that view, the church replaced Jesus on earth and has a mission to instruct its followers and ensure their salvation. Millennial groups that expected the return of Jesus to earth, nonetheless, emerged during the Middle Ages, drawing on messianic passages in biblical books, such as Daniel and Revelation, often refusing to accept the standard exegeses of the texts and predicting the imminent end of the world as we know it.[4]

A burst of apocalyptic expectations, which often initiated new translations of the sacred Scriptures and encouraged a fresh reading of the texts followed the Protestant Reformation in the sixteenth century.[5] Looking at the Old Testament in a new manner, a number of Protestant groups expected the Jews to play an important role in the imminent events of the end times. These groups came from both the left wing of the Reformation and the more mainstream Reformed tradition. The English Revolution in the mid-seventeenth century also stirred messianic hopes and gave rise to premillennialist groups that were interested in the Jewish people and

---

2. Norman Cohn, *The Pursuit of the Millennium* (New York: Oxford University Press, 1970).
3. Bart Ehrman, *Jesus: Apocalyptic Prophet of the New Millennium* (New York: Oxford University Press, 1999).
4. Cohn, *The Pursuit of the Millennium*.
5. George Williams, *The Radical Reformation* (Philadelphia: Westminster, 1970).

the prospect of their return to Palestine. Messianic hopes played a part in the deliberations on the return of the Jews to England in the 1650s.[6] Likewise, premillennialist Christians in Britain and Holland followed with interest the Jewish messianic movement stirred by Shabbatai Zvi in the mid-seventeenth century, hoping that it would bring about the return of the Jews to Palestine.[7]

Already at this stage one could notice characteristics of Christian interest in the Jewish return to Palestine on behalf of a messianic faith grounded in a certain mode of reading the Bible. Such Christians tended to read their sacred Scriptures in a more literal manner, oblivious to traditional mainstream Christian exegetical traditions that began with the fathers of the church. In contrast to older branches of Christianity, they saw the Jews as descendants of the biblical sons of Israel, heirs to the covenant between God and Abraham, and the object of biblical prophecies about a restored Davidic kingdom in the land of Israel. In their messianic scenarios, the return of the Jews to Palestine was the first step in the advancement of the messianic time table. Their image of the Jews, which was based on Scripture and not on encounters with actual Jews was, however, often mixed and ambivalent.

Christian biblical proto-Zionism resurfaced with much vigor in the early decades of the nineteenth century with the rise of the evangelical movement in Britain and a new wave of fascination with prophecy and the prospects of the arrival of the messianic times.[8] Two types of Christian messianic faiths gained prominence in the nineteenth century, "historical" and "futurist," differing as to when the events of the end time were to begin. For the most part, these two messianic schools shared views of the role of the Jews and the Holy Land in God's plans for humanity.[9] Adherents of both schools became supporters of Zionist agendas as well as of

---

6. David Katz, *Philosemitism and the Return of the Jews to England* (Oxford: Clarendon, 1982).

7. Gershom Scholem, *Shabbatai Zvi: The Mystical Messiah* (New York: Schocken Books, 1970).

8. Yaakov Ariel, "The French Revolution and the Reawakening of Christian Messianism," *The French Revolution and it Impact* (ed. Richard Cohen; Jerusalem: Zalman Shazar, 1991), 319-38.

9. Ernest Sandeen, *The Roots of Fundamentalism: British and American Millenarianism, 1800-1930* (Grand Rapids: Baker Book House, 1978).

missionary activity among the Jews.[10] In Europe, the predominant messianic school was historical, identifying current events with biblical passages, while the premillennialist faith in its futurist, dispensationalist form became widely accepted in America in the latter decades of the nineteenth century. Dispensationalism aligned itself with a conservative evangelical manner of reading the Bible, as well as a conservative Christian outlook on contemporary society and culture. It has provided evangelicals with a pessimistic critique of culture and a philosophy of history that divided divine economy and human experiences into different eras, offering, among other things, reassurance in the face of uncertainty.[11]

Liberal Christians have often viewed the evangelical messianic faith as arbitrary, based on an unsophisticated, if not idiosyncratic, reading of the biblical texts.[12] Pietists and evangelicals are certain, however, that their messianic faith derives from an unbiased straightforward reading of chapters and verses in the Hebrew and Greek Bibles, the Old and New Testaments. Each act, stage, and player in the messianic scenario is accompanied by biblical prophetic lines.[13] The role of the Jews and the Holy Land has been tied to the larger outlook on the sacred Scriptures and history, revolutionizing conservative Christian attitudes toward the Jews. According to the dispensationalist reading of biblical passages, God has different plans for the Jews, the church, and the rest of humanity. Premillennialist

---

10. For example, Barbara Tuchman, *Bible and Sword: England and Palestine from the Bronze Age to Balfour* (London: Macmillan, 1983), 80–101.

11. A. G. Mojtabai, *Blessed Assurance: At Home with the Bomb in Amarillo, Texas* (Boston: Houghton Mifflin, 1986).

12. James Barr, *Fundamentalism* (Peabody: Trinity International, 2010).

13. For example, John Walvoord, *Israel in Prophecy* (Grand Rapids: Zondervan, 1962); Elwood McQuaid, *It Is No Dream: Bible Prophecy: Fact or Fanaticism* (Bellmawr, N.J.: Friends of Israel Gospel Ministry, 1978); Alvin Showalter, *New Chronological Harmony of History and the Bible* (Cape Town: n.p., 1988); John Walvoord, *Major Bible Prophecies* (Grand Rapids: Zondervan, 1991); Timothy Tow, *Prophescope on Israel* (Singapore: Christian Life Publishers, 1992); Harold Sevener, *God's Man: The Visions and Prophecies of Daniel* (Charlotte: Chosen People Ministries, 1994); David Larsen, *Jews, Gentiles and the Church: A New Perspective on History and Prophecy* (Grand Rapids: Discovery House, 1995); Mal Couch, ed., *Dictionary of Premillennial Theology* (Grand Rapids: Kregel, 1996); Kendell Easley, *Living with the End in Sight: Meditations on the Book of Revelation* (Nashville: Holman Bible, 2000); Tim LaHaye, Jerry Jenkins, and Sandi Swanson, *The Authorized Left Behind Handbook* (Wheaton: Tyndale House, 2005); Dan Bruce, *Lifting the Veil on the Book of Daniel* (n.p.: The Prophecy Society, 2012).

Christians define the church as the body of the true believers, composed of those who have undergone inner experiences of conversion, have accepted Jesus as their personal Savior, and have taken it upon themselves to live saintly Christian lives. They alone will be saved and spared the turmoil and destruction that will precede the arrival of the Messiah. Jews are, in many ways, a special category, since, while not yet redeemed, they are also not cast out and thus deserve more good will and devotion on the part of true Christians than do other unconverted people.

The dispensationalist school of Christian messianic thought, which has become prominent in our era, views the Bible as a book holding God's plans for all categories of humanity in all eras, including apocalyptic times. The end times, they believe, will begin with the rapture of the church (based, among other reasoning on 1 Thess 4:17). The true believers will be snatched from earth and meet Jesus in the air. Those believers who die prior to the rapture will rise from the dead and will also join the living in heaven. These saintly persons will remain with Jesus for seven years (according to some versions, for three and a half years) and thus be spared the turmoil and miseries that will be inflicted on those who remain on earth during that period. For the latter, this period will be marked by natural disasters such as earthquakes, floods, and famines, as well as wars and murderous dictatorial regimes (based on Dan 12:1; Matt 24:21; Luke 18:7; 2 Pet 3:2–4). By the time Jesus returns to earth, about two thirds of humanity will have perished.[14]

For the Jews, the seven years that stand between the current era and messianic times will be known as the "time of Jacob's trouble." The Jews will return to their ancient homeland "in unbelief," without accepting Jesus as their Savior. They will establish a political commonwealth there, not the millennial Davidic kingdom, but nonetheless a necessary step in the advancement of the messianic timetable. Living in spiritual blindness, the Jews will let themselves be ruled by the antichrist, an impostor posing as the Messiah. The antichrist will inflict a reign of terror, directed at, among others, Jews who will accept the belief in Jesus during this period. The arrival of Jesus at the end of the great tribulation will end the antichrist's rule. Jesus will crush this satanic figure and his armies and will establish the millennial kingdom. Those Jews who survive the turmoil and terror

---

14. For details on this eschatological hope, see, e.g., Hal Lindsey's best seller *The Late Great Planet Earth* (Grand Rapids: Zondervan, 1971).

of the great tribulation will accept Jesus as their Savior. There will follow a period marked by the righteous rule of Christ on earth, with the Jews inhabiting David's ancient kingdom and Jerusalem serving as the capital of the entire world.

Messianic Faith and Christian Support for the Zionist Cause

The Christian Protestant messianic reading of the Bible can well explain the interest those holding such beliefs have shown in the Jews and the prospect of their national restoration. Beginning in the nineteenth century, premillennialist Christians have come up with a series of initiatives intended to bring about or promote the national restoration of the Jews in Palestine. The initiatives of Christian Zionists predated the rise of political Zionism. The most outstanding of them was William Blackstone. An evangelist and promoter of the dispensationalist messianic faith, Blackstone visited Palestine in 1889 and was deeply impressed by the developments that the first wave of Zionist immigration had brought about in a country he had considered to be a desolate land. He viewed the agricultural settlements and the new neighborhoods in Jerusalem as "signs of the time," indicating that an era was ending and the great events of the end times were to occur very soon.[15]

Blackstone decided to take an active line and help bring about Jewish national restoration to Palestine. In 1891 he organized a petition urging the president of the United States to convene an international conference of the world powers that would give Palestine back to the Jews. More than four hundred prominent Americans—congressmen, governors, mayors, publishers and editors of leading newspapers, notable clergymen, and leading businessmen—signed Blackstone's petition. Although it failed to bring the American government to take a meaningful action regarding its request, the petition reflected the warm support that the idea of the Jewish restoration to Palestine could receive among Protestants influenced by a biblical messianic outlook on the Jews and Palestine.[16]

Blackstone devised a theory that has become a cornerstone of American Christian supporters of Zionism and Israel ever since. He asserted that

---

15. See Blackstone, *Jesus Is Coming* (3rd ed.; Los Angeles: Bible House, 1908), 211–13, 236–41.

16. See Yaakov Ariel, "An American Initiative for a Jewish State: William Blackstone and the Petition of 1891," *Studies in Zionism* 10 (1989): 125–37.

the United States has a special role and mission in God's plans for humanity: that of a modern Cyrus, to help restore the Jews to Zion (see, e.g., 2 Chr 36:22-23; Isa 45:13). God has chosen America for that mission on account of its moral superiority over other nations, and America will be judged according to the way it carries out its mission.[17] This theory enabled American evangelicals to combine their messianic belief and understanding of the course of human history with their sense of American patriotism. Although they have often criticized contemporary American culture, they have remained loyal citizens of the American commonwealth.

When Theodore Herzl began his efforts in the mid-1890s to secure international recognition for the idea of a Jewish state, Pietists and evangelicals showed much interest in the new movement and offered support. William Hechler, a German-British believer in the imminent second coming of Jesus, became an advisor to Herzl and his liaison to the Protestant Christian rulers of Europe.[18] Hechler introduced Herzl to the Grand Duke of Baden, who reacted sympathetically and promised to support the Zionist cause. The Grand Duke, in turn, introduced Herzl to the German Emperor, whom Herzl wished to turn into a patron of the Zionist cause. When the first Zionist Congress convened in Basil in 1897, a number of Christians came as guests to show support.

The characteristics of the relationship between Christian supporters of a biblical messianic faith and Jewish Zionist leadership were laid down at that time. Herzl did not comprehend what motivated Christians like Hechler to become supporters of the fledgling Zionist movement. But he became satisfied that Hechler was genuinely a friend, and that was all that mattered to him. The Jewish Zionist leaders were not familiar with Pietist or evangelical biblical exegeses and did not take the premillennialist theology seriously. Rather, they viewed it as a somewhat eccentric conviction and focused instead on the actual support its adherents provided for their cause.[19] Christian Zionists, for their part, had mixed feelings about the Zionist movement. Their immediate reaction to the Zionist endeavor

---

17. In a letter to Woodrow Wilson, November 4, 1914, and in a telegram to Warren G. Harding, December 10, 1920. Blackstone Personal Papers at the Billy Graham Center, Wheaton, Illinois.

18. On Hechler and his relationship with Herzl, see Amos Elon, *Herzl* (Tel Aviv: Am Oved, 1975), 212-19, 296, 321-23, 438; Paul Merkley, *The Politics of Christian Zionism, 1891-1948* (London: Frank Cass, 1998), 3-43.

19. See Yaakov Ariel, "William Blackstone and the Petition of 1916: A Neglected

was enthusiastic, and their reports on the rise of the Zionist movement and the developments in Palestine were reminiscent of those of Jewish supporters of the Zionist cause. They were, however, disappointed by the secular character of the movement and saddened that the Zionists were unaware of what they considered to be the real significance of the Jewish return to Palestine.

As the Zionist movement grew and became better organized, evangelical supporters began coordinating their work with the Jewish Zionist leadership. Receiving endorsement for his plan from major Protestant churches and coordinating his efforts with those of the American Zionist leadership, Blackstone organized a second petition in 1916 calling upon the president of the United States to help restore Palestine to the Jews. American Zionist leaders, like Louis Brandeis, Steven Wise, Jacob de Haas, and Nathan Straus, saw the Christian efforts as beneficial to the Zionist cause and established a warm relationship with Blackstone. The American evangelist did not keep his premillennialist motivations secret from his Jewish friends, but the Zionist leaders were not bothered by his prediction that great suffering was awaiting the Jews when the events of the end times would begin to unfold. They did not expect the rapture to take place, and they saw the help that Blackstone was providing them as the only concrete outcome of his messianic faith. This time, Blackstone's efforts were more effective, for he and his friends succeeded in convincing President Wilson to allow the British to issue the Balfour Declaration. Wilson himself did not want his negotiations with Zionist leaders and their Christian supporters to become public knowledge: he preferred to make pro-Zionist moves behind closed doors.[20]

Evangelical Christians welcomed the Balfour Declaration and the British takeover of Palestine, interpreting these developments as further indications that the ground was being prepared for the arrival of the Messiah. Their joy over the new regime in Palestine dominated two conferences on biblical prophecy that took place in Philadelphia and New York in 1918.[21]

Chapter in the History of Christian Zionism in America," *Studies in Contemporary Jewry 7* (1991): 68–85; Merkley, *The Politics of Christian Zionism*, 75–96.

20. Ariel, "William Blackstone and the Petition of 1916."

21. William L. Pettingill, J. R. Schafler, and J. D. Adams, eds., *Light on Prophecy: A Coordinated, Constructive Teaching, Being the Proceedings and Addresses at the Philadelphia Prophetic Conference, May 28–30, 1918* (New York: Christian Herald Bible House, 1918); Arno C. Gaebelein, ed., *Christ and Glory: Addresses Delivered at the New*

Evangelical and Pietist Christians maintained a profound interest in the events that were taking place in the life of the Jewish people and especially in the development of the Jewish community in Palestine. They saw the struggles and turmoil that befell the Jewish nation in the period between the two world wars and during World War II in light of prophecy and the biblical predictions about "the time of Jacob's trouble."[22] Evangelical and Pietist journals with pro-Zionist leanings, such as *Our Hope, The King's Business, The Moody Monthly*, and the pentecostal *Evangel*, regularly published news on developments in the life of the Jewish people, the Zionist movement, and especially the Jewish community in Palestine. They were encouraged by the new wave of Zionist immigration to Palestine in the years of the British administration of the country, and events like the opening of the Hebrew University in 1925 and the new seaport in Haifa in 1932 were publicized in their periodicals. They interpreted these developments as signs that the Jews were energetically building a commonwealth in their ancient land and that the great events of the end times were to occur very soon.[23] Excited by the prospects of an imminent second coming of Jesus to earth, they expressed dismay at the restrictions on Jewish immigration and settlement that the British were imposing. They also criticized the Arabs for their hostility toward the Zionist endeavor and for their violence against the Jews. They saw attempts at blocking the building of a Jewish commonwealth in Palestine as equivalent to putting obstacles in the way of God's plans for the end times. Such attempts, they asserted, were futile, and the Arabs would pay dearly for their rebellious attempts.[24]

Evangelical and Pietist efforts and protests did not shape British policy in Palestine, although they might have had some influence on modifying it since their views on the Jewish presence there were so sportive. During that period conservative evangelical and Pietist political power was on the decline, and the political influence of Christians influenced by biblical narratives and premillennialist messianic faith, both in Britain and in

---

York Prophetic Conference, Carnegie Hall, November 25–28, 1918 (New York: Publication Office, "Our Hope," 1919).

22. For example, Arno Gaebelein, "The Shadows of Jacob's Trouble," *Our Hope* 38 (1932): 102.

23. See, e.g., George T. B. Davis, *Fulfilled Prophecies That Prove the Bible* (Philadelphia: Million Testaments Campaign, 1931); and Keith L Brooks, *The Jews and the Passion for Palestine in Light of Prophecy* (Los Angeles: Brooks Publications, 1937).

24. James Gray, "Editorial," *Moody Bible Institute Monthly* 31 (1931): 346.

America, weakened considerably. In Britain, the evangelical movement was just a shadow of what it had been a century earlier; and in America, after the Scopes trial in 1925, conservative evangelicals withdrew to a large degree from the public arena. Evangelical leaders did not see themselves as influential national figures whose voices would be heard by the policymakers in Washington or as people who could advance a political agenda on the international level. On the European continent, the rise of the Nazis to power subdued, if not completely crushed, pro-Zionist Pietist activity. At a very crucial moment in the life of the Jewish people, its Christian supporters were weak. Such supporters would resurface after World War II and the birth of the State of Israel and would play again an important role in mustering political support, especially in America, for the new Jewish state.

Biblical Prophecies, Christian Supporters, and a Jewish State

Evangelical response to the establishment of the State of Israel in 1948 was enthusiastic. Evangelical journals published sympathetic articles and followed the young Jewish state with great interest in an attempt to interpret its significance for the unfolding of biblical prophecy and the advancement of God's plans in the ages. While they were not happy with the secular character of Israeli government and society, some of the things they saw, such as the mass emigration of Jews to Israel in the 1950s from Asian, African, and East European countries enhanced their messianic hopes.[25] Although evangelicals criticized the Arab hostility against Israel and supported the Israeli state in its struggles with its Arab neighbors, they expressed a belief that the land of Israel could maintain an Arab population alongside its Jewish population and that Israel had an obligation to respect human rights and treat Arabs with fairness.[26] In striving to reconcile premillennialist teachings with the hopes and fears of Arab congregants and potential converts, they emphasized that the ingathering of the Jews in the land of Israel and the eventual reestablishment of the Davidic kingdom did not necessitate the banishment of Arabs from that land. In spite of such

---

25. Louis T. Talbot and William W. Orr, *The New Nation of Israel and the Word of God* (Los Angeles: Bible Institute of Los Angeles, 1948); M. R. DeHaan, *The Jew and Palestine in Prophecy* (Grand Rapids: Zondervan, 1954); Arthur Kac, *The Rebirth of the State of Israel: Is It of God or Men?* (Chicago: Moody Press, 1958); and George T. B. Davis, *God's Guiding Hand* (Philadelphia: Million Testaments Campaign, 1962).

26. John Walvoord, *Israel in Prophecy* (Grand Rapids: Zonderman, 1962), 19.

reassurances, only rarely did Pietist or evangelical Arabs become supporters of Zionism and Israel.[27] The June 1967 war had a dramatic effect on evangelical and Pietist political and messianic views. The dramatic Israeli victory, and the territorial gains it brought with it, strengthened the conviction that Israel was created for a mission in history and was to play an important role in the developments that were to precede the arrival of the Messiah.[28] During the 1970s and to the present, conservative evangelicals have been among Israel's most ardent supporters in the American public arena.[29] Likewise, the growing evangelical population in Latin America has become, by the beginning of the twenty-first century, a powerful constituency that has developed, among other things, a very favorable attitude toward Israel. In addition, evangelical and Pietist groups in countries such as Holland or Finland have served during that period as pro-Israel lobbies, counterbalancing anti-Israel sentiments in their nations. The growth of the evangelical community in Korea has also turned the Christian community in that country into a pro-Israel stronghold. Christian supporters all around the globe involved themselves in such causes as the demand to facilitate Jewish immigration from the Soviet Union and later on in the transporting and absorbing of Soviet Jews in Israel.

Especially in America, evangelicals motivated by a more literal reading of biblical passages have turned into a pro-Israel lobby that uses its political power to promote policies favorable to the interests of the Jewish state. The decades following the June 1967 war were marked by massive American support for Israel in terms of money, arms, and diplomatic backing. For many conservative Christians in America, their pro-Israel stand was an appreciation of the importance of the State of Israel for the advancement of prophecy while also going hand in hand with American interests.[30]

---

27. On Palestinian-Arab Christian Zionists, see Sahri Huri, *Udat al Masiah* [Arabic] (Jerusalem: El Mia el Hia, 1939).

28. E.g., L. Nelson Bell, "Unfolding Destiny," *Christianity Today*, July 21, 1967, 1044–45.

29. See, e.g., Peter L. Williams and Peter L. Benson, *Religion on Capitol Hill: Myth and Realities* (New York: Oxford University Press, 1986); Allen D. Hertzke, *Representing God in Washington* (Knoxville: University of Tennessee Press, 1988); Mark Silk, *Spiritual Politics* (New York: Touchstone, 1989); and Michael Lienesch, *Redeeming America: Piety and Politics in the New Christian Right* (Chapel Hill: University of North Carolina Press, 1993).

30. Stephen Spector, *Evangelicals and Israel: The Story of American Christian Zionism* (New York: Oxford University Press, 2009).

The years following the 1967 Middle East war saw a dramatic rise in evangelical influence in America. Growing in numbers and self-confidence, evangelicals have become more visible and aggressive. In 1976, when Jimmy Carter was elected president, many Americans who identified with liberal causes discovered to their surprise that evangelicalism had grown considerably and was much more influential than they had assumed. The liberal Carter was, however, a disappointment to conservative evangelicals. Carter did take an interest in the Middle East and brought Egypt and Israel to sign a peace treaty, but the role he played was that of a progressive American statesman rather than a "Bible-believing" evangelical Christian. He did not consider Israel to fulfill a biblical messianic role. He was not concerned with the messianic hope of paving the way for the Davidic kingdom, and he did not give preference to Israeli interests over and against Arab ones.

Ronald Reagan, who replaced Carter as president in 1981, was influenced in forming his Middle East policy by conservative evangelical pressure, if not by his own premillennialist understanding of the course of history.[31] Reagan's policy toward Israel was adopted by his successor, George H. W. Bush, who was also close to pro-Israel evangelicals and relied on their support. A friendly attitude toward Israel has been part and parcel of the evangelical vision for America's global policy.[32] While other considerations determined Reagan's and Bush's policy toward Israel, the evangelical favorable attitude toward that country and the insistence that America should assist the Jewish state played an influential part.[33] Bill Clinton's relationship with Israel has to be judged very differently than that of Reagan or Bush. Although nominally an evangelical Christian himself, Clinton was not a conservative Bible believer and did not receive much support from evangelicals, who saw him as representing liberal values to which they have been opposed. While in Arkansas, Clinton had remained, however, a member of a Southern Baptist church. When he was elected president, his pastor delivered a sermon that included the message that the newly elected president should not neglect his obligation to protect

---

31. See Martin Gardner, "Giving God a Hand," *New York Review of Books*, August 1987, 22. On American presidents and Israel, see Paul Merkley, *American Presidents, Religion and Israel: The Heirs of Cyrus* (Westport, Conn.: Praeger, 2004).

32. Timothy Weber, *On the Road to Armageddon* (Grand Rapids: Baker, 2004); Spector, *Evangelicals and Israel*.

33. On American presidents, religion, and Israel, see Merkley, *American Presidents*.

Israel. This tells us perhaps more about the manner Baptists in Little Rock, Arkansas read the Bible than it does about Clinton's personal faith. Yet it is important to note that the roots and cultural background of the American president who opened his administration to Jews more than any president before and who showed a deep concern for Israel were in the Bible Belt, in a church that promoted a special attitude toward Israel.

George W. Bush's administration was also strongly influenced by evangelical, pro-Israeli sentiments. A committed conservative Christian himself, Bush relied heavily on conservative support and, in addition to extending political and financial support to the Jewish state, was reluctant to initiate diplomatic moves that might upset evangelical supporters of Israel. Barak Obama and his wife were members for many years of a charismatic African American church; but while the congregation and its pastor promoted a direct reading of the Bible, their conclusions were somewhat different than those of evangelicals with dispensationalist leanings. Most African American conservative churches have not embraced a pro-Israel outlook, although some pastors and groups have followed that line of biblical exegesis and messianic hope.

The evangelical premillennialist understanding of Israel has influenced, sometimes more openly than at other times, the attitudes of other prominent American public figures toward Israel. One notable example is that of Jesse Helms, who served as a United States Senator from North Carolina during the 1980s, 1990s, and early 2000s. A convinced premillennialist, Helms, who as chair of the Senate's Foreign Affairs Committee labored to limit American financial support abroad, approved of the extensive financial support that the United States offered Israel. Helms's attitude was not unique. From the 1970s to the present, dozens of pro-Israel Christian organizations emerged in the United States and other countries. Besides mustering political support for Israel, their leaders have also lectured in churches, distributed material on Israel, and organized tours to the Holy Land. A number of such groups have also been engaged in evangelization efforts directed toward Jews. The years following the June 1967 war also saw an increase in the actual presence and activity of evangelical Christians in Israel. Tours of evangelical and Pietist groups to that country increased, as did the numbers of field-study seminars and of volunteers coming to kibbutzim. Evangelical Christians even established institutions of higher education in Israel, one of these being the Jerusalem University College set up by Douglas Young, an evangelical theologian with a pro-Zionist orientation.

One of the better-known Christian organizations in support of Israel is the International Christian Embassy in Jerusalem (ICEJ). Its story tells us a great deal about conservative Christian pro-Israel activity and about the relationship that has developed between the Christian evangelical and Pietist communities and Israeli society and government. In the 1970s, evangelical and Pietist activists in Jerusalem founded a local fellowship that aimed to muster support for Israel. The participants met weekly, prayed, sang, and discussed means to promote Christian support for Israel in order to counterbalance anti-Israel sentiments in the Christian world.[34] One of the founding leaders of the group, the Dutch minister Jan Willem van der Hoeven, suggested organizing large annual gatherings of Christian supporters of Israel from all over the world during Sukkoth (the Feast of Booths or Tabernacles), the Jewish fall harvest festival commemorating the temporary dwellings of the Israelites in the wilderness after the exodus. His theological rationale was that according to the Bible (Zech 14:15) Gentiles were also commanded to gather in Jerusalem during the festival. In 1979 the group launched its first yearly Tabernacles festival, a weeklong assembly of Christian supporters of Israel highlighted by a biblical meal on the shore of the Dead Sea and a march through the streets of Jerusalem.

In 1980, the Israeli parliament, the Knesset, passed the "Jerusalem Law," which declared the whole of the city of Jerusalem to be the capital of the State of Israel. In protest, almost all countries with embassies and consulates in Jerusalem moved their diplomatic staffs to Tel Aviv. This evacuation provided a dramatic point at which the Christian activists announced the creation of the International Christian Embassy as an act of support for Israel.[35] The Embassy chose as its logo two olive branches hovering over a globe with Jerusalem at its center. "This symbolizes the great day when Zechariah's prophecy will be fulfilled, and all nations will come up to Jerusalem to keep the Feast of Tabernacles during Messiah's reign on earth."[36] Israeli officials, including the mayor of Jerusalem, Teddy Kollek, noted the propaganda value of the Embassy's creation and welcomed the new organization. It made the point, they believed, that even though many

---

34. On the Christian world and Israel, see Paul Merkley, *Christian Attitudes towards the State of Israel* (Montreal: McGill University Press, 2001).

35. James McWhirter, *A World in a Country* (Jerusalem: B.S.B. International, 1983), 160–74.

36. Van der Hoeven, "If I Forget Thee O Jerusalem," 4.

countries had removed their embassies and consulates from Jerusalem because of Arab pressure, the Christian world backed Israel.

The Embassy has promoted support for Israel among conservative Protestants worldwide and collected funds for philanthropic programs in Israel. It seeks to represent all true Christians and has made efforts to open branches and gain supporters in as many countries as possible. In the United States, its branches are mainly situated in the Bible Belt, while in Europe, representatives of the Embassy can be found in traditionally Protestant nations. There are also volunteers for the Embassy in predominantly Catholic countries. In recent years, representatives have also worked for the Embassy's interests in Eastern Europe.[37] There are also representatives in Australia, New Zealand, South Africa, Zaire, and Nigeria, enhancing the international image of the Embassy. ICEJ has also received support from the growing number of Latin American evangelicals, thousands of whom participate in the annual tours of the Holy Land sponsored or initiated by the Embassy. There has also been an attempt to attract supporters in South Asia.

Embassies around the globe distribute ICEJ journals, brochures, leaflets, and CDs of "Davidic music" and sermons. Embassy representatives also collect money for the Embassy's philanthropic enterprises in Israel. Aware that many Jews are suspicious of Christian charitable enterprises, ICEJ often distributes its parcels through Israeli public agencies.[38] Along with the International Fellowship of Christians and Jews, the Embassy is one of the few Christian institutions to systematically donate money to Israeli enterprises. Most evangelical pro-Zionist groups have traditionally collected money intended for missionary work among the Jews.

During the 1980s–2000s, Jan Willem van der Hoeven, the Embassy's ideologue, emerged in the conservative Protestant camp as one of the better known spokespersons on Israel and its role in history.[39] Van der Hoeven

---

37. A typewritten list of ICEJ international representatives, dating to February 1992, includes representatives from Florida, Georgia, Mississippi, South Carolina, Texas, Maryland, California, and Wyoming.

38. On the various activities of the Embassy, see its brochure, "The Ministry of the International Christian Embassy Jerusalem" (Jerusalem: International Christian Embassy, 1992); Arlynn Nellhaus, "Go Tell It on the Mountain," *Jerusalem Post Magazine*, October 1992, 6–7.

39. On van der Hoeven's views on Israel, see his book, Jan van der Hoeven, *Babylon or Jerusalem* (Shippensburg, Pa.: Destiny Image, 1993).

shares the Christian premillennialist vision of Israel as a transitory but necessary vehicle on the messianic road. According to that view, the Jewish political entity will exist in rebellious unbelief until the arrival of Jesus. At the same time, its existence and security are a positive, even reassuring, development in the unfolding of history; it is therefore pertinent to protect Israel against forces that would undermine it. In his view, Palestinian organizations hostile to the Israeli project have been instruments of Satan, while Arabs who are true Christian believers support the Israeli cause.[40] Van der Hoeven's attitude toward the Jews has been ambivalent. He has expressed the firm belief that the Jews are the heirs of biblical Israel, God's chosen people, destined for a glorious future in the messianic age; but he also has harbored feelings of frustration and disappointment. He expressed bitterness, for example, that so many Israelis have been unwilling to support a more firm political agenda. In order to be accepted by the liberal West, he complained, they were willing to compromise their national aspirations and, in so doing, betray their purpose in God's plans for the end times. For him, "land for peace" is not a pragmatic political strategy aimed at enhancing the well-being of the region; rather, such a decision could impede the divine plan for human redemption. The Jews are not just another people who can make choices according to their political needs; they have a burden to carry, a duty and purpose in history. A second refusal to accept Jesus, or to prepare the ground for his arrival, would be even worse than the first, for the Jews would miss their second opportunity for redemption.

Arabs and pro-Arab Christian churches and leaders have resented the theology and agenda of groups like the International Christian Embassy.[41] The Israeli leadership, on the other hand, has welcomed its unexpected allies with open arms.

Israelis and Christian Supporters

Israeli leaders have not always comprehended the nature of the special attitudes of Christian Bible believers toward the new state and have

---

40. *Le Maan Tzion Lo Echeshe* (Jerusalem: International Christian Embassy, 1990), 13.

41. Regina Sharif, *Non-Jewish Judaism: Its Roots in Western History* (London: Zed, 1983); Stephen Sizer, *Christian Zionism: Road Map to Armaggedon* (Leicester: Intervarsity, 2004); Victoria Clark, *Allies for Armaggedon: the Rise of Christian Zionism* (New Haven: Yale University Press, 2007).

therefore overlooked elements in the Christian messianic theology and activity to which, in principle, they should have objected. Israeli officials could not tell the difference between its mainline Christian supporters, mostly during the 1940s to1960s, who showed sympathy for Israel on the basis of political or humanitarian considerations, and its conservative evangelical supporters, whose attitudes have been rooted in a biblical messianic faith.[42] They were unaware of the details of the Christian eschatological hopes and had never heard of such terms as "the great tribulation" or the "time of Jacob's trouble." Israel's first prime minister, David Ben-Gurion, is a case in point. Ben-Gurion believed that Christian supporters viewed the establishment of the State of Israel as the ultimate fulfillment of biblical prophecies rather than as a stepping stone toward the realization of such prophecies. He expressed his views in an address he wrote for the opening of an international pentecostal conference that convened in Israel. Israeli officials who sat at the opening session were puzzled by the coolness of the pentecostal reactions to the prime minister's speech.[43] They certainly were not aware that messianic hopes encouraged not only support for Zionism and for Israel but also aggressive missionary activity among the Jews.

A major feature of conservative Pietist and evangelical relations to the Jews has been their evangelism. Since the rise of the Pietist movement in central Europe at the turn of the eighteenth century and the evangelical movement in Britain at the turn of the nineteenth century, missions to the Jews have occupied an important place on the premillennialist Christian agenda and have come to characterize the messianic-oriented Christian interaction with the Jews even more than pro-Zionist activity. Its meaning for evangelicals and Pietists has gone far beyond attempts to capture Jewish souls. They have seen missionizing the Jews as taking part in the divine drama of salvation. Propagating Christianity among the Jews meant teaching the people of God how to read biblical passages properly and learn

---

42. A striking example of this failure to understand can be found in Michael Pragai's book *Faith and Fulfillment* (London: Valentine Mitchell, 1985). The author, who served as the head of the department for Christian churches and organizations in the Israeli Ministry of Foreign Affairs, demonstrated a lack of knowledge of the nature of the evangelical support of Zionism and of the differences between conservative and mainline/liberal churches.

43. Yona Malachy, *American Fundamentalism and Israel* (Jerusalem: Institute of Contemporary Jewry, 1978), 106–11.

about their role and purpose in history, as well as saving some of them from the turmoil of the great tribulation. When at the turn of the nineteenth century a strong evangelical premillennialist movement came into being, it gave rise to Zionist initiatives, as well as to a large and resourceful missionary movement. Throughout the nineteenth century, evangelicals established numerous missions to the Jews, operating all around the Jewish Diaspora.[44] Often, the same persons would be active on both fronts, promoting support for Zionism and evangelism of Jews at the same time.

The best-known of today's evangelical missions, Jews for Jesus, also works to promote pro-Zionist sentiments, calling its music band the "Liberated Wailing Wall."[45] The rise of Jews for Jesus took place in the same years that Messianic Judaism, another Christian-Zionist movement associated with the missionary movement, emerged. A movement of Jewish converts to evangelical Christianity, Messianic Jews see themselves as overcoming the historical differences between Judaism and Christianity and amalgamating the Christian faith with Jewish identity, symbols, and causes. Like evangelical Christians, Messianic Jews relate strongly to both the Hebrew and Greek Bibles; and while following Christian views that see the Old Testament as pointing toward the New Testament, they have also promoted the idea of the covenant relationship between God and Israel and the special status of the Jews as the chosen people. The Messianic Jewish ideology has strongly influenced the missionary movement, transforming its ideology and rhetoric. Missions to the Jews have emphasized since the 1970s that becoming Christian does not work to eradicate Jewish identity. On the contrary, it turns Jews into "complete Jews," true to the real goal and purpose of the Jewish people. From the 1970s to the present, more than four hundred messianic congregations were established in Israel, Britain, Argentina, South Africa, and other countries with substantial Jewish communities. Both messianic groups and missions to the Jews have as their goals increasing support in the Christian community for the premillennialist idea of the centrality of the Jews in God's plans for humanity, and also evangelizing the Jews. For institutions like the American Messianic Fellowship or the Friends of Israel, the two aims are inseparable.[46]

---

44. A. E. Thompson, *A Century of Jewish Missions* (Chicago: Fleming H. Revell, 1905).

45. Yaakov Ariel, "Counterculture and Missions: Jews for Jesus and the Vietnam Era Missionary Campaigns," *Religion and American Culture* 9 (1999): 233–57.

46. Interview with Reverend William Currie, former head of the American

Since the late 1970s, as the evangelical pro-Zionist influence on American political life has become more apparent, the Israeli government has taken measures to establish contact with evangelical Christians.[47] Israeli officials speak at evangelical conferences, and evangelists meet with Israeli leaders as part of their touring schedules in Israel. From the 1980s to the present, Israeli officials have relied on the International Christian Embassy as a vehicle to reach the Protestant Christian community, believing that it represents a large segment of Christianity.[48] Israeli leaders meet frequently with Embassy leaders and have granted the ICEJ permission to hold gatherings in the courtyard of the Knesset, as part of its Tabernacles celebrations.[49] In April 1990, the speaker of the Knesset presented the Embassy with the Quality of Life Award for its positive role in Israeli life. Ironically, many of the more enthusiastic allies of pro-Israel Christians are in the nationalist-religious wing of Israeli society. In 1988 the magazine *Nekuda* ("Settlement"), an organ of the Jewish settlements in Judea and Samaria, published a favorable article on the International Christian Embassy in Jerusalem entitled "Without Inhibitions: Christians Committed to Judea and Samaria." Emphasizing that the Embassy had no missionary intentions, *Nekuda* described the Embassy as a Christian pro-Israel group that, unlike many Jews, realized that the Bible authorized the Jews to settle their land.[50]

One example of the Israeli ignorance of the biblical-messianic nature of Christian interest in Zionism related to Israel is the attempt to combat missionary efforts, an activity in which Christian supporters of Israel have long been engaged. One of the Begin government's earliest acts of legislation, in the late 1970s, was intended to restrict missionary activity, not realizing that this activity was carried out by the same elements in Christianity with whom it was trying to establish a friendly relationship. When the proposed law was being debated, prior to the enactment

---

Messianic Fellowship, Jerusalem, September 1991. Currie had little appreciation for the Embassy.

47. "Israel Looks on U.S. Evangelical Christian as Potent Allies," *Washington Post*, March 23, 1981.

48. "Israel's Leaders Greet the Embassy," in *Prepare Ye the Way of the Lord* (Jerusalem: International Christian Embassy, 1991).

49. For a photograph of such a gathering, see Tzipora Luria, "Lelo Tasbichim: Notztim Mechuiavim LeYesha," *Nekuda* 128 (1989): 31.

50. Ibid., 30–34.

of the legislation in 1978, many evangelists were worried that the law might bring their activity to an end. They were relieved when they saw the wording of the law, which forbids the offering of economic incentives in exchange for conversion, since it clearly did not place restrictions on the sort of work they did. Contrary to Jewish myths, missionaries were not "buying" converts, and at any rate, the Israeli government was reluctant to enforce the law.[51]

In the 1990s antimissionary sentiments were again running high, and a number of Orthodox and non-Orthodox members of the Knesset came out with initiatives to outlaw missionary activity.[52] In 1996, an initial, first-round proposal to curtail missionary activity passed in the Knesset. But then the complex and paradoxical nature of the relationship between the evangelical community and Israeli society became unprecedentedly clear. Missionaries operating in Israel called upon their supporters around the globe to raise their voices against the impeding law. One of their appeals reads:

> We call upon the international Christian community to join us in our opposition to this law as Christian believers in the God of Israel and in Jesus the Messiah and Savior of the world, we have a special respect and appreciation for the Jewish people and the nation of Israel. We seek and pray for the welfare of all of God's people in the land. We view with grave concern the erosion of Israel's democratic freedom by this proposed law.[53]

Israeli embassies and consulates in countries with evangelical populations were virtually flooded with letters of protest against the law. Many wrote directly to the prime minister in Jerusalem. The standard letters emphasized that they were written by friends of Israel who wished the country well and were writing to warn the government that the passing of such a law would turn its current supporters against it. Prime Minister Benjamin Netanyahu, who at first offhandedly supported the bill, changed his mind and promised evangelical activists he would oppose it.[54] The aborted

---

51. Yaakov Ariel, *Evangelizing the Chosen People: Missions to the Jews in America 1880–2000* (Chapel Hill: University of North Carolina Press, 2000), 277–78.

52. Daniel Ben Simon, "Doing Something for Judaism," *Haaretz*, December 18, 1997, English Edition.

53. E.g., a letter circulated through the internet by Noam Hendren, Baruch Maoz, and Marvin Dramer, March 1997.

54. Ibid.

attempts at curtailing missionary activity in Israel highlighted the paradoxical nature of the relation of Bible-believing evangelical Christians toward Jews: the evangelization of a people they see as chosen and whose country they strongly support. It also points to the nature of Israeli *real politik*.

Biblical Prophecies and the Building of the Temple

One of the outcomes of the June 1967 war for Christians expecting the second coming of Jesus has been the Israeli takeover of the Temple Mount on which the temple could be rebuilt. The prospect of rebuilding the temple excited premillennialist Christians, often considering the building project as the one event standing between this era and the next.[55] A striking demonstration of the prominence of the temple in Christian messianic thought can be found in Hal Lindsey's *The Late Great Planet Earth*, an evangelical Christian bestseller of the 1970s. Lindsey was strongly impressed by the June 1967 war and its consequences, and he placed Israel at the center of the eschatological drama.[56] For him, the rebuilding of the temple and the rise to power of the antichrist were major components of the great tribulation, without which the coming of the Messiah could not take place. There remained, however, a number of obstacles to the advancement of this stage in the prophetic timetable. Many Israelis understood the outcome of what they have come to call the Six Day War in messianic terms, but most of them did not wish to rebuild the temple.[57] There was the unavoidable reality that the Temple Mount was a Muslim site, complete with magnificent mosques and administered by Muslims. The Israeli Minister of Defense at the time, Moshe Dayan, designed a policy that insisted on maintaining the status quo on the Temple Mount as well as in other Muslim and Christian sites. In addition, a number of rabbis declared that Jews are forbidden to enter the Temple Mount. Most rabbinical authorities have viewed the Temple Mount as being as sacred as it was when the temple was standing.[58]

---

55. Raymond L. Cox, "Time for the Temple?" *Eternity* 19 (1968): 17–18; Malcolm Couch, "When Will the Jews Rebuild the Temple?" *Moody Monthly* 74 (1973): 34–35, 86.

56. Lindsey, *The Late Great Planet Earth*, 32–47.

57. Gideon Aran, "From Religious Zionism to Zionist Religion: the Roots of Gush Emunim," *Studies in Contemporary Jewry* l 2 (1986): 118.

58. See *m. Kelim* 1:8. See also "Har HaBayit" [Temple Mount], *HaEncyclopedia HaTalmudit* 10:575–92.

All Jews are required to purify themselves with the ashes of a red heifer before entering the Mount, and there are no red heifers to be found (Num 19). Rabbis also feared that Jews might walk into restricted sacred space, such as the holy of holies, which ordinary Jews and even ordinary priests are not allowed to enter.[59]

An Australian premillennialist, Dennis Michael Rohan, decided to change the existing reality. After spending some time as a volunteer in an Israeli kibbutz, Rohan visited Jerusalem in July 1969 and there, convinced that God had designated him for that task, planned and executed the burning of the El-Aqsa Mosque on the Temple Mount in an attempt to secure the necessary ground for the building of the temple.[60] The mosque was damaged and Arabs in Jerusalem rioted. Rohan was arrested, put to trial, found insane, and sent to Australia to spend the rest of his life in an asylum.[61] Most premillennialist Christians have not taken the law into their own hands but have sought legal and peaceful means to advance their agenda. A number of Christian premillennialist groups and individuals in the 1970s to the present have promoted the building of the Jewish shrine through a variety of activities, most of them centered on encouraging Jews to prepare for the building of the temple.[62] Such Jews, who are studying temple rituals, manufacturing utensils to be used for sacrificial purposes according to biblical or talmudic texts, or trying to breed a new brand of heifers, serve to sustain the Christian messianic imagination, serving as "signs of the time," indications that the current era is ending and the apocalyptic events of the end times are near.[63]

Many Christian Bible-believers have embraced the theory that the location of the temple was between the two major mosques, El-Aqsa and the Dome of the Rock. The temple, they have concluded, could there-

---

59. Ehud Sprinzak, *The Ascendance of Israel's Radical Right* (New York: Oxford University Press, 1991), 279–88.

60. I am indebted to Avinoam Brog for sharing with me information and impressions on Rohan's stay in the kibbutz and his motive for burning the mosque.

61. See Jerusalem District Court Archive, Criminal File 69/173.

62. On the Jewish groups aiming at building the temple, see Ehud Sprinzak, *The Ascendance of Israel's Radical Right* (New York: Oxford University Press, 1991), 264–69, 279–88.

63. Grant R. Jeffrey, *Armageddon: Appointment with Destiny* (Toronto: Frontier Research Publications, 1988), 108–50. For example, Don Stewart and Chuck Missler, *The Coming Temple: Center Stage for the Final Countdown* (Orange, Calif.: Dart, 1991), 157–70.

fore be rebuilt without destroying the existing mosques, thus providing a "peaceful solution" to the dilemma of how to build the temple at a site that is holy to the Muslims.[64] These Christian proponents of building the temple have not limited their efforts to discovering the exact site of the temple. Some have searched for the lost ark, a quest that inspired a number of novels and a movie based in part on a real life figure.[65] Some evangelical Christians have also searched for the ashes of the red heifer, while others have supported attempts to breed red heifers.[66] A new interest has arisen in Christian conservative circles in the temple building, its interior plan, and its sacrificial works, as well as in the priestly garments and utensils.[67] The rebuilt temple has also played an important role in novels and fictions. The most popular has been the series *Left Behind*, which was published in the late 1990s and early 2000s and has sold tens of millions of copies. The novels take place in the aftermath of the rapture, describing the struggles of those left behind, not least of them the rise to power of the antichrist, one of whose "achievements" is orchestrating the removal of the mosques to New Babylon.[68]

Among the Israeli groups that have established a working relationship with evangelical Christians has been the Temple Mount and Land of

---

64. See Yisrayl Hawkins, *A Peaceful Solution to Building the Next Temple in Yerusalem* (Abilene: House of Yahweh, 1989).

65. On the premillennialist fascination with the lost ark, see Doug Wead, David Lewis, and Hal Donaldson, *Where Is the Lost Ark?* (Minneapolis: Bethany House, 1982); Don Stewart and Chuck Missler, *In Search of the Lost Ark* (Orange, Calif.: Dart, 1991).

66. Lawrence Wright, "Forcing the End," *The New Yorker* 74 (1998); Peter Ephross, "Approaching the Millennium: Mississippi Preacher Devotes Life to Birthing Red Heifer in Israel," *Jewish Telegraph Agency*, September 2, 1999. Online: http://www.jta.org/1999/09/02/life-religion/features/approaching-the-millennium-mississippi-preacher-devotes-life-to-birthing-red-heifer-in-israel.

67. For example, Charles W. Slemming, *These Are the Garments: A Study of the Garments of the High Priest of Israel* (Fort Washington, Pa.: Christian Literature Crusade, 1974); Wead, Lewis, and Donaldson, *Where is the Lost Ark?*; Stewart and Missler, *In Search of the Lost Ark*; Thomas Ice and Randall Price, *Ready to Rebuild* (Eugene, Oreg.: Harvest House, 1992).

68. Tim LaHaye and Jerry B. Jenkins, *Left Behind* (Wheaton, Ill.: Tyndale House, 1995). The series has sold more than twenty million copies. On the temple, see, e.g., LaHaye and Jenkins, *Left Behind*, 415; LaHaye and Jenkins, *Nicolae: The Rise of Antichrist* (Wheaton, Ill.: Tyndale House, 1997), 369; LaHaye and Jenkins, *Tribulation Force* (Wheaton, Ill.: Tyndale House, 1996), 208, 277.

Israel Faithful. Pat Robertson, the renowned leader of the 700 Club and a one-time presidential hopeful, offered his support and hospitality to Gershon Solomon, the founder of the group. In August 1991, the 700 Club aired an interview with Solomon. Robertson described Solomon's group as struggling to gain the rightful Jewish place on the Temple Mount. "We will never have peace," Robertson declared, "until the Mount of the House of the Lord is restored."[69] Solomon, for his part, described his mission as embodying the promise for a universal redemption of humanity. "It's not just a struggle for the Temple Mount, it's a struggle for the ... redemption of the world," he declared.[70] The evangelical-Jewish relationship relates to other religious groups as well. Radical conservative evangelicals, such as Hal Lindsey or Jan-Willem van der Hoeven, take a negative attitude toward Islam and refuse to accept the sovereignty of Muslims on the Temple Mount.

The negotiations between the Israelis and the Palestinians over a peace agreement have caused alarm among some premillennialist Christians,[71] but for most Christians expecting the second coming of Jesus, their hopes for the rebuilding of the temple have remained strong.[72] One cannot tell what would happen if, from a radical evangelical perspective, Israel works against God's will and the unfolding of prophecy by giving up its official control of the Temple Mount. Some fear that such an act might stir Jewish and Christian extremists to take steps that would "secure" the Jewish and Christian presence on the mountain.

Conclusion

Evangelical pro-Zionist and pro-Israel activity has been an extraordinary development in the history of relationships between religious communities. To my knowledge, in no other case have members of one religious community considered another religious community to hold a crucial role in God's plans for human redemption and to be God's first nation. Likewise, it is unique that Christians view a foreign country as holy and as the ground zero of apocalyptic and messianic times without claiming

---

69. Robert I. Friedman, *Zealots for Zion* (New York: Random House, 1992), 144.
70. Friedman, *Zealots for Zion*, 144–45.
71. See articles in the *Middle East Intelligence Digest*, a publication of the International Christian Embassy in Jerusalem in the 1990s.
72. For example, the series *Left Behind*.

it as their own. The unique nature of such attitudes is highlighted when one bears in mind that for most of its history the major trends in Christianity have seen Judaism as replaced by the church. The explanation of the almost incredible evangelical and Pietist relationship lies, to a large degree, in the nature of conservative, premillennialist, evangelical reading of Christian Scriptures; in the centrality of the Hebrew Bible in addition to the New Testament; in the more literal reading of sacred texts; and in meshing their interpretation of the Bible with a premillennialist faith. Such Bible-believing Christians have perceived the rebuilding of the Jewish state and the temple by the Jews as necessary stages toward the realization of the messianic age. At the same time there has been a dissonance between their biblical and theological perceptions of the role of the Jews in the unfolding of prophecy and the cultural perceptions of the Jews held by many of them.

The phenomenon of Christians supporting the Israeli cause on behalf of their faith is therefore embodied with paradoxes. Evangelical attitudes toward Israel and Israeli culture have been characterized by two conflicting sentiments, one supportive and appreciative, and the other critical and patronizing. In general, evangelical opinions of the Jews have improved considerably in the last generation, due to the larger interaction between the two groups and extensive evangelical involvement with Israel.[73] While, in principle, evangelicals do not engage in interfaith dialogue, evangelical and Jewish activists have met for conversations and exchanged opinions.[74]

In no other realm has the paradoxical nature of the relation of evangelical Bible-believers to Jews demonstrated itself as in the Christian attempts to help traditionalist Jews rebuild the temple. Such Christians have formed historically unprecedented friendships and alliances with Jews that would have been difficult to imagine at other times and places. The unique relationship that has developed between Jews and Christians over the building of a Jewish state in Palestine and also the hopes that such Christians have placed on Jews preparing the ground for the arrival of the Messiah have brought about scenes that are almost surreal, including Christians marveling at and receiving reassurance for their messianic faith

---

73. Charles Y. Glock and Rodney Stark, *Christian Beliefs and Anti-Semitism* (New York: Harper Torchbooks, 1966); L. Ianniello, Anti-Defamation League press release, January 8, 1986.

74. Byron Johnson and Nancy Isserman, eds., *Uneasy Allies: Evangelical and Jewish Relations* (Lanham, Md.: Lexington Books, 2007).

from Orthodox Jews who are taking steps toward the reinstatement of the sacrificial system.

In the last analysis, Christian interest in the Jewish resettlement of Palestine and support for the State of Israel have derived first and foremost from their messianic hope and their mode of interpretation of biblical passages. One must conclude that their support of the Israeli cause represents an attempt to promote their own agenda. Pro-Israel sentiments derive from the perceived function of a Jewish commonwealth in biblical prophecies and the advancement of history toward the arrival of the Lord. Christians advocating and acting on such views see themselves as supporting and working toward a great cause: the unfolding of prophecies and the establishment of the kingdom of God on earth.

# PART 2
THE BIBLE, AMERICA'S FOUNDING ERA, AND AMERICAN IDENTITY

Does America Have a Biblical Heritage?

John Fea

What do we mean when we say that America has a "biblical heritage?" Is the question a historically valid one? What is the relationship between the Bible and the vision of the United States set forth by the founding fathers? What role has the Bible played in shaping American institutions, movements, and the lives of the men and women who have led them? While a sister question, "Was America founded as a Christian Nation?," has been thoroughly debated through a host of books, articles, blog posts, and media outlets, rarely do we hear any discussion—at least in the so-called culture wars—about the influence of the Bible on the American founding or on American history more broadly.[1]

This, of course, does not mean that Americans are not interested in the question. Consider, for example, the Pennsylvania House of Representatives. In 2012 it passed a resolution declaring that year the "Year of the Bible" in the Commonwealth. The resolution affirmed the Bible's "formative influence" over the nation and the state. Borrowing much of its language from Ronald Reagan's 1983 national "Year of the Bible" resolution, it declared that "biblical teachings inspired the concepts of civil government that are contained in our Declaration of Independence and the Constitution of the United States." It reminded the people of the Commonwealth that "this nation now faces great challenges that will test it as it has never been tested before; and whereas renewing our knowledge of and faith in God through holy scripture can strengthen us as a nation and a people."[2]

---

1. For an introduction to the topic of whether or not the United States was founded as a Christian nation, see John Fea, *Was America Founded as a Christian Nation? A Historical Introduction* (Louisville: Westminster John Knox, 2011).

2. Commonwealth of Pennsylvania, *Legislative Journal*, 196th Gen. Assemb., Janu-

Or consider the work of Christian nationalist writer David Barton. When he is not claiming that Thomas Jefferson was an orthodox Christian or an abolitionist at heart, Barton is convincing tens of thousands of Americans, through his wildly popular books, videos, radio shows, and appearances on the Glenn Beck radio program that America indeed has a biblical heritage. Barton, for example, believes that virtually everything in the United States Constitution is based directly upon a biblical concept. For example, the framers' idea for three branches of government comes directly from Isa 33:22 where the prophet proclaims: "The LORD is our judge. The LORD is our lawgiver. The LORD is our King." Article II, Section 1, which discuss the qualifications for the office of the presidency, comes from Deut 17:15: "Thou shalt in any wise set him king over thee, whom the LORD thy God shall choose: one from among they brethren shalt thus set king over thee, thou mayest not set a stranger over thee, which is not thy brother." And who knew that tax-exempt status for clergy came directly from Ezra 7:24: "We certify you, that touching any of the priests and Levites, singers, porters, Nethinims, or ministers of this house of God, it shall not be lawful to impose toll, tribute or custom upon them"? Scholars ensconced safely in their ivory towers might dismiss Barton's ideas and balk at his influence, but anyone who spends time at PTA meetings, evangelical megachurches, or local gatherings of the Republican Party or Tea Party will find his views about the Bible, the founding, and the Christian roots of America alive and well.[3] Indeed, in 2005 *Time* magazine named him one of the twenty-five most influential evangelicals in America.[4]

Or consider an organization called American Vision that is very popular with many conservative evangelicals. Led by popular radio commentator and author Gary DeMar, American Vision sets out to equip "Christians to apply the Bible to every aspect of life in order to restore America to her Biblical foundation."[5] The future of America will again be

---

ary 24, 2012, 87. Online at http://www.legis.state.pa.us/WU01/LI/HJ/2012/0/20120124.pdf#page=15.

3. Barton's two most influential books are *The Jefferson Lies: Exposing the Myths You've Always Believed About Thomas Jefferson* (Nashville: Thomas Nelson, 2012) and *Original Intent: The Courts, The Constitution, and Religion* (Aledo, Tex.: WallBuilders, 2008).

4. David Van Biema et al, "The 25 Most Influential Evangelicals in America," *Time*, February 7, 2005, 34–45.

5. Mission statement taken from The American Vision's official Facebook page: https://www.facebook.com/americanvision.

a "city on a hill" drawing all nations to the Lord Jesus Christ and teaching them to subdue the earth for the advancement of his kingdom. Much of the mission of American Vision has been informed by the late Christian Reconstructionist Rousas J. Rushdoony, a Calvinist philosopher who had a profound influence on the early leaders of the Christian Right and the Christian homeschool movement and who advocated that Old Testament law should be applied to modern society.

Indeed, the idea that America has a biblical heritage has many defenders, but in our current religious, cultural, and political climate it appears that the only people who are interested in the question are those who ally themselves with the Christian Right. Those who sing the praises of America's biblical "heritage" today are really talking more about the present than the past. The purpose of heritage, writes historian David Lowenthal, is to "domesticate the past" so that it can be enlisted "for present causes." It is a way of approaching the past that is fundamentally different than the discipline of history. History explores and explains the past in all its fullness and complexity. Heritage calls attention to the past to make a political point. Since the purpose of heritage is to cultivate a sense of collective or national identity, it is rarely concerned with nuance, paradox, or complexity. As Lowenthal writes, devotion to heritage is a "spiritual calling"—it answers needs for ritual devotion.[6]

Of course any serious student of American history cannot ignore the powerful role that the Bible has played in the collective life of the nation, but we should also be wary about approaching that history with a celebratory mindset informed by the heritage crusade. For example, John Winthrop, invoking Matt 5:14, told the colonists of Massachusetts Bay that their new settlement would be a "city upon a hill," a shining model of what a society might look like if it were built on the teachings of Scripture. Of course, the Bible was also used to persecute, and in a few cases even execute, anyone in the city on a hill who was unwilling to conform to Puritan orthodoxy. The Bible, as we will see, was used to both support and condemn the American Revolution. It was used to promote the abolitionism of slavery and the moral defense of slavery. In his second inaugural address, a speech filled with biblical illusions and theological insight, Abraham Lincoln reminded his hearers on that wet Washington morning

---

6. David Lowenthal, *The Heritage Crusade and the Spoils of History* (New York: Viking, 1997), 1.

that "both read the same Bible and pray to the same God, and each invokes His aid against the other." The Bible was employed on behalf of women's rights and civil rights, but it was also used as a basis for Jim Crow laws and the harsh treatment of Native American populations. When American Protestantism and American democracy came together in the early nineteenth century, the result was a free-wheeling approach to biblical interpretation that led to some of America's brightest moments and some of its darkest moments.

My task in this essay is to briefly explore the role the Bible played in the founding of the United States, particularly among the Protestant clergymen who may have had the most influence in spreading revolutionary ideas.[7] I have argued before that it is difficult to make the case that the United States was founded as a Christian nation; but what about a biblical nation?[8] What role did the Bible play in the founding era—the years leading up to the American Revolution, the Revolution itself, and the Revolution's immediate aftermath? My goal is to cut through the political rhetoric of the Christian heritage crusaders and try to make some historical sense of the complicated ways in which eighteenth-century patriots, founders, and loyalists utilized the Bible in the midst of the imperial crisis with England.

Political scientist Donald Lutz, in a massive study of the authors most cited by the founding fathers, concluded that they cited the Bible more than any other source during the 1770s and 1780s.[9] This is significant, for it shows how important the Bible was to the revolutionary generation. For example, Thomas Paine, in his popular 1776 tract *Common Sense*, a work that convinced many colonists to support the cause of independence, used the Bible extensively to argue against monarchial rule. Paine was no friend of Christian orthodoxy, but he knew his audience well and communicated to them in a language that they could understand.[10] One would be hard-pressed to find a founding father—Washington, Adams, Jefferson, Madi-

---

7. James P. Byrd, *Sacred Scripture, Sacred War: The Bible and the American Revolution* (New York: Oxford University Press, 2013).

8. Fea, *Was America Founded*.

9. Donald S. Lutz, "The Relative Influence of European Writers on Late-Eighteenth-Century American Political Thought," *American Political Science Review* 78 (1984): 189–97, esp. 190.

10. Thomas Paine, *Common Sense* (Lancaster, Penn: Francis Bailey, 1776). Online: http://www.ushistory.org/paine/commonsense/.

son, Franklin, Witherspoon, Henry, Jay—who did not believe a knowledge of the moral teachings of the Bible, especially the moral teachings of Jesus of Nazareth, could contribute to the building of a virtuous American Republic.[11] Of course, such statistics about the use of the Bible in the writings of the founding fathers must be considered carefully. Lutz concluded that the founders cited from the combined wisdom of Enlightenment, Whig, and classical authors more than twice as much as they cited the Bible. And though the founders cited the Bible more than any other source during the 1770s and 1780s, when one compares the number of citations to Enlightenment, Whig, and classical authors during these decades, the number exceeds that of the Bible.[12]

Another way of examining the use of the Bible in the revolutionary-era is to see how the Old and New Testaments were used by clergy. Historian Gordon S. Wood has said that "it was the clergy who made the Revolution meaningful for most common people," because "for every gentleman who read a scholarly pamphlet and delved into Whig and ancient history for an explanation of events, there were dozens of ordinary people who read the Bible and looked to their ministers for an interpretation of what the Revolution meant."[13] Historian James P. Byrd has analyzed over seventeen thousand biblical citations in over five hundred religious sources (mostly sermons) from the period and found that ministers used the Bible to justify and oppose war, articulate the political idea of republicanism, support and oppose independence, and rail against the Stamp Act, Boston Massacre, and Coercive Acts. His study reveals that between 1763 and 1800 eight biblical verses were cited more than any other. They were Rom 13 (Paul on obedience to civil rulers), Exod 14–15 (parting of the Red Sea), Gal 5 (Paul's teaching on freedom in Christ), Judg 4–5 (the "Curse of Meroz"), 1 Pet 2 ("fear God and honor the King"), 1 Kgs 12 (the division of David's kingdom), Ps 124 (David's thanksgiving prayer for Israel's salvation), and Matt 5 (Jesus's Sermon on the Mount).[14]

Indeed, colonial clergy were consumed with the political issues of the day. It was quite common for ministers to blend Whig politics with biblical

---

11. Fea, *Was America Founded*, 171–242.
12. Lutz, "The Relative Influence of European Writers," 190.
13. Gordon S. Wood, "Religion and the American Revolution," in *New Directions in American Religious History* (ed. Harry S. Stout and D. G. Hart; New York: Oxford University Press, 1997), 175, cited in Byrd, *Sacred Scripture, Sacred War*, 173.
14. Byrd, *Sacred Scripture, Sacred War*, 170.

themes. In 1773 Baptist clergyman John Allen, preaching to the Second Baptist Church in Boston, fashioned himself as a modern-day Micah, the Old Testament prophet who challenged the tyrannical reign of King Ahaz of Judah. Referring to 2 Chr 28, Allen showed that when Ahaz "did not that which was right in the sight of the LORD" (v. 1),[15] Ahaz's failure to conform to the moral standards that God required of all monarchs prompted Micah to stand up for the "liberties and happiness of the people above the authority of the King." At one point in the sermon, Allen even described Micah as a "son of liberty." Based on this interpretation of 2 Chronicles and other episodes in Israel's history, Allen concluded that God had indeed established monarchs to rule over Israel, but such kings—including David, Saul, and Solomon—were "made for the people, and the people for them." Allen did not hesitate to make the comparison between this view of the Old Testament monarchy and the reign of George III in England. By unfairly taxing the people of the colonies and taking away their liberties, George III was departing from the "royal standard" that God had placed on all kings through history. With such a view of monarchy affirmed, Allen concluded his sermon with a healthy dose of Whig politics: "The Parliament of England cannot justly make any laws to oppress, or defend the Americans, for they are not the representatives of America, and therefore they have no legislative power either for them or against them."[16] This was a bold, but common interpretive leap. Allen moved from the sins of Ahaz, to a lesson on a king's responsibility to serve the people, to a political plea for "no taxation without representation."

In a 1776 sermon on the occasion of his appointment as a chaplain to a New Jersey militia, Enoch Green, the minister of the Deerfield Presbyterian Church, grounded his understanding of colonial rebellion in the history of British liberties, arguing that the "king derives his power from the people." He continued with a history lesson on the English Civil War and the Puritan resistance to Charles I: "Little better than a century ago," he preached, the people "resisted and opposed a Tyrant, King Charles ... and they took ... their rights and vanquished the Tyrant." George III's newfound "Tory" sentiments prompted Green to encourage his listeners to begin making gunpowder in preparation for war. The language Green

---

15. Unless otherwise noted, all biblical translations follow the KJV.

16. John Allen, "An Oration on the Beauties of Liberty" (1773), in *Political Sermons of the American Founding Era, 1730–1805* (ed. Ellis Sandoz; Indianapolis: Liberty Fund, 1991), 315–18, 320–24.

employed in this sermon was similar to a message on tyranny and liberty he had preached at Deerfield six years earlier. In this sermon Green noted, "Because we were enslaved" and had become "Slaves to Sin—to ye Tyrant Satan ... we are all fond of Liberty." He added, "as long as we are out of Christ, we are enslaved to ye worst kind of Bondage, enthralled by ye Tyrant of Hell." By the time of the American Revolution, Green's theological and biblical understanding of tyranny and liberty had taken on a new political meaning. The enslaver and tyrant was no longer Satan but George III and his army. Liberty was no longer the freedom from sin and the right to enjoy God's presence forever in heaven, but the individual rights secured to all the people. The champion of liberty was not Christ but the New Jersey militia, for which Green would serve as chaplain.[17]

Many clergy were more explicit in their use of the Bible to justify rebellion against England. Two such sermons are worth treating in some depth. The first, Abraham Keteltas's "God Arising and Pleading His People's Cause," was preached in 1777 to Dutch and Huguenot Christians in Jamaica, New York. Based on Ps 74:22 ("Arise, O God, plead thine own cause"), Keteltas's sermon is a classic example of the way ministers made the Bible conform to Whig ideas. Keteltas began by reminding his hearers that God demands righteousness of his people. God requires Christians to love, worship, and please him and to obey his "will and commandments." Christians are to show their love for God by leading lives of benevolence, justice, charity, integrity, truth, and kindness. They are to love their neighbors and hate sin. A society that practices this kind of righteousness will always be pleasing to God. Keteltas assumed that colonial America was this kind of Christian society.

Keteltas affirmed that "the righteous" would always have God's protection. "When the true believer is injured, oppressed, persecuted, plundered, imprisoned, tormented, and murdered," he argued, God will "look upon their cause as his own." God views injuries and threats to God's righteous followers as if they were done to him. This is why, for example, God punished Nebuchadnezzar, the Babylonian king who persecuted God's righteous people. He concluded that God has proven throughout biblical history to intercede "in behalf of his elect." Jesus is "our merciful High Priest"

---

17. Enoch Green, "Upon His Appointment as Chaplain of the New Jersey Militia," sermon, 1776, Firestone Library, Dept. of Rare Books and Special Collections, Princeton University; Green, "Titus 2:14," sermon, Presbyterian Historical Society, Philadelphia.

and will always make intercession on behalf of the righteous who call to him for aid.

Based on this biblical and theological evidence, Keteltas asserted that "the cause of this American continent, against the measure of cruel, bloody, and vindictive ministry, is the cause of God." If the colonies were indeed God's "elect" people, as Keteltas believed, then any such war carried out against them must be "unjust and unwarrantable." His conclusion was a powerful one:

> Be therefore of good courage, it is a glorious cause. It is the cause of truth, against error and falsehood; the cause of righteousness against the oppressor; the cause of pure and undefiled religion, against bigotry, superstition, and human inventions. It is the cause of the reformation, against popery; of liberty, against arbitrary power, of benevolence, against barbarity, and of virtue against vice. It is the cause of justice and integrity, against bribery, venality, and corruption. In short, it is the cause of heaven against hell—of the kind of Parent of the universe, against the prince of darkness, and destroyer of the human race.

If this was not enough to convince his hearers, Keteltas added that the cause of the American Revolution was the cause "for which the Son of God came down from his celestial throne, and expired on a cross."[18] There was little difference between the gospel and the resistance to English tyranny or between the church and the colonies.

The second sermon worth discussing at length is Samuel Sherwood's "The Church's Flight into the Wilderness: An Address on the Times." Sherwood, the Congregational minister in Weston, Connecticut, blended millennial themes from the book of Revelation with contemporary political ideas. His sermon was based on Rev 12:14–17, the story of a woman who, with the help of eagle's wings, flies into the wilderness to find protection from an evil serpent (dragon). When the serpent cannot drown the woman with the flood pouring from its mouth, it decides instead to make war on the woman's "seed" who "keep the commandment of God, and have the testimony of Jesus Christ." Like most commentators on the book of Revelation—past and present—Sherwood interpreted this story as a metaphor. The serpent is an agent of Satan who from the beginning of time has

---

18. Abraham Keteltas, "God Arising and Pleading His People's Cause" (1777), in Sandoz, *Political Sermons*, 584–99, 603.

used his "subtlety and malice to defeat the purposes of divine grace, and to destroy Christ's kingdom on earth." But for Sherwood this evil dragon is a very specific manifestation of Satan's minions: "Among all his crafty and subtle interventions, *popery*, which exalts the principal leaders and abettors of it ... seems most cunningly devised, and best adapted to answer his purpose; and has proved the most formidable engine of terror and cruelty to the true members of Christ's church."[19]

What exactly did Sherwood mean when he equated the dragon of Rev 12 with "popery?" Ever since the Reformation, Protestants have connected the evil forces of the book of Revelation with the leader of the Roman Catholic Church. It was especially common for Protestant Bible commentators to declare that the pope was the "great whore of Babylon" from Rev 17. As Protestantism grew, especially in the English-speaking world, it became convenient for clergy to define themselves politically and religiously against the so-called papists who were loyal to Rome. By the eighteenth century, Protestant nations such as England saw themselves as "free" nations. Religiously, they could read the Bible and interpret it as they saw fit without any interferences from popes, bishops, or priests. They quickly connected this kind of religious liberty with the civil rights they enjoyed as British subjects and, as we have seen, compared the freedom of England to the religious and political tyranny of Catholic France.

Sherwood expanded this definition of "popery" beyond the Catholic Church to include any government or power that threatens civil and religious freedom:

> This popish mysterious leaven of iniquity and absurdity ... has not been confined to the boundaries of the Roman empire, nor strictly to the territory of the Pope's usurped authority and jurisdiction, but has spread in a greater or less degree, among almost all the nations of the earth; especially amongst the chief rulers, the princes and noblemen thereof.[20]

In other words, "popery" was synonymous with religious and political tyranny. It was not merely confined to France, but could also be applied to some of the seventeenth-century Stuart monarchs (Charles I and James II)

---

19. Samuel Sherwood, *The Church's Flight into the Wilderness: An Address on the Times* (New York: Loudon, 1776), 36, 9, 10.

20. Sherwood, *Church's Flight*, 10–11.

who threatened the religious liberties of England. Popery could be found anywhere that a "corrupt system of tyranny and oppression" was in place.

Such a broad definition of "popery" allowed Sherwood to apply the lessons of Rev 12 to the cause of the American Revolution: "I am of the opinion that the Church of Christ in every age, may find something in this book applicable to her case and circumstances; and all such passages that are so, may lawfully be applied and improved by us accordingly." Sherwood was prepared to put an American spin on Rev 12. The woman, whom Sherwood now identified as the "Church of Christ," fled to a "wilderness," which he now identified as the English American colonies. Here the woman would be nourished by God in the "quiet enjoyment of her liberties and privileges, civil and religious." But the serpent, or Parliament, was threatening. In a strange blend of political vocabulary and biblical interpretation, Sherwood described the "despotism," "arbitrary power," "dominion," "tyranny," and "corruption" that this English "serpent" was enforcing on the woman in the wilderness. The woman was representative of some combination of the "Church of Christ" and the English colonies as a whole. Sherwood's conclusion brought it all home:

> Liberty has been planted here; and the more it is attacked, the more it grows and flourishes. The time is coming and hastening on, when Babylon the great shall fall to rise no more, when all wicked tyrants and oppressors shall be destroyed forever. These violent attacks upon the woman in the wilderness, may possibly be some of the last efforts, and dying struggles of the man of sin. These commotions and convulsions in the British empire, may be leading to the fulfillment of such prophecies as relate to his downfall and overthrow, and to the future glory and prosperity of Christ's church. It will soon be said and acknowledged, that the kingdoms of this world, are become the kingdoms of our Lord, and of his Christ. The vials of God's wrath begin to be poured out on his enemies and adversaries; and there is falling on them a noisome and grievous sore.[21]

In writing about the use of the Bible in Revolutionary America, historian Mark Noll has suggested, "To be sure, patriotic ministers often applied biblical texts to support their cause. But now, after the passage of time, these efforts look more like comical propaganda than serious bibli-

---

21. Sherwood, *Church's Flight*, 18, 25, 49.

cal exposition."[22] Many clergy took great liberties with biblical passages in order to make them fit with the dominant political idea of the day.

Today some of the most ardent defenders of the notion that America has a "biblical heritage" or was "founded as a Christian nation" are conservative evangelicals and fundamentalists who claim to interpret the Bible at face value, without relying too heavily on metaphor. This is ironic, because the closest thing one might find to a biblical literalist during the time of the American Revolution was a Loyalist, a minister who used the Bible to oppose the cause of liberty. As Byrd has shown, it was Rom 13:1–7 and 1 Pet 2:13–17 that drew the most discussion and debate among the clergy during this era.

When taken at face value, these passages suggest that all rulers are "ordained by God" and are worthy of "honour." First Peter 2:13–17 exhorts believers to "fear God," "honour the king," and "submit yourselves to every ordinance of man for the Lord's sake." Romans 13 states clearly that one who resists such authority will receive "damnation." These passages also require Christians to pay their taxes ("tribute"). When taken literally, they seem to be teaching complete submission to government authorities with no exceptions or caveats.

This is exactly the way in which many Loyalists, mostly Anglican ministers, interpreted the meaning of these passages of Scripture. Jonathan Boucher no doubt had Rom 13 in mind when he wrote, "to resist and to rebel against a lawful government, is to oppose *the ordinance of God*, and to injure or destroy institutions most essential to human happiness."[23] New York Anglican Samuel Seabury thought his sermon on 1 Pet 2:17 was necessary "to wipe off those Asperations and ill Impressions which the Ignorances and foolish Men had brought upon the Christian Religion, by pretending that their Christian Liberty set them free from Subjection to Civil Government."[24] Another New York Anglican, Charles Inglis, believed that the Christians' obedience to government was what "distinguish[ed]

---

22. Mark A. Noll, Nathan O. Hatch, and George M. Marsden, *The Search for Christian America* (2nd ed.; Colorado Springs: Helmers & Howard, 1989), 81.

23. Jonathan Boucher, *A View of the Causes and Consequences of the American Revolution in Thirteen Discourse, Preached in North America between the Years 1763 and 1775* (London: G. G. & J. Robinson, 1797; repr. New York: Russell & Russell, 1967), 422–23.

24. Samuel Seabury, *St. Peter's Exhortation to Fear God and Honor the King* (New York: Hugh Gaine, 1777), 5–6.

themselves from others and manifest[ed] the native Excellence and Spirit of their Religion.[25]

These Anglican Loyalists affirmed that obedience to civil authority was required of Christians regardless of the form of government or behavior of the government. Christians must obey the government, Seabury argued, "whether it be exercised by KINGS as Supreme, or by Governors sent by them and acting by their Authority." He reminded his readers:

> When St. Peter and St. Paul wrote their Epistles, they were under the Government of Heathen Emperors and Magistrates, who persecuted them, and the other Christians--depriving them of their Possessions, beating and banishing and killing them—without any Crime proved against them, but merely because they were Christians. And yet it was to these Emperors and Magistrates—even to *Nero and Caligula*—that the Apostles commanded Honor and Respect, at all Times, and whenever it could be done consistently with Obedience to God, Duty and Submission.[26]

Similarly, Inglis noted that Peter wrote his epistle at a time when Nero was the emperor of Rome. He stressed that "the personal Character of the Magistrate was not to interfere with the Civil Duty of the Subject. Even when bad, it did not dissolve the Obligation of the latter."[27]

The patriots used phrases such as "passive obedience" and "unlimited submission" to describe this Anglican view of the relationship between Christians and civil authority. They spent hundreds of pages trying to counter it. The most outspoken defender of such a patriotic interpretation of Rom 13 and 1 Pet 2 was Jonathan Mayhew, the minster at Boston's West Church. Mayhew was a liberal Congregationalist and forerunner of the Unitarian movement in New England. He was committed to interpreting the Bible predominantly through the grid of natural law and reason. His sermon on Rom 13, "A Discourse Concerning Unlimited Submission and Non-Resistance to the Higher Powers," was preached in 1750 on the celebration of the one hundred anniversary of the execution of Charles I during the English Civil War. Despite the fact that Mayhew's sermon was published a quarter century prior to the outbreak of revolutionary hostility in Boston, John Adams, reflecting on the causes of the Revolu-

---

25. Charles Inglis, *The Duty of Honouring the King, Explained and Recommended* (New York: Hugh Gaine, 1780), 10.

26. Seabury, *St. Peter's Exhortation*, 5–6, 12.

27. Inglis, *Duty of Honouring the King*, 11.

tion, wrote in 1818: "If the orators on the fourth of July really wish to investigate the principles and feelings which produced the Revolution, they ought to study ... Dr. Mayhew's sermon on passive obedience and non-resistance."[28]

Mayhew began his sermon by affirming that Rom 13 required Christians to be obedient to government, regardless of whether the government was a monarchy, republic, or aristocracy. But the real issue at hand was the *extent* to which such "subjection to higher powers" should be practiced. Mayhew concluded that sometimes resistance to civil authority might be justified. According to Mayhew, Rom 13 could not be advocating unlimited submission to government, because such a practice did not conform either to the true meaning of the passage or to the dictates of reason. Paul's primary audience in this passage was those in the first-century Roman church who did not show proper respect to civil authority and were of a "licentious opinion and character." Moreover, Rom 13 could not conceivably require submission to all rulers, but only to those rulers who were "good." Rulers who "attend continually upon the gratification of their own lust and pride and ambition, to the destruction of the public welfare" were not worthy of a Christian's submission. Mayhew argued, "rulers have no authority from God to do mischief." It is "blasphemy," he continued, to "call tyrants and oppressors God's ministers." It follows that when a ruler becomes tyrannical, Christians "are bound to throw off our allegiance to him, and to resist; and that according to the tenor of the apostle's argument in this passage." Perhaps the most ironic thing about Mayhew's argument is the way he managed to transform Rom 13 from a verse teaching submission to authority into a verse justifying the execution of Charles I and, for that matter, all rebellion against tyrannical government. Charles I, he concluded, had failed to respect the "natural and legal rights of the people, against the unnatural and illegal encroachments of arbitrary power." As a result, resistance was absolutely necessary in order to preserve the nation from "slavery, misery, and ruin."[29]

---

28. Jonathan Mayhew, *A Discourse Concerning Unlimited Submission and Non-Resistance to the Higher Powers* (Boston: D. Fowle and D. Gookin, 1750). For the Adams quote, see John Adams, *The Works of John Adams* (ed. Charles Francis Adams; 10 vols; Boston: Little, Brown, 1850–1860), 10:301, cited in Claude Halstead Van Tyne, "The Influence of the Clergy and of Religious and Sectarian Forces on the American Revolution," *American Historical Review* 19 (1913): 50.

29. Mayhew, *Discourse Concerning Unlimited Submission*, 18, 21, 23, 24, 30, 44,

For Mayhew, it was "obvious" to any rational person exercising common sense that Rom 13 and 1 Pet 2 did not teach submission to a government perceived to be tyrannical. How could God require his people to live under oppression? God had promised his people freedom. But such an interpretation required ministers like Mayhew to move beyond a plain reading of these texts. In order to turn these passages into revolutionary manifestos, Mayhew needed to interpret them with a strong dose of the ideas of political philosophers such as John Locke. In his famous *Two Treatises on Government* (1689), a pamphlet designed to explain why the glorious Revolution (the removal of English monarch James II from the throne) was justified, Locke taught that individuals had the right to overthrow tyrannical governments that violated their natural rights to life, liberty, and property. His justification for resistance to government had a profound influence on the leaders of the American Revolution, but it ran counter to the teachings of Rom 13 and 1 Pet 2. This tension did not stop clergy from interpreting these passages through the grid of Locke's revolutionary teachings.[30]

The liberal or "Lockean" interpretation of these biblical passages was a minority position in the history of the Christian church and was relatively new in the history of Protestantism. According to political scientist Steven Dworetz: "Basing revolutionary teaching on the scriptural authority of chapter 13 of St. Paul's Epistle to the Romans must rank as one of the greatest ironies in the history of political thought." Romans 13 served as "the touchstone for passive obedience and unconditional submission from Augustine and Gregory to Luther and Calvin." Martin Luther, the father of the Protestant Reformation, wrote that resistance to civil rulers is "a greater sin than murder, unchastity, theft, and dishonest, and all these may include."[31]

John Calvin, the Genevan reformer who had the most influence on the theology of the colonial clergy, taught that rebellion against civil government was never justified:

> If we keep firmly in mind that even the worst kings are appointed by this same decree which establishes the authority of kings, then we will never

---

45. Also see Steven M. Dworetz, *The Unvarnished Doctrine: Locke, Liberalism, and the American Revolution* (Durham, N.C.: Duke University Press, 1994), 160.

30. Dworetz, *Unvarnished Doctrine*, 155–72.

31. Dworetz, *Unvarnished Doctrine*, 155.

permit ourselves the seditious idea that a king is to be treated according to his deserts, or that we need not obey a kind who does not conduct himself towards us like a king.

Calvin added: "we must honour the worst tyrant in the office in which the Lord has seen fit to set him," and "if you go on to infer that only just governments are to be repaid by obedience, your reasoning is stupid." He taught that Christians must "venerate" even those rulers who were "unworthy" of veneration.[32] In the end, many patriotic clergy may have been more influenced in their political positions by Locke than the Bible.

Was the Bible important at the time of the founding of the United States? Of course it was. American patriotic clergy used their pulpits to promote the cause of independence by infusing biblical interpretation with the predominant Whig political thinking of the day. Biblical terms such as "slavery" and "freedom" took on new political meanings. Clergy protested against British taxation using political language that was baptized with the conviction that God was always on the side of liberty. The long-standing Puritan view that the people of America were the chosen people of God—a new Israel—was used to show that God must be on the side of the patriots. Bible passages that had historically been employed to teach the importance of submission to government authorities were now being interpreted to justify revolution. The Bible, as proclaimed from American pulpits, played a prominent role in the coming of the American Revolution, but those who argue that the American Revolution was a Christian event or that the United States has a "biblical heritage" need to reflect deeply on the ways in which the Bible was interpreted by those responsible for teaching it to ordinary Christians in this time of political crisis.

---

32. John Calvin, "Of Civil Government," in *Institutes of the Christian Religion*, 4.20.27, quoted in Gregg Frazer, "The Political Theology of the American Founding" (Ph.D. diss., Claremont Graduate University, 2004), 359–60.

"God's New Israel": American Identification with Israel Ancient and Modern

Shalom Goldman

At the 2012 Democratic National Convention in Charlotte, North Carolina, delegates voted to put God (or, in any case, the word *God*) back in the party platform, "amending a section about the government's role in helping people reach their 'God-given potential.'"[1] Republicans had noticed that God was missing from that statement, and Democrats responded with alacrity, concerned that they might be perceived as "ungodly."

On the same day, the party reinstated in the platform the line "Jerusalem is and will remain the capital of Israel," a line that had been in the 2008 Democratic platform. According to the *New York Times*, President Obama himself had urged party leaders to restore this statement. Republicans had been touting the Bush administration's support of Israel and the principle that Jerusalem is Israel's "undivided and eternal capital" in Prime Minister Ariel Sharon's words (ca. 2000). Democrats could not but remind voters that they, too, were supportive of Israel. Against this background, it might seem that the title of this essay, "God's New Israel," might be from the Republican or Democratic platforms or from the website of the American Israel Public Affairs Committee (AIPAC).

But actually the phrase is from a sermon by Ezra Stiles, pastor of the Congregational Church in Newport, Rhode Island, at the time of the American Revolution. Stiles, who went on to become president of Yale University at the end of the eighteenth century, was articulating a sentiment and metaphor widespread in the American colonies. The colonists wishing to free themselves from the British yoke were modern children

---

1. This quotation and those in the next paragraph are taken from Mark Landler, "Pushed by Obama, Democrats Alter Platform Over Jerusalem," *New York Times*, September 5, 2012.

of Israel, George III of England was the Pharaoh, and God had destined the colonists for a God-fearing life in the promised land, a "land flowing with milk and honey" in the words of the Hebrew Bible.[2] So closely did Stiles identify the new American nation with the ancient Hebrew theocracy "that he imagined them both consisting of equal numbers of citizens in covenant with God." Stiles wrote that

> the history of the Hebrew theocracy shows that the secular welfare of God's ancient people depended upon their virtue, their religion, their observance of the holy covenant with Israel entered into with God on the plains at the foot of Nebo on the other side of Jordan. Here Moses, the man of God assembled three millions of people, the number of the United States, recapitulated and gave them a second publication of the sacred judicial institute, delivered thirty-eight years before with most awful solemnity at Mt. Sinai.[3]

The implication of Stiles's statement is that there is theological meaning to the "fact" that the number of Israelites who came out of Egypt (three million according to eighteenth-century estimates; see Exod 12:37) and the United States' population of Stiles day were roughly equal. For both Israelites and Americans are a "covenantal people," and therefore the welfare of the new American people is dependent upon this early American identification with the Israelites, an identification that preceded Stiles, lived on after him, and would have far-reaching and for the time unimaginable geopolitical results. For it was this identification that laid the groundwork for what in the twentieth century would become the much-vaunted and sometimes condemned United States alliance with Israel. Contrary to the assertions of many social scientists, the United States–Israel alliance is not the product of colonialism, the Cold War and its aftermath, or other political manifestations; rather, it is the result of a continuous and unbroken series of identifications and engagements between the United States and the idea and reality of Zion. Here I am arguing against the contention of John Mearshimer and Stephan Walt in *The Israel Lobby and U.S. Foreign Policy* that "the lobby" is the principal reason for the United States' "lavish support of Israel."[4] Rather, the

---

2. E.g., Exod 3:8; Lev 20:24; Num 13:37; Deut 6:3; Josh 5:6; Jer 11:5; Ezek 20:6.

3. From a 1783 sermon, cited in Conrad Cherry, *God's New Israel: Religious Interpretations of American Destiny* (Englewood, N.J.: Prentice Hall, 1971), 82–83.

4. John J. Mearsheimer and Stephan M. Walt, *The Israel Lobby and U.S. Foreign Policy* (New York: Farrar, Straus & Giroux, 2008), 7.

reasons for United States support are various and complex; as I have written elsewhere, "No one explanation, including a 'Biblical' one, is sufficient."[5] But all explanations ultimately lead back to the biblical one.

While the rhetoric of the United States as "God's American Israel" may have waned in the first half of the nineteenth century, American interest in the future of the Holy Land and the place of the Jews in its future did not. Even as the rhetoric of the early American Republic became more secularized, the tie to an idea of Zion remained strong. A long-standing theological interest in the Holy Land and the restoration of the Jews to that land was eventually transmuted into a political and diplomatic interest, an interest that never lost its theological underpinnings.

The biblical trope of enslavement, liberation, and covenant was understood as a metaphor for the American experience, and that metaphor exerted so much force that in the minds of many Americans it took on a certain reality. If the British colonists in the New World were the children of Israel, they should then emulate their biblical antecedents in more ways than one. For Stiles and his colleagues at Yale, studying Hebrew and examining the history of the Holy Land were ways of expressing American identification with ancient Israel and its people. This identification had a mythic power that exerted considerable influence during the subsequent two American centuries. As literary critic Sacvan Bercovitch noted:

> Nothing more clearly attests to the power of the American Puritan imagination that [this] mythico-historiography. The emigrants had fled England as from certain destruction. Behind them, they believed, lay the failure of European Protestantism—and before them, as their refuge, what they called "wilderness," "desert." ... The New World, according to that image, was the modern counterpart of the wilderness through which the Israelites reached Canaan, of the desert where Christ overcame the tempter. More than counterpart, it was antitype: the journey then was a foreshadowing of the journey now by a *Christian* Israel to the long-awaited "new heavens and a new earth."[6]

---

5. See Shalom Goldman, "U.S.-Israel Relations," *Jewish Quarterly Review* 99 (2009): 603–8.

6. Cited in in Shalom Goldman, *Hebrew and the Bible in America: The First Two Centuries* (Brandeis Series in American Jewish History, Culture, and Life; Hanover, N.H.: University Press of New England, 1993), xvi–xvii.

The New England colonists' identification with ancient Israel began in England, and it was expressed in intellectual endeavors. And they carried on these endeavors during the voyages to America. On the Mayflower there were two Hebraists (scholars of Hebrew), William Bradford and William Brewster. Bradford was governor of the Plymouth Colony and author of colonial America's first narrative history, *Of Plymouth Plantation*.[7] His colleague Brewster, who was both teacher and preacher at Plymouth, is regarded by many as leader of the Pilgrims. Both men, busy as they were in the early years of settlement, set time aside each day for the study of the Bible and the sacred tongue. In the original manuscript of his history of the colony, *Of Plymouth Plantation*, Bradford included eight pages of Hebrew vocabulary notes. These were his "Hebrew exercises," a list of over one thousand Hebrew words and phrases and their English equivalents. As historian Egal Feldman notes, "Bradford was driven to study Hebrew in order to catch a glimpse of Israel's past, a past he wished to recreate in New England."[8]

In later American historiography, the "new Israel" dimension of the colonists' vision is somewhat muted. Many Americans today know that the American colonists sought to build "a city upon a hill" in the New World. But what is often elided from that historical memory is that the author of that phrase, Governor John Winthrop of the Massachusetts Bay Colony, opened his sermon saying that "the God of Israel in among us." Winthrop was implying that because the God of Israel was among them they had to build the city referred to by Jesus in the Gospel of Matthew (Matt 5:14).[9] Winthrop's reference to Matthew serves to remind us that for the New England elites and their Puritan predecessors, identification with "Zion" was based on New Testament references as well as on Old Testament narratives. The land where Jesus walked was Israel, a land still imbued with sanctity.

For African American slaves, the Israelite slavery and liberation story in Exodus became a way of narrating their own experience and a means of expressing hope for future freedom. Slave narratives and abolitionist

---

7. William Bradford, *Of Plymouth Plantation, 1620–1647* (Boston: Massachusetts Historical Society, 1856).

8. Egal Feldman, *Dual Destinies: The Jewish Encounter with Protestant American* (Urbana: University of Illinois Press, 1990), 15.

9. Cherry, *God's New Israel*, vii. See also the comments in David Morgan's essay ("The Image of the Protestant Bible in America") in this volume, 99–100.

tracts are replete with biblical allusions from both the Old and New Testaments. And for some in the black churches, the Holy Land became more than a metaphor; it was an actual place yearned for and constantly evoked in prayer and sermons. After the Civil War a number of African American clergymen traveled to Palestine to visit the holy sites and "walk where Jesus walked."[10]

For the Church of Latter Day Saints, which emerged in the United States in the 1830s and 1840s, the experience of ancient Israel served as a template for its political and religious development. Joseph Smith taught that "the whole of America is Zion itself from north to south."[11] The history of the Mormon Church was written so as to connect members of the church in a direct and concrete fashion to Judea in the time of Jesus. To link the ancient and the modern, the connection between the emerging church of the Latter Day Saints and the Israelites had to be made explicit; it had to move from the abstract to the concrete. To accomplish this, the Mormon prophet Joseph Smith sent his disciple Orson Hyde to Jerusalem in 1841. Hyde arrived after an arduous three month journey, and on a ridge facing the walls of Jerusalem's Old City he prayed for the return of Jews to their ancestral home. With the 1948 establishment of Israel, Mormon support of Zionism became explicit and forceful. A few years after the 1967 Six-Day War and the Israeli conquest of Jerusalem, the Mormon Church acquired a prized tract of land in Jerusalem. There it built a campus of Brigham Young University. The campus is situated above the ledge where Hyde prayed in 1841.[12] While the Mormon experience is but one part of the vast religious mosaic of the United States, it is an important and emblematic part. As literary critic Harold Bloom notes in *The American Religion*, "Insofar as there is an American Religion … then Joseph Smith may be considered to be in many respects its unacknowledged forerunner."[13]

---

10. Lester I. Vogel, *To See a Promised Land: Americans and the Holy Land in the Nineteenth Century* (University Park: Pennsylvania State University Press, 1993), 18–19.

11. Joseph Smith Jr., *Teachings of the Prophet Joseph Smith Taken from His Sermons and Writings as They are Found in the Documentary History and Other Publications of the Church and Written Or Published in the Days of the Prophet's Ministry* (Salt Lake City: Deseret News, 1938), 6.362.

12. Shalom Goldman, *God's Sacred Tongue: Hebrew and the American Imagination* (Chapel Hill: The University of North Carolina Press, 2004), 301.

13. Harold Bloom, *The American Religion: The Emergence of the Post-Christian Nation* (New York: Simon & Schuster, 1992), 111.

What I am arguing is that the American obsession with the modern State of Israel in particular, and with the Middle East in general, cannot be fully understood without an in-depth analysis of the biblically-based view that many, if not most, American citizens brought to the issue, first during the Revolutionary period and the years of the early Republic, and subsequently throughout later American history.

This is not to claim that identification with ancient Israel was the only model that influenced American political thought. The classical traditions of Greece and Rome were often invoked by American elites of the founding era and the early Republic. But with time, the Roman Republic model lost its appeal and the biblical model was more often appealed to. As Eran Shalev has noted, "The Old Testament, specifically the history of biblical Israel, provided a productive intersection between politics and religion." In the expanding American nation biblical names dotted the landscape. By naming their towns and cities Salem, Hebron, Bethlehem, and Pisgah, eighteenth- and nineteenth-century Americans were declaring the New World a biblical area. While the theologically-based identification with ancient Israel declined in the mid-nineteenth century, interest in the "land of Israel" as depicted in the Bible did not. With the participation of American scholars in geographic and early archaeological research in Palestine, such interest increased. Among the most talented and creative Palestine explorers were Americans Edward Robinson and Eli Smith, whose book *Biblical Researches in Palestine* was a bestseller in the early 1840s, the same decade that Mormon identification with ancient Israel and advocacy for Israel's return to its land was solidified.[14]

A relatively unknown chapter in the United States' relationship with the Middle East in general, and with nineteenth-century Palestine in particular, is the story of American Christian colonization efforts in the region. In the late 1840's the first of these groups, led by Adventist "prophetess" Clorinda Minor, settled in the port area of Jaffa. They called their settlement Mount Hope. Their intention was to "prepare" the Holy Land for the return of the Jews to their land, an intention shared by subsequent groups of American Protestant colonists. Aided by a Jewish convert to Christianity, John Meshullam, Clorinda Minor went on to establish another colony

---

14. Eran Shalev, *American Zion: The Old Testament as A Political Text from the Revolution to the Civil War* (New Haven: Yale University Press, 2013), 12; Shalom Goldman, *Zeal for Zion: Christians, Jews and the Idea of the Promised Land* (Chapel Hill: University of North Carolina Press, 2009), 11.

near Bethlehem in the town of Artas. Though these American colonists did not stay in Palestine for longer than a few years, they did encourage European Jewish colonists to engage in agriculture and light manufacture; thus they advanced the Zionist cause. Other American Christians were inspired by Minor's example and made the arduous journey to Palestine, intending to introduce American farming and manufacturing methods to the Holy Land, a land to which Jews were slowly returning. In the 1850s, Minor publicized her farming experiments in the American press. She wrote that the Holy Land, "in harmony with the improving prospects of its scattered people, is showing symptoms of returning to life."[15]

In 1865, when steamship travel enabled Americans to reach Jaffa is a mere three weeks, a new Christian settlement effort, the largest and strangest of them all, began in Maine and New Hampshire. At the urging of charismatic preacher George Adams, 160 New Englanders embarked to start a colony in Palestine. On a ship outfitted with timber for building and packed with supplies for farming in Palestine, they set sail for Jaffa. The colonists settled in that port city and intended to use the seeds, trees, and farm implements they brought with them from New England to establish an American-style working farm. The erratic behavior of Pastor Adams, who had a weakness for "demon rum," combined with the harsh weather of that Jaffa summer, brought their efforts to a disastrous end within a few months. Many of the American colonists, especially the young children, died of malaria, and most of the surviving remnant returned to the United States. Readers of Mark Twain's *Innocents Aboard* will recall his humorous and touching account of meeting with those few who remained in the Holy Land.[16]

The most influential and longest lasting of these American Christian Palestine settlements efforts was the American Colony, founded in 1881. Arriving in the same period as the European Jewish pioneers of the "First Aliya" (emigration), the American Colony group, which joined forces with a group of Swedish Christians resident in Jerusalem, soon established clinics, infirmaries, and light manufacturing projects for Jerusalem's inhabitants, regardless of religious affiliation. Some of these Jerusalemites, aided by the Americans, eventually converted to Protestant forms of Christian-

---

15. Cited in Barbara Kreiger and Shalom Goldman, *Divine Expectations: A Nineteenth Century American Woman in Palestine* (Athens: Ohio University Press, 1999), 37.

16. See chapter 57 of Mark Twain, *Innocents Abroad: Or The New Pilgrim's Progress* (New York: Harpers, 1911).

ity; others did not. United States State Department officials were unhappy with these American expatriates, many of whom exhibited "religious enthusiasms." Selah Merrill, the United States consul in Jerusalem during the last quarter of the nineteenth century, complained bitterly about the American Colony and its Jewish beneficiaries. In an 1891 letter to the State Department, Merrill stated that "the Jews are not ready for Palestine, and Palestine is not ready for the Jews."[17] A major American journal of the time, *Appleton's Magazine*, sent a journalist to Jerusalem to report on the American Colony. He dubbed them "an undaunted body of American citizens; a body that, with the hands of its own government repeatedly and inexplicably raised against it, has persevered to the end."[18]

That many influential Americans, and not only the few Christian colonists who went to Palestine, were deeply attached to the idea of a restored Jewish homeland was evident in the Blackstone Memorial of 1891. This petition to President Harrison called on the president to convene an international conference to support Jewish claims in Palestine. It posed this question to the president, "Why not give Palestine back to them again? According to God's distribution of nations, it is their home, an inalienable possession from which they were expelled by force." Four hundred and thirteen prominent American politicians, philanthropists, and clergymen signed this document. A full century after Stiles of Yale College had dubbed the Republic "God's New Israel," the elites of that republic were calling on their president to reestablish ancient Israel, the primary model of America's self-concept.[19]

And what, one might ask, of American Jews? Aren't they part of this story of the American identification with ancient Israel? Not in the first American century. In this formative period of the American self-concept, there were very few Jews living in the United States, and those who did live here had very little to do with public life and the shaping of public opinion. For the most part, Jews were excluded from it. To be specific, in the early Republic there were, as Stiles noted, three million people in the colonies: colonists, African Americans, Native Americans, and one thousand people of Jewish descent. European Jewish immigration started in the mid-nineteenth century and rose in the late nineteenth century. Thus,

---

17. Cited in Goldman, *Zeal for Zion*, 69.

18. Alexander Hume Ford, "Our American Colony at Jerusalem," *Appleton's Magazine* 8 (December 1906): 645.

19. On the Blackstone Memorial, see Goldman, *Zeal for Zion*, 24.

we are speaking of the Hebrew or ancient Israelite component in the Protestant American self-concept, not a Jewish one.[20]

But once Jewish communities were established in the United States and members of those communities rose to positions of prominence and influence, opinions about a "return to Zion" were strongly expressed. Some of these opinions were in favor of Zionism, others were not. When the Blackstone Memorial was drafted in 1891, the great majority of its signatures were Protestant; some Catholic clergy and laymen also signed. Jewish names were few and far between in that document. And, in fact, some of the more prominent Jewish clergy and lay leadership of that era campaigned against the petition. Rabbi Emil Hirsch of Chicago's Sinai Congregation, a Reform temple, called for a boycott of the Blackstone Memorial. Consistent with the ideas expressed in Reform Judaism Pittsburgh Platform of 1885, Rabbi Hirsch reminded his fellow Jews that

> we modern Jews do not wish to be restored to Palestine. We have given up hope in the coming of a political personal Messiah. We say "the country wherein we live is our Palestine and the city where in we dwell is our Jerusalem."... There is no cause for Zionism in America. Let those who favor a return to Jerusalem go there if they will.[21]

Rabbi Hirsch's opinion on the "Palestine Issue" was not representative of general American Jewish opinion on the question. But it was representative of many Reform congregations. Hirsch's attitude, that "America is our Zion" reflected an anxiety that informed many American Jewish conversations about Zionism. Would such support weaken Jews hard-won claims for a secure place in the American social and political landscape? This anxiety was often expressed. Reform Jewish opposition to Zionism would wane in the mid-twentieth century, and late in that century Reform Judaism would become as ardently Zionist as the other Jewish denominations. But that opposition, as well as the opposition of other Jewish groups (socialist, internationalist, and ultra-Orthodox), serves as a reminder that Zionism's hold on the modern Jewish imagination was, until recently, more tenuous than might be imagined.[22]

---

20. See the comments of Rabbi Isaac Meyer Wise in Cherry, *God's New Israel*, 218–28.
21. Cited in Goldman, *Zeal for Zion*, 25.
22. Goldman, *Zeal for Zion*, 272–73.

President Harrison did not act on the recommendations of the Blackstone Memorial of 1891. Twenty-five years later, in 1916, the memorial was submitted again, this time to President Wilson. The new document was cosponsored by the official Zionist movement, a movement founded in 1897, midway between the drafting of the two versions of the memorial. The first Blackstone effort was spearheaded and supported by Christians. The second was ardently supported by Jews, among them Louis D. Brandeis, Supreme Court Justice and American Zionist spokesman. While President Wilson did not respond directly to the new Blackstone Memorial, he did signal his support of Zionism when he endorsed Britain's Balfour Declaration of 1917. In 1918 the United States House and Senate also endorsed the Declaration.[23]

In the nineteenth and early twentieth centuries, those American Christians who were inspired by the Holy Land ideal but were unable to settle in a colony in Palestine or make a pilgrimage to its sacred sites found substitutes in the American landscape. In the mid-1870s, thousands of visitors from all over the United States flocked to Palestine Park in Chautauqua, New York. There they could dip into the park's own "Jordan River," climb its "Judean Hills" and see a model of the Jerusalem temple. A larger and more spectacular "Palestine" with a constructed-to-scale Old City of Jerusalem was built for the St. Louis World's Fair of 1904. The model of the Church of the Holy Sepulcher was the fair's most popular exhibit. These substitute Holy Lands still thrive in American culture, as witnessed by the success of the Orlando, Florida, "Holy Land Experience."[24]

Thus we can see that "God's New Israel" is a concept that ebbs and flows in the arc of American history—and a concept that returned to full power in the twentieth century with the emergence of political Zionism. It enabled Protestant identification with the idea of ancient Israel reborn. In 1948, the metaphor of the Promised Land was, in the mid-twentieth century, transformed into a reality—the State of Israel. In contextualizing President Harry Truman's 1948 decision, against State Department advice,

---

23. Yaakov Ariel, *On Behalf of Israel: American Fundamentalist Attitudes toward Jews, Judaism, and Zionism, 1865–1945* (Brooklyn: Carlson, 1991), 70.

24. Goldman, *Zeal for Zion*, 14. See also Mark Pinsky, "Not Another Roadside Attraction: The Holy Land Experience in America," in *Archaeology, Bible, Politics, and the Media: Proceedings of the Duke University Conference, April 23–24, 2009* (eds. Eric M. Meyers and Carol Meyers; Duke Judaic Studies Series 4; Winona Lake, Ind.: Eisenbrauns, 2012), 245–58.

to recognize the government of the newly declared State of Israel, Truman biographer David McCullough wrote that "beyond the so called 'Jewish vote' there was the country at large, where popular support for a Jewish homeland was overwhelming. As would sometimes be forgotten, it was not just American Jews who were stirred by the prospect of a new nation of Jewish people.... it was America."[25]

After the establishment of the State of Israel in 1948, and even more so after the 1967 War, Conservative Evangelicals moved toward a full embrace of Israel. As Yaakov Ariel notes,

> The mass emigration of Jews to Israel in the late 1940s and 1950s from many parts of the world was one cause for encouragement. In evangelical opinion this was a significant development, one that had been prophesied in the Bible, and a clear indication that the present era was terminating and that the events of the end of the age were beginning to occur.[26]

To return to my opening remarks on the Democratic and Republican platforms of 2012: These political entities were not the first groups to recognize the power of the idea of Zion. From David Ben Gurion onward, the political leadership of the State of Israel recognized the power that biblically-referenced ideas have in the United States. As I pointed out in *Zeal for Zion*:

> That Israel's leaders recognize the power of Israeli territorial claims on the imagination of the Western world is clear from Prime Minister Ehud Barak's comments at the United Nations Millennium Summit in September 2000: "I believe that the very words 'Temple Mount,' in every Western language, carry the real story of this place. When we think of Jesus walking in the streets of Jerusalem, what he saw there was not a mosque, nor even a Christian church. What he saw was the Temple—the Second Temple of the Jews." Barak, military hero, and exemplar of Israeli secularism, was as ideologically distant from his Jewish coreligionists of the Temple Mount faithful as he was from Christian Zionists. It may have struck some in his United Nations audience as strange that the Israeli prime minister was invoking the name of Jesus. But like all Israeli leaders from Ben-Gurion onward, Barak recognized the power exerted

---

25. David McCullough, *Truman* (New York: Simon and Schuster, 1993), 596.
26. Yaakov Ariel, *An Unusual Relationship: Evangelical Christians and Jews* (New York New York: University Press, 2013), 173.

by ancient images and ideas on the religious and political imaginations of Christians the world over.[27]

It is the sense that "Israel in its land" is the fulfillment of God's will, combined with the self-concept of many Americans that the United States is "God's American Israel," that makes the United States' support for Israel a powerful and enduring force. Contrary to the claims of many journalists and political pundits, it is not end-time speculation and Armageddon imagery that moves most Americans to embrace Israel. The book of Revelation from which this speculation and imagery derives is far less significant for most American Protestants than the book of Genesis. In 2013, the claim of the Blackstone Memorial to President Harrison remains as persuasive to most Americans as it was in 1891: "According to God's distribution of nations, it is their home, an inalienable possession from which they were expelled by force."[28]

---

27. Goldman, *Zeal for Zion*, 308.

28. William E. Blackstone, "Blackstone Memorial," cited in Goldman, *God's Sacred Tongue*, 232.

The Image of the Protestant Bible in America

David Morgan

Whatever the Bible may be as a text or collection of texts, it also exhibits a career as an image. This consists of the history of representations circulating in advertisement and commerce, entertainment, religious instruction, devotional literature, and proselytism. I would like to trace the history of the image of the Bible in a variety of visual forms from seventeenth-century America to the present day, focusing attention on how the image of the book was put to use in popular piety from the private home to the public square.

Martin Marty once aptly described the Bible as an object easily overlooked by those inclined to miss it: "In the corner, under a layer of dust, there is a leather-bound, gilt-edged, India-papered object, a Bible, revered *as* object, *as* icon, not only in Protestant churches but in much of the public congregation as well."[1] This "icon of the republic," as Marty called it, both object and image, was one of the most widely recognized and readily evoked symbols of authority throughout late colonial and early national American life. It also served as the emblem of evangelical piety and devotional practice. And from the early seventeenth century to the present, its prophecies have been understood to endorse a special covenant between God and Americans. After the Revolutionary War, the Bible was used in American public classrooms to form patriotic ideals and induce national loyalty among children. But the place of the book in American culture was not destined to remain unchanged. For a number of reasons, the Bible was eventually eclipsed by the American flag as the icon of national unity, which underwent intense sacralization in the last decades of the

---

1. Martin E. Marty, *Religion and Republic: The American Circumstance* (Boston: Beacon, 1987), 143.

nineteenth century. Concerns about the sacred character of both have remained points of controversy.

The Colonial Era: Puritanism and the New Israel

The visibility of the Bible in colonial America operated in several different registers: in the domain of social authority (in meetinghouses, on the desk of the schoolmaster, and on the bench of the civil magistrate); in the domain of domestic life (as a genealogical document recording the births and members of a family, as an heirloom, as an object of display, as a precious possession, as a textbook for teaching children to read); and in the domain of devotional practice (as the device for studying, teaching, and preaching the Protestant religion, in particular, the evangelical version of it that arose in Puritanism). The book was read, invoked, and recited endlessly, but it was also revered as a power object—used to protect its owners from evil influence and as a tool in practices of divination.[2] Of course, all of these uses were not discrete spheres in colonial American life, but underscore that the book was not only read and heard, but visually contemplated and represented as an image.

This is doubly at work in an early portrait of Puritan preacher Richard Mather (fig. 1), issued as a woodcut shortly after his death in 1669. The clergyman had arrived in Boston in 1635 and quickly became prominent in New England Puritanism and a leader in the Congregationalist cause of separating from the Church of England. As author and clergyman, Mather is pictured holding a text in his hand, which may be the Bible or may be the Bay Psalm Book, a translation of the book of Psalms, which he coauthored in 1640. The link between the Bay Psalm Book and the Bible was quite immediate in the seventeenth century. What may be the first book published in the colonies, the Bay Psalm Book was often bound by its owners with the Bible.[3] In either case, as the Bible or as part of it, the

---

2. See David D. Hall, *Worlds of Wonder, Days of Judgment: Popular Religious Beliefs in Early New England* (Cambridge: Harvard University Press, 1989), 25–26; on the Bible in early American education, see W. Clark Gilpin, "The Creation of a New Order: Colonial Education and the Bible," in *The Bible in American Education: From Source Book to Textbook* (ed. David L. Barr and Nicholas Piediscalzi; Philadelphia: Fortress, 1982), 5–23.

3. John Alden, "The Bible as Printed Word," in *The Bible and Bibles in America* (ed. Ernest S. Frerichs; Atlanta: Scholars, 1988), 13.

text in the woodcut serves to honor Mather as an emblem of his stature as scholar and clergyman. The book is both an image vouching for the piety of the individual and a badge of his social station. Yet as an honorific portrait of the deceased, an important member of the New England community of nonconformist divines, the book is perhaps more a testament to Mather's significance for a colonial society in which Puritan clergymen exercised unparalleled social power in conducting the civil experiment of a Christian commonwealth that understood itself to be prophetically prescribed as the new Israel.

The Bible as a purely evangelical image appears at the opening of John Bunyan's *Pilgrim's Progress*, one of the most adored and widely read books

Fig. 1. Attributed to John Foster, *Richard Mather*, ca. 1670, woodcut. Courtesy American Antiquarian Society.

in colonial New England. Christian, the protagonist of Bunyan's allegory, appears in the famous frontispiece, just above the figure of the dreaming author. Walking staff in one hand and open Bible in the other, Christian makes his solitary way toward the heavenly Jerusalem led there by what he reads. He also appears holding a Bible in the book's second illustration (fig. 2). What he reads troubles him greatly, precipitating an agonizing crisis of evangelical awakening. At the outset of his long pilgrimage, Christian is pictured with "a great burden upon his back," greeting the evangelist, who hails him at the moment of his departure from the "world," the state or "city" of ruin.[4] The pilgrim has opened the book and read it, and he found himself convicted of sin and deserving the harsh judgment of the Almighty. A paradigm of evangelical introspection and conversion, Christian's case is carefully visualized by the dreaming Bunyan in an allegory of the evangelical path to rebirth and salvation. "Now I saw, upon a time," Bunyan narrates, "when he was walking the fields ... reading his Book, and greatly distressed in his mind; and as he read, he burst out, as he had done before, crying, *What shall I do to be saved?*"[5] The travail was sparked by reading the Bible, which was the proper evangelical preparation to receive the word of the Evangelist, who directs him toward the narrow gate of faith as his only hope against "the wrath to come." The path to redemption, in other words, begins in reading the Bible, which means internalizing its message to the end of spiritual regeneration or rebirth. It is not a disinterested perusal, but an excruciating consumption of sacred writ and one that launches the long ordeal that ends with entry into the Heavenly Jerusalem.

As figures 1 and 2 suggest, during the colonial period two modes of representation tended to frame the portrayal of the Bible: as an emblem or accouterment of social station, and as the instrument of spiritual devotion and the evangelical quest for holiness. Two additional forms of depiction became important during the antebellum era. The extension of the Bible as a tool for regeneration can be traced to the rise of the missionary enterprise in the first two decades of the nineteenth century and in domestic iconography of the Bible as the means for shaping Christian children over the first three and four decades. Proselytism and child-rearing were both evangelical concerns par excellence. Evangelicals were never content to save only them-

---

4. John Bunyan, *The Pilgrim's Progress* (New York: Barnes & Noble, 2005), 13.
5. Bunyan, *Pilgrim's Progress*, 14.

Fig. 2. *Christian speaks with the Evangelist*, from John Bunyan, *The Pilgrim's Progress* (4th ed; London: Nath. Ponder, 1680). Photo by author.

selves. Saving others was the next step after securing one's own soul. Thus, Bunyan's first part of Christian's spiritual trek culminating in heaven was followed by part two: the pilgrimage of his wife, Christiana, and her children, who together stood for the true church of Christian believers. In the late eighteenth and early nineteenth century, after generations of evangelical revival since the 1730s, Protestant groups in continental Europe and North America followed the example of British dissenters in forming missionary, tract, and Bible societies, whose purpose was the production of inexpensive pious print and its national and increasingly international distribution.

The Bible appears in illustrations to these publications as the seal of the preacher's authority. Figure 3 is an image of a missionary that appeared in

Fig. 3. J. G. G, *The Missionary*, 1854, wood engraving, from *The Family Christian Almanac for 1855* (New York: American Tract Society, 1854). Photo by author.

the American Tract Society's *Family Christian Almanac* in 1855. An evangelist orates before a group of Native Americans who calmly listen to the young missionary as his coat unfurls in the stirring wind of his homily. The closed Bible held in the preacher's hand is not something from which he reads, but is the source of his preaching, the authorization of what he says. More than that, it is clasped as a power object, with its binding visible to the viewer and its front cover visible to the Native Americans. They listen to the missionary but also gaze raptly on the sacred tome, which the speaker grips not as a book to be opened and read aloud, but as a talisman, as something he wants to *show* his listeners. Their gaze locks on the object, which becomes the visual counterpart of what they hear and perhaps (the image might have us believe) what they feel as the breath or aura of the man's inspired discourse. Writing, speaking, hearing, and seeing intermingle as the integrated means of transmitting faith. Or so the Tract Society would like to have it. In the business of deploying texts with effects, the Tract Society never tired of recounting stories of the moving reception of their printed matter.[6] Reviv-

---

6. For further discussion of this point see David Morgan, *The Lure of Images: A History of Religious Visual Media in America* (London: Routledge, 2007), 31–36.

alist Evangelicalism needed to show the efficacy of its special measures, its technology of spiritual awakening. The Bible became a powerful instrument, a talisman whose display alone exerted emotional influences. This certainly helps account for the popularity of displaying Bibles in parlors. And it is important to recognize that figure 3 signals the fact that many Native Americans converted to Catholicism and Protestantism. But dispatched within the reams and reams of print rolling from Protestant presses, images were crucial to evangelicals for their capacity to register the effect of words in the mute medium of print. Word and image were made to collaborate such that images served to enact the iconicity of sacred text.[7] And the image of the Bible helped materialize its power in the new print culture, especially as secular rivals such as newspapers and the penny press multiplied.

The image of the Bible also became a symbol of domestic piety and the formation of children during the antebellum period in the United States. The gradual movement of male employment out of the home and into the countryside, factory, and growing towns made mothers increasingly responsible for the spiritual formation of children. The republican mother, the domestically bound woman charged with the task, became the target of tracts, sermons, and advice literature. She was often shown on illustrated covers and engraved pages of Protestant material reading to her children from scripture or pious literature.[8] Images of missionaries and mothers with Bibles engaging indigenous peoples and children put to work the conversion embodied by Christian in Bunyan's allegory of the Christian's life. Evangelicals are as evangelicals do, so it is important to see the Bible reader and the Bible preacher as either side of a single coin in the age of mass print and revivalism.

The expansion of the American Republic simultaneously occasioned another, but for evangelicals an intimately related, social function of Scripture: the concern to secure the new republic as Christian (read: Protestant) by deploying the Bible as a moral influence in restraining immoderate human nature and making good citizens. The notion that the New World was blessed by God in a special way and charged with a noble mission was not a new idea by the time of the American Revolution. Indeed, the seventeenth-century immigrants from England had launched their

---

7. Morgan, *The Lure of Images*, 15.

8. For a discussion of this iconography, see David Morgan, *The Sacred Gaze: Religious Visual Culture in Theory and Practice* (Berkeley: University of California Press, 2005), 191–206.

enterprise with the idea in mind. The Puritans had considered England the new Israel; when that did not take place, some decamped for the New World to find it there. When John Winthrop was about to set sail for the New World in 1630, John Cotton preached a sermon based on 2 Sam 7:10, "I will appoint a place for my people Israel and will plant them, so that they may dwell in their own place, and be disturbed no more" (ESV). The idea, as Mark Valeri and John F. Wilson have argued, was to develop an alternative to the *old* England, the land where the reform of the church had not succeeded.[9] The Puritan cause, at least for some, focused on "New England" as the second chance. Winthrop's iconic sermon, "A Model of Christian Charity," preached aboard ship en route to Massachusetts Bay in 1630, called the colonists to the task of creating a "city upon a hill" whose light would shine to the world as a new Israel.[10] The group, he claimed, was joined together in a covenant with God, attesting to the social force of their faith in a new world that would test them to the limit.

THE NINETEENTH CENTURY: VISUAL CONSTRUCTIONS OF THE NATION

Although many left England to gain religious freedom in the New World, most wasted no time in creating colonies that enforced an established religious citizenship. It took rancorous debate at the new nation's constitutional convention and the political leadership of James Madison and Thomas Jefferson to secure the disestablishment of religion in the First Amendment to the Constitution. This innovation frightened conservative Protestants, who saw in it the loss of leverage over conduct and popular sentiment, the downhill slide from republic to democracy. But once evangelicals found that the formation of voluntary associations such as tract, Bible, Sunday school, and missionary societies could mobilize print and proselytizers on an unprecedented scale, the logistics of revival shifted and expectations brightened.[11] The Reverend Lyman Beecher confessed in his

---

9. Mark Valeri and John F. Wilson, "Scripture and Society: From Reform in the Old World to Revival in the New," in *The Bible in American Law, Politics, and Political Rhetoric* (ed. James Turner Johnson; Philadelphia: Fortress, 1982), 22–23.

10. John Winthrop, "A Model of Christian Charity," in *American Religions: A Documentary History* (ed. R. Marie Griffith; New York: Oxford University Press, 2008), 16–19.

11. Nathan O. Hatch, *The Democratization of American Christianity* (New Haven: Yale University Press, 1989); R. Laurence Moore, *Selling God: American Religion in*

Plea for the West (1835) that he had been unable to take seriously Jonathan Edwards's expectation that the millennium would commence in America until he realized the way in which constitutionally guaranteed religious liberty had suited the nation for this lofty millennial office. In effect, the Puritan peculiarity of the nation was salvaged, but we find an unmistakable element of national bravado, the penchant for superlatives familiar to anyone listening to presidential State of the Union speeches today.

> What nation is blessed with such experimental knowledge of free institutions, with such facilities and resources of communication, obstructed by so few obstacles, as our own? There is not a nation upon earth which, in fifty years, can by all possible reformation place itself in circumstances so favorable as our own for the free unembarrassed application of physical effort and pecuniary and moral power to evangelize the world.[12]

Divine election also meant secular national destiny as global leader. America, Beecher confidently asserted, was "destined to lead the way in the moral and political emancipation of the world."[13] The nineteenth century was a time of updating and adjusting old prophecies as the United States entered and came to shape the modern world.

At the end of the eighteenth century, Protestant Americans came to regard the Puritans as their forebears precisely because of the group's enmity with England as religious dissenters, many of whom, most famously the sect of the Pilgrims, found their way to religious freedom in the colonial world of New England. It is ironic, to be sure, that such a rigidly strict strain of Christianity as the dissenting Puritans would come to stand for the national quest for religious liberty, but by the end of the eighteenth century the phrase "Pilgrim fathers" had entered the national lexicon.[14] A spate of publications, songs, poems, prints, and paintings multiplied the

---

the Marketplace of Culture (New York: Oxford University Press, 1994); Peter J. Wosh, *Spreading the Word: The Bible Business in Nineteenth-Century America* (Ithaca: Cornell University Press, 1994); Paul Gutjahr, *An American Bible: A History of the Good Book in the United States, 1777–1880* (Stanford, Calif.: Stanford University Press, 1999); David Morgan, *Protestants and Pictures: Religion, Visual Culture, and the Age of American Mass Production* (New York: Oxford University Press, 1999), 123–58.

12. Lyman Beecher, *Plea for the West* (Cincinnati: Truman and Smith, 1835), 10.

13. Beecher, *Plea for the West*, 10.

14. According to Albert Matthews (*The Term Pilgrim Fathers* [Cambridge: Wilson & Son, 1915], 352), the first appearance of the term was 1799.

nomination of the Pilgrims, or more generally the Puritans, for the honor. With the growing arrival of Catholics in the 1820s, Protestants launched a battle for national ethos, for the character of the country, in fear that the political instruments of the nation's peculiarly Protestant identity and mission would be compromised and its covenant broken. So the Bible was at the heart of the enterprise, deployed as a symbol of piety, identity, purpose, race, and cultural dominance.

A popular example of the Bible used to signify the piety of Puritan forefathers was George Henry Boughton's painting, *Pilgrims Going to Church* (1867; fig. 4). Widely admired and reproduced in the nineteenth century, the image portrays a solemn procession of early seventeenth-century New Englanders clad in period costume, accompanied by armed escorts, walking through a wintry forest on their way to worship. Each member of the company conspicuously carries a thick sacred volume. Even the guards hold a Bible in one hand and a musket in the other. As a nineteenth-century vision of Puritan faith and life, Boughton's painting portrays a people who balance piety and violence in the single mission of nation building.[15] The octavo (9 x 6 inches)- and duodecimo (7 3/8 x 5 inches)-sized volumes that the figures carry in Boughton's scene may suggest that they are copies of the Geneva Bible (translated in 1560), which was published in the smaller formats before the King James Version (KJV) was. The Pilgrims used the Geneva version rather than the Authorized Version since they separated themselves from the Church of England, and it was King James who authorized the later translation as the official version used by the Church of England. Harry Stout has shrewdly argued that the Geneva Bible suited Pilgrim theology better than the KJV since the Geneva Bible's marginal notes accommodated the Pilgrim understanding of grace as personal rather than the KJV's emphasis on a national or federal covenant of grace.[16] The New England Puritans embraced the idea that God had formed a covenant with them as a new Israel, a "peculiar people" set on the hill that Winthrop hymned in his sermon.

---

15. For more on the image see David Morgan, "Painting as Visual Evidence: Production, Circulation, Reception," in *Using Visual Evidence* (eds. Richard Howells and Robert W. Matson; Maidenhead, England: Open University Press, 2009), 8–23.

16. Harry S. Stout, "Word and Order in Colonial New England," in *The Bible in America: Essays in Cultural History* (ed. Nathan O. Hatch and Mark A. Noll; New York: Oxford University Press, 1982), 19–38.

Fig. 4. George Henry Boughton, *Pilgrims Going to Church*, 1867, oil on canvas. Collection of The New York Historical Society, The Robert L. Stuart Collection, on permanent loan from The New York Public Library, 1944.

Yet Boughton's picture was originally titled "Early Puritans of New England going to worship armed, to protect themselves from Indians and wild beasts." The subsequent switch to "Pilgrims" may reflect the late nineteenth-century association of Pilgrims with Thanksgiving, which became the principal feast of American civil religion after Lincoln officially called for a day of national thanksgiving on the last Thursday of November in 1863. Not surprisingly, his formal proclamation, issued in the midst of the Civil War, called on Americans to "implore the interposition of the Almighty Hand to heal the wounds of the nation."[17] The earlier title seems more fitting since the picture conveys a communal covenant in action, and this may have struck Boughton's contemporaries as an apt representation of the original spirit of the nation. The fact that Boughton's picture was painted in 1867 further argues for the relevance of the image to an ideal that many Protestants applauded in the nineteenth century: that America was a Christian nation. Coming so quickly after the Civil War, when violence nearly destroyed the nation, but ultimately redeemed it in the words of Lincoln's second inaugural address ("until every drop of blood drawn with the lash shall be paid by another drawn with the sword"), Boughton's picture may have appealed for its affirmation of the

---

17. Abraham Lincoln, "Proclamation of Thanksgiving" (proclamation, Washington, D.C., October 3, 1863). Abraham Lincoln Online. Online: http://www.abrahamlincolnonline.org/lincoln/speeches/thanks.htm.

American theory of redemptive violence that kept an imperiled nation together and would continue to do so in the ritualized, mythologized memories of the nation's origins.

His painting was popular because it celebrated the idea of Anglo Protestant national origins that made Bible religion fundamental to American identity. The picture did so by envisioning a moment far in advance of the fractious violence of the Civil War. In so doing, the picture offered something common to which to return, positing a common enemy that actually occupied American public consciousness in headline after headline during the 1860s and 1870s as pioneers, ranchers, railroads, and immigrants battled with Native American groups on the western and southwestern plains. If the American Tract Society's image of a passive Native American acceptance of the Anglo missionary's message seemed attractive in the 1850s (see fig. 3), newspapers and many politicians sensationally stoked a different response as the United States Army fought Comanche, Sioux, and Apache warriors from Texas to Canada in the decade following the end of the war.

Boughton's picture may have appealed to white Americans as much for what it did not visualize as for what it did. The heart of the American project, it seemed to say, was an Anglo Protestantism fiercely dedicated to its well-being. The divisive forces of nineteenth-century America—slavery, sectionalism, and Catholic immigration—were absent from this colonial evocation. What was implied was the intrepid march of Anglo civilization in the face of a deadly enemy. Yet for many Protestants there was a more menacing challenge in the nineteenth century than Native Americans. Protestant Nativists who understood national identity and mission as divinely sanctioned and rooted in the Puritan past might have updated Boughton's picture by seeing the West as a wilderness endangered as much by Catholic immigrants as by hostile Native Americans. One of many Protestant alarmists regarding Catholic inroads was the Reverend John Dowling, who published in successive editions of his vitriolic *History of Romanism* an account of a Catholic friar who publicly burned a number of Bibles in Champlain, New York in 1842 (fig. 5). Entering the city from Quebec, the brother put to fire several copies of Bibles distributed among local Catholics by a Protestant Bible society.[18] For Dowling and many of

---

18. Reverand John Dowling, *The History of Romanism: From the Earliest Corruptions of Christianity to the Present Time* (6th ed.; New York: Edward Walker, 1845), 613.

his sympathetic readers, the event represented an incursion on American soil by the international forces of Rome, and a direct challenge to the religious liberty enshrined by the First Amendment, proof that Catholic immigrants made dubious citizens in a democratic republic.

Fig. 5. *Burning of Bibles, by Romish Priests, at Champlain, N.Y.*, from Reverend John Dowling, *The History of Romanism, 1845: From the Earliest Corruptions of Christianity to the Present Time* (6th ed.; New York: Edward Walker, 1845), 441. Photo by author.

One sympathizer of Dowling's cause was the nation's first Jewish congressman, Lewis Charles Levin, a Know Nothing agitator whose speeches incited some of the anti-Catholic riots in Philadelphia of 1844, which resulted in the destruction of several Catholic churches and a monastery (for which Levin was arrested and fined). In 1848, as a third-term Pennsylvania congressman, Levin spoke passionately against a bill before Congress to establish a diplomatic mission at the Vatican. He cited the Champlain case reported by Dowling and deplored that "we have lived to see the Bible driven from our public schools and BURNT IN THE PUBLIC STREETS! That Bible so inseparably interwoven with the genius and spirit of American institutions." He closed his screed with this salvo: "Pass your bill, and from that hour NATIVE AMERICANISM means only the defence of Protestant rights and Protestant freedom against Papal tyranny and Jesuit aggression.... GOD SAVE THE REPUBLIC!"[19]

Dowling's example of Catholic iconoclasm as violence to the (Protestant) Bible was intensified by Thomas Nast, the well-known cartoonist whose work decrying the feared influence of Catholicism in the American public sphere was regularly featured in *Harper's Weekly*, including during a much publicized controversy in Cincinnati over the role of the (King James) Bible in public school instruction. In one image (fig. 6), Nast envisioned what many Protestants feared would soon happen: a public classroom transformed into a Roman Catholic catechetical session, presided over by priests who drill the children in Romanist doctrine especially offensive to Protestant republicans such as the recently promulgated teaching of papal infallibility. In Nast's cartoon, a priest sweeps away a large volume labeled "Bible" and along with it a "Reader," presumably a *McGuffey's Reader*, which included references to the Bible and the Protestant version of the Lord's Prayer and was presented as evidence against the role of the Protestant Bible in the classroom in the Cincinnati case.[20]

While the Protestant majority was busy applauding the KJV in public schools, others were intent on dismantling the Bible as a straightforward narrative. In order to be properly understood and put to use, in order to harvest the value embedded in it as historical record, some felt the Bible was in need of surgical intervention. For Thomas Jefferson, the Bible could not be taken at face value without removing its substantial apparatus of myths, legends, miracle reports, and outdated customs. The result was his slender edition of the New Testament put together with scissors and paste about 1820 as *The Life and Morals of Jesus*. In a letter of that year, he described his method in treating the teachings of Jesus: "I separate, therefore, the gold from the dross; restore to Him the former, and leave the latter to the stupidity of some, and roguery of others of his disciples."[21] Jefferson's

---

19. Lewis Charles Levin, *Speech of Mr. L. C. Levin, of Penn., on the Proposed Mission to Rome, Delivered in the House of Representatives, March 2, 1848* (Washington, D.C.: J. & G. S. Gideon Printers, 1848), 15–16.

20. Robert Michaelsen, "Common School, Common Religion? A Case Study in Church-Relations, Cincinnati, 1869–70," *Church History* 38 (1969): 201–17; Morgan, *Sacred Gaze*, 228–30.

21. Quoted in F. Forrester Church, "Thomas Jefferson's Bible," in *The Bible and Bibles in America* (ed. Ernest S. Frerichs; Atlanta: Scholars Press, 1988), 159.

Fig. 6. Thomas Nast, "Foreshadowing of Coming Events in Our Public Schools," *Harper's Weekly Magazine*, April 16, 1870, 256. Photo by author.

Bible is pared down to the biography and moral teachings of Jesus. It is not a Bible to be thumped, because it has little more than the substance of a thick pamphlet. The girth of sacred revelation has been replaced by the leaner frame of a moral guide. Jefferson found in Jesus's teachings what he could—not the historical Jesus, as one scholar has pointed out, but the one whom he found intelligible.[22]

Thomas Jefferson never published "his" Bible. It did not appear in print until 1904. For a man who was obsessed with his posterity and the negative use to which his enemies might put his writings, it is not hard to understand why. But the impact of the Enlightenment on biblical studies that reverberates in his redaction had already begun to challenge the stability of the text before Jefferson put scissors to paper. The scholarly analysis of text along grammatical and historical lines of inquiry contrasted sharply with the tendency to sacralize the Bible as a uniform, even infal-

---

22. Church, "Thomas Jefferson's Bible," 160.

lible record of divine revelation. The modern challenge to the sacrosanct status of the text collided with the belief that the Bible was a single, unified text rather than a collection of widely dated, diversely authored, and variously received productions, an unintegrated accumulation of texts held together by tradition rather than authorial consistency or singularity of purpose. As scholars of modern bent tended to see it, the Bible was not a book, but a library. Its putative unity collapsed when they scrutinized the text with stylistic and archaeological tools that refused to presume a single author, a single message, or an obediently compelled and uniform readership. Once the Bible was no longer written by one author (God), no longer read as bearing one message, and no long read by a sympathetic and related audience, the book became something else. For many scholars that meant a complex historical record.[23]

Protestants responded in different ways to modern scholarship. For the Adventist William Miller, like many Fundamentalists after him, preserving the integrity of Scripture meant deploying a very artful deconstruction of its surface. The truth was all there, but discerning and vindicating it took some rather elaborate doing. Having toyed with Deist thought as a young man, Miller later renounced Deism's critique of the Bible, which had considered the book full of mistakes and self-contradiction.[24] Where Thomas Paine, Ethan Allen, or Thomas Jefferson saw errors, Miller wanted to see a complex set of texts that could be harmonized as a system of symbolic internal references. Miller believed that he resolved the inconsistencies and contradictions of the biblical texts by ceasing to interpret them in a straightforward narrative sense, reading them instead as symbols to be properly decoded as part of a sprawling network of corresponding passages. He overlaid the Old Testament books of Daniel and Ezekiel with the New Testament book of Revelation. Rather than read any text as grounded in its own time and place, a product of one historical situation, bearing its own perspective, concerns, and audience, Miller's hermeneutic recast the entire Bible as a system of intertextual linkages. Passages were rendered meaningful by association with entirely different sites in the book. Rather than a library or a faulty hodgepodge, the Bible was a coded, inte-

---

23. Grant Wacker has regarded this shift, especially as conducted by late nineteenth-century modernist biblical scholarship, as the basis for what he calls "The Demise of Biblical Civilization," in *The Bible in America: Essays in Cultural History* (ed. Nathan O. Hatch and Mark A. Noll; New York: Oxford University Press), 121–38.

24. See Morgan, *Protestants and Pictures*, 123–58.

grated network. It was visualized in the charts that Miller and his cohort of Adventists developed as tools for teaching and preaching (fig. 7). What we see in this set of symbolic figures and texts is something like a schematic diagram of how to read the biblical prophecies as chronological markers

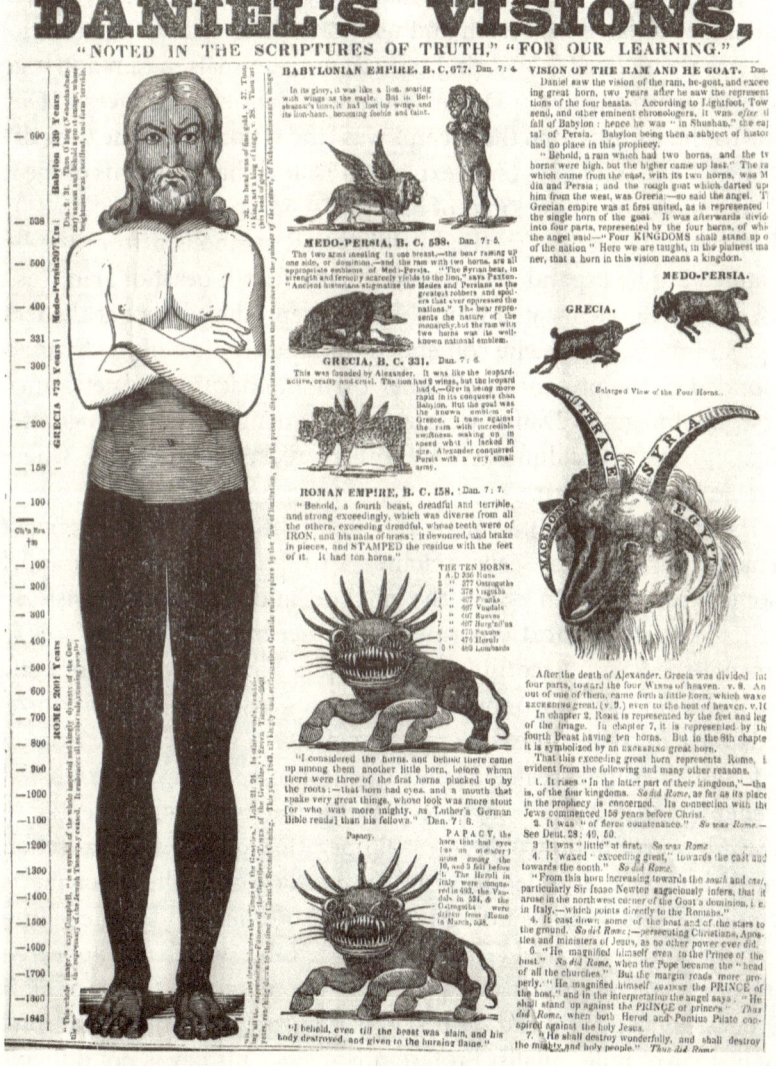

Fig. 7. *Daniel's Visions*, New York Tribune, March 2, 1843. Photo by the author.

leading to Miller's own day. This chart, in other words, is what the Bible *really* looks like in Adventist hermeneutics.

Key to the Adventist calculation of the second coming of Jesus was the "great image" from Nebuchadnezzar's dream (fig. 7), which the prophet Daniel famously recited and interpreted (Dan 2:31–45). Miller interpreted the figure as a chronology by linking it to another dream, this one Daniel's own, about four beasts—a winged lion, a bear, a leopard, and an unidentified beast with large iron teeth and ten horns (Dan 7:4–7). An additional layer was then added, consisting of two more animals, a ram and a goat, from the eighth chapter of Daniel. The angel Gabriel announces to Daniel that what he witnessed in the dreams was "the vision … for the time of the end" (8:17, ESV) and goes on to explain to Daniel that the horns of the ram and goat represented the kings of Media, Persia, and Greece (8:20–21). So Miller could derive this method of historical symbolism from the book of Daniel, but he expanded it by treating the fourth beast of Dan 7 as the beast of Rev 17. He located it on the chart reproduced here at the feet of the great image, because he contended that the clay feet of the figure corresponded to the present day. Rather than an obscure, hermetic ancient vision, the images of Daniel were ways of parsing the chronology of historical epochs that culminated, by Miller's reckoning, in 1843, when he expected Jesus to return.

The elaborate Adventist method of interpreting scripture was invested in charts that served as visual rejoinders to rationalist criticism and Jeffersonian redaction. In effect, the method and the charts transformed the Bible into a hypertext, a permeable surface of text that interfaces with layers of other texts. According to this view, a Bible passage is not a single textual record, referring only to a past event, a historical referent. Instead, words melt into other texts in reticular patterns of reference. Ironically, like Jefferson, Miller created a new text—not by reducing the original, but by redeploying it. Miller sought to preserve the historical referentiality of the text by turning it into an internal operation of hypertextual reticulation. Although Jesus failed to show up in 1843, or in the following year after a desperate recalculation, Miller's method transcended the failure of his prediction. The Scofield Chain Reference Bible, which first appeared in 1909, operates in a similar way, placing in the margins a cluster of biblical references by which to read the text at hand. And Miller's influence on the long history of millennialist Protestantism since his day is not difficult to discern. Even his chart's imagery remains in circulation, being used by Seventh-day Adventists, Jehovah's Witnesses, dispensationalists, and the

Church of God.[25] If Miller longed to secure the Bible's integrity, he demonstrated its plasticity in doing so. The acrobatics of conservative Protestant hermeneutics have not ceased.

FLAG VENERATION AND THE QUEST FOR NATIONAL UNITY

With the disestablishment of religion and the rise of the public school as the principal public institution responsible for forming American citizens, the social career of the Bible continued to change. Revolutions in the technology and commerce of print production also made the Bible affordable and eventually a mass commodity. But the growing diversity of the nation urged groups outside of the Protestant mainstream to question Protestant hegemony as expressed in the use of the King James Bible in public classrooms. With a growing number of court cases concerning the Bible in public schools, the ever expanding numbers of Catholics, the steady increase of new religious movements, and the ongoing competition among the many different Protestant sects for religious consumers, Christianity looked less and less like the unifying element that many of its adherents wanted for the nation. As American nationalism developed in the wake of the Civil War and the nation's emergence on the global stage, investment in symbols of national loyalty and unity began to shift from the Bible to the flag.[26]

Beginning in the 1880s, as the aging generation of Civil War veterans began to dwindle, hereditary organizations and patriotic groups turned to the sacralization of the American flag in the quest for a compelling icon of national identity. Groups such as the Daughters of the American Revolution (DAR) and the Grand Army of the Republic (GAR) were dedicated to making the memory of the war dead (the Revolutionary War and the Civil War, in these two primary examples) definitive of the nation's values and mission. Most of these avoided taking strong stands on religious issues since their members were varied and the purpose of the organizations was national unity in patriotic terms. Religion, after all, was easily sectarian and ethnic—two tribal forces that veterans and hereditary organizations came increasingly to regard as a problem to be overcome by the unified and puta-

---

25. Ibid., 161–77 and 265–67.
26. An excellent history of American flag culture is Scot M. Guenter, *The American Flag, 1777–1924: Cultural Shifts from Creation to Codification* (Cranbury, N.J.: Associated University Presses, 1990).

tively unifying veneration of the flag, the observance of national holidays, and the cult of memory dedicated to the nation's wars and those who died in them. It is not difficult to see the ritualism, sacralizing practices, and taboos promoted by national fraternities such as the DAR and GAR as "almost religious," as one historian of the organizations has put it.[27] Hereditary organizations endorsed the adoption of flag veneration in public schools and pushed legislation to support this as well as laws that regulated the proper use of the flag and forbade its desecration.[28] Manuals appeared to direct compliance with new statutes of venerating the flag in schools.

The Pledge of Allegiance, written in 1892 by Baptist clergyman Francis Bellamy for the national celebration of Columbus Day, quickly became a principal feature of the daily rites, visible in this photograph (fig. 8), which shows school children in 1899 delivering the pledge with hands placed over hearts.[29] The very celebration of Columbus Day as the discovery of America nudged the nation away from the Pilgrims and Thanksgiving foundation narrative, toward the spirit of global exploration by an Italian explorer sponsored by a Spanish monarchy. Columbus was embraced by Italian-Americans and certainly represents a concession to the new American immigrant. Bellamy himself later confirmed that American patriotism was not defined by race or blood, as it had long been in Europe: "Outside of our dwindling Colonial stock, American ancestry is from many races and languages. Consequently the composite patriotism of our masses is mostly the result of a definite education, and its exercise is a matter of reasoning."[30] This sentiment is closer to Thomas Jefferson than to John Winthrop. His Pledge of Allegiance was not a mystical ritual of devotion, but a conscious affirmation that acknowledged difference. To be sure, it was collectively experienced by children and therefore almost inescapably coercive. But making the pledge a test of loyalty and a means of exclusion that invested the flag with totemic power was not what Bellamy had intended. Neverthe-

---

27. Wallace Evan Davies, *Patriotism on Parade: The Story of Veterans' and Hereditary Organizations in America 1783-1900* (Cambridge: Harvard University Press, 1955), 217.

28. On the history of litigation and legal controversy regarding the flag, see Robert Justin Goldstein, ed., *Desecrating the American Flag: Key Documents in the Controversy from the Civil War to 1995* (Syracuse: Syracuse University Press, 1996).

29. On the history of the pledge, see Richard J. Ellis, *To the Flag: The Unlikely History of the Pledge of Allegiance* (Lawrence: University Press of Kansas, 2005), esp. 9–23.

30. Quoted in Ellis, *To the Flag*, 214.

Fig. 8. Frances Benjamin Johnston, *Pledge of Allegiance*, Washington, D.C., 1899(?). Courtesy Library of Congress.

less, fashioning the pledge into a sacralization of the flag whose collective devotion would stoke patriotic fervor among children was the civil piety that took over responsibility for promoting national cohesion.

Patriotic organizations helped by strongly endorsing the pledge, by sponsoring national holidays, and by not hesitating to object to any group that conducted its exercises or activities on patriotic occasions. Thus, Methodists in San Francisco were asked by the local GAR branch not to hold picnics on Memorial Day. In Portland, Methodist Sunday schools that advertised an excursion on Memorial Day were taken to task by the GAR.[31] Other proponents of flag veneration in public schools could even be caustic in their anxiety about the competition that sectarian religion provided to the nation's patriotic piety. One Civil War veteran who authored a manual on patriotism in 1890 that set out rituals for daily veneration of the flag in public schools charged that Lutheran, Catholic, Presbyterian,

---

31. Davies, *Patriotism on Parade*, 218.

Quaker, and Jewish schools promoted sectarian intolerance and resistance to the singularity of "American ideas and institutions."[32]

Others could be less harsh but still convey the view that the religion of patriotism now served in the place of the biblical faith of an earlier day as the basis for bolstering the nation's bonds of affection. At the annual meeting of the Minnesota Educational Association in 1898, one speaker asked how Minnesota schools could promote patriotism and "meet the requirements of citizenship."[33] His address answered the question by arguing that the old idea "that we were a sort of chosen people under the special care of Divine Providence has been more slowly giving way to the view that we are not exempt from the consequences of ignorance, folly, dishonesty, and that, if we would avoid these consequences, some special effort must be made to train the boys and girls of the rising generation in something else than the noble art of looking out for themselves."[34] That was the task of inculcating patriotism: the restraint of self-interest by the love of country. American exceptionalism's roots in the covenant that Winthrop hailed as the basis of the Massachusetts Bay Colony, dependent on providence for its sense of mission, was to be replaced by a more or less secular patriotism. The conference was next addressed by the mayor of St. Paul, who opened with the anodyne assertion that "the symbols of modern civilization are the school house and the church," and then offered an encapsulated history of the nation that celebrated the place of the Bible in the colonial household and the steeple's replacement of tepees in the nineteenth-century West. Yet when his honor came to the contemporary day, Christianity vanished entirely in the steamy clouds of patriotic fervor. "Into your hands," he told the state's educators, "is committed the care of the shield of the nation. Its hope is centered in the public schools. Its safeguard is the intelligence and education of the masses. Teach the youth to aim high and hit somewhere above the horizon. Teach them patriotism. Teach them loyalty to the old flag, and teach them how great are the privileges and duties of citizenship under that flag."[35]

---

32. Colonel George T. Balch, *Methods of Teaching Patriotism in the Public Schools* (New York: D. Van Nostrand, 1890), xviii.

33. Dr. G. O. Virtue, "Normal Schools," in *Proceedings of the Thirty-Sixth Annual Session of the Minnesota Educational Association, Saint Paul, December 27, 28, and 29, 1898* (Minneapolis: School Education Company, 1899), 26–30.

34. Virtue, "Normal Schools," 26.

35. Hon. A. R. Kiefer, "Address," in *Proceedings of the Thirty-Sixth Annual Session of the Minnesota Educational Association*, 32.

The ascendance of the national flag as a sacred object is apparent in its entry into church sanctuaries in the early twentieth century and in the creation of a Christian flag designed in 1907 by a Sunday school superintendent on the basis of the American flag: a red cross in a blue field, in the upper left corner of a white field. The colors of the national flag were easily morphed into symbols of Christian faith: red was the blood of Jesus, blue the water of baptism, and white the color of purity. A pledge of allegiance to the Christian flag appeared in the 1908, written by a Methodist pastor, and was once again modeled on the Pledge of Allegiance to the flag: "I pledge allegiance to my flag and the Savior for whose kingdom it stands; one brotherhood uniting all mankind in service and love."[36] Churches around the country eventually adopted the use of the Christian flag in sanctuaries and Sunday school rooms, as in the photograph reproduced here (fig. 9) from the Sunday school of a Lutheran church in Iowa, which shows the Christian flag flanking one side of an altar and the American flag the other, with Warner Sallman's *Head of Christ* hanging behind a cross. Such an arrangement allowed Protestants to honor nation and church in a way that sutured what many considered their undue separation by secularizing interpretations of the First Amendment to the United States Constitution. But the arrangement may also adhere in Lutheran settings like this one, because of the two world wars during which German Americans found their patriotism on trial.

American flag piety easily became a litmus test of belonging, a brash proclamation of loyalty that could be applied effectively, its proponents preached, to the task of social engineering that the public school was assigned to undertake. One can readily imagine the visceral pressures brought to bear on children in the classroom standing at attention as in fig. 8, delivering the Pledge of Allegiance. Who would dare not stand and deliver the sacred vow? In fact, a few did—members of religious minorities who regarded the flag as an idol. In 1940 the Supreme Court heard the case of twelve-year-old Lillian Gobitas and her younger brother William,

---

36. The best discussion I have found on the history of the Christian flag is by Mark Sidwell, "The Christian Flag: A Fundamentalism File Research Report." Online: http://lgdata.s3-website-us-east-1.amazonaws.com/docs/474/231457/SidwellMark-Christian_Flag.pdf. Other, much briefer sources online include Elesha Coffman, "Do You Know the History of the Christian Flag?" Christian History.net. Online: http://www.christianitytoday.com/ch/asktheexpert/jul13.html; "The Christian Flag." Online: http://www.auburn.edu/~allenkc/chrflag.html

Fig. 9. *Church Flag and American Flag*, Sunday school fellowship hall, Zion Lutheran Church, Ogden, Iowa, 1991. Photograph by Phillip Morgan.

who were members of Jehovah's Witnesses and had been expelled from a Pennsylvania public school for refusing to recite the pledge. The Jehovah's Witnesses offered an alternative pledge, one that ended, "I pledge allegiance and obedience to all the laws of the United States that are consistent with God's law, as set forth in the Bible." But that concession failed to satisfy their opponents. In several different cases, school boards enforced the expulsion of young members of the Jehovah's Witnesses and set as the condition of their readmission to school the willingness to participate in the pledge.[37] The Third Circuit Court of Appeals upheld the district court decision in favor of the Gobitas children, but its decision was overturned by the United States Supreme Court, which refused to "exercise censorship over the conviction of legislatures that a particular program or exercise will best promote in the minds of children who attend the common schools an attachment to the institutions of their country."[38] But the court went a different direction three years later in a case once again involving a member of the Jehovah's Witnesses, this time in West Virginia. The majority opinion argued against the 1940 opinion, which had asserted that "national unity is the basis of national security."[39] The court overruled the 1940 case, countering the anxiety for unity with the sober assertion that "those who begin coercive elimination of dissent soon find themselves exterminating dissenters. Compulsory unification of opinion achieves only the unanimity of the graveyard."[40]

The rows of saluting bodies and joined voices in the photograph reproduced here (see fig. 8) practiced a discipline of martial unity in the concerted gaze and marching diction of their daily ritual. Loyalty meant doing what everyone else was doing and feeling part of the group. In the late nineteenth century the anxiety to stabilize an immigrant nation whose religious diversity was expanding rapidly, to form the "unum" from "pluribus," came to substitute a civil religion of flag piety and patriotism for the

---

37. Ellis, *To the Flag*, 91–99.

38. *Minersville School District v. Board of Education*, 310 U.S. 586. Online: http://www.law.cornell.edu/supct/html/historics/USSC_CR_0310_0586_ZS.html. Note that the family name was misspelled in the court's published opinion. For discussion of the case, see Ellis, *To the Flag*, 99–105.

39. *Minersville School District v. Board of Education*, 595.

40. *West Virginia State Board of Education v. Barnette*, 319 U.S. 624, 641. Online: http://www.law.cornell.edu/supct/html/historics/USSC_CR_0319_0624_ZO.html#319_US_624.

Bible piety that had claimed to represent the heritage and original unity of the nation. By the end of the century, Protestant Americans were investing their hopes less in the Bible as the overt symbol of national unity than in the flag as national talisman and cult object. Religion, many, perhaps most agreed, exerted a powerful binding effect, but Christianity had become sectarian and only one religion among many others. If a religious sentiment was to gather the nation together and secure in its young an embodied affection for something larger than the self, the tribe, the ethnic clan, or the sect, it was to be the civil religion practiced by devotion to the flag. But for many Christians, of course, there was no tension between love of country and biblical faith. As a result, Christianity in America, especially Protestantism, came to look increasingly like patriotism. Nothing could articulate the kinship better than the Christian flag.

Yet the rise of the flag as national icon did not eclipse the Bible. In the late twentieth century a fresh assertion of Christian nationhood was occasioned by the Supreme Court's 1973 *Roe v. Wade* decision, which came to represent to many conservative Protestants a judiciary uncoupled from a Protestant Christian heritage. Evangelical authors issued a rising tide of pamphlets, sermons, articles, and books that argued the "founding fathers" of the nation were "Bible-believing Christians."[41] For Evangelicals, the Bible never lost its power to represent the true identity of the nation and its installment at the foundation of the American project. This was certainly the claim of Alabama state Supreme Court Chief Justice Roy Moore, who in 2001 installed a 5,280 pound granite sculpture of the Ten Commandments in the rotunda of the judicial building in Montgomery. On August 1, 2001, Moore dedicated the monument: "Today a cry has gone out across our land for the acknowledgment of that God upon whom this nation and our laws were founded.... May this day mark the restoration of the moral foundation of law to our people and the return to the knowledge of God in our land."[42] Two years later, he was relieved of office when he refused to obey a federal court order to remove the monument. His fellow judges then had it moved from its perch in the rotunda to a storage room. Moore wasted little time before organizing an itinerant career for the Ten Commandments: loaded aboard a flatbed semi-trailer, the monument traveled

---

41. See, for instance, D. James Kennedy with Jerry Newcombe, *What If America Were a Christian Nation Again?* (Nashville: Thomas Nelson Publishers, 2003), and Pat Robertson, *The Ten Offenses* (Nashville: Integrity, 2004).

42. Joshua Green, "Roy and His Rock," *The Atlantic* (October 2005): 70–82.

across the country to rallies and audiences who shared its owner's longing to restore the nation's rightful biblical heritage. Today the object sits in a church in Moore's hometown.[43] Judge Moore has since regained a seat on the Alabama Supreme Court, but has said that he will not return the Ten Commandments to the judicial building.[44]

Efforts from Protestant extremes have in recent years captured the attention of media by destroying copies of the Qur'an.[45] These sensational public rituals enrage Muslims in other parts of the world, but domestically do little more than convey the desperation of those who used to insist on the centrality of the Bible for national identity. Nowadays they resort to the iconoclastic destruction of other sacred texts, mimicking unwittingly what they claim has happened to their own. Their desperation is evident in their dependence on secular media, without which they would likely go quite unnoticed. Their extreme gestures betray a frustration that the nation no longer belongs to them and that it largely does not care about what they believe. It is a frustration well-founded. Yet something of the biblically-revealed specialness of the American people persists in the fondness of American presidents and their applauding audiences for superlatives when describing the nation and its aims (the best, the bravest, the most courageous, the most inventive, the most successful, the most powerful). Such proud assertions sound like a secular descendent of the old exceptionalism inherited from Puritan Boston.

---

43. Joshua Green, "What Happened to Roy Moore's Ten Commandments Monument?" *The Atlantic* (March 2011). Online: http://www.theatlantic.com/politics/archive/2011/03/what-happened-to-roy-moores-ten-commandments-monument/73221/. The case of Judge Moore and its legal implications have been further discussed in Claudia Setzer and David A. Shefferman, eds., *The Bible and American Culture: A Sourcebook* (London: Routledge, 2011), 85–87.

44. Ryan J. Reilly, "'Ten Commandments Judge' Roy Moore Wins Back Alabama Supreme Court Seat," Talking Points Memo, November 7, 2012. Online: http://tpmmuckraker.talkingpointsmemo.com/2012/11/roy_moore_ten_commandments_victory.php.

45. For an overview of the events see Tricia Escobedo, "Timeline of Florida's Quran-Burning Pastor," CNN Belief Blog, April 1, 2011. Online: http://religion.blogs.cnn.com/2011/04/01/timeline-of-floridas-quran-burning-pastor/.

Part 3: The Bible and Popular Culture

Holy Words in Hollywood: DeMille's *The Ten Commandments* (1956) and American Identity*

Adele Reinhartz

As a child, I loved Walt Disney movies, especially *Bambi*, *Cinderella*, and *Snow White and the Seven Dwarves*. But the two films that I watched frequently, one might say, religiously, over a period of many years on our small black and white television were *The Wizard of Oz* and *The Ten Commandments*. *The Wizard of Oz* (1939) delighted and frightened in equal measure and for a young girl also provided a powerful role model in the plucky Dorothy, who not only had marvelous adventures but could sing up a storm. Nevertheless, as a young Jewish girl, *The Ten Commandments* (1956) had a special place in my heart. I knew that *The Wizard of Oz* was pure fantasy—*my* shoes never took me anywhere when I clicked them together—but *The Ten Commandments* was history, and not just any history but my history and that of all the Jewish children and parents I knew. I viewed DeMille's epic as a faithful rendering of the story of Moses and the exodus from Egypt that we learned about in detail at the Jewish school I attended every day after school and that we recalled every year at our Passover seders. Some decades later, I introduced my own children to this movie, which they watched over and over, now with the help of a new technology called VHS. They particularly loved the part where Bithia, the Pharaoh's daughter, takes baby Moses out of the water, but the parting of the Red Sea was pretty fine too; they would rewind and play those scenes numerous times.

By then, of course, I realized just how much DeMille had amplified and embroidered his account, and it was not long before my children did

---

* Permission to make use of material from Adele Reinhartz, *Bible and Cinema: An Introduction* (London: Routledge, 2013), 36–44 is gratefully acknowledged.

too, though this did not spoil our enjoyment. Eventually, the movie lost its grip on our household, and the VHS made its way to the basement to join the other abandoned toys, audiotapes, and videotapes. Even after I began teaching and writing about the Bible and film, I did not return to this one on the grounds that my students would find more relevance in more recent, less epic fare.

And so DeMille's film languished in our storage room and the forgotten recesses of our minds until a couple of years ago, when my work on Bible and film led me back to the epics of the 1950s. Our VCR long broken, I bought the DVD and settled down to watch. I expected to spend a pleasant three hours of over-the-top spectacle and grand emotion, tinged with mild nostalgia for my now-grown children's childhood and my own. Instead, I was arrested from the opening credits to Moses's final gaze across the river Jordan. My interest was held not by the epic elements of the film that had enchanted me decades ago as a child and young mother, but by the film's blatant political and theological messages. How could I have missed them before?

Many have commented on DeMille's anticommunist and Cold War agenda.[1] This point does not require particular insight, for it is made explicit by DeMille himself in his film's prologue, in which he steps out from behind the curtain to declare that "the theme of this picture is whether men ought to be ruled by God's law or whether they ought to be ruled by the whims of a dictator like Rameses. Are men the property of the State or are they free souls under God? This same battle continues throughout the world today." In this way, DeMille not only asserts the historicity of his account but also instructs the viewers to view the analogies between the Exodus story and the struggle against world-wide Communism that threatens the freedom of America and the progress of global democracy.

But the film offers more than a Cold War diatribe against the Soviet menace. In refashioning Moses as a Jesus-like redeemer figure and the Israelites as freedom-loving Americans, DeMille turns the Exodus story into

---

1. For example, see Jonathan P. Herzog, *The Spiritual-Industrial Complex: America's Religious Battle against Communism in the Early Cold War* (New York: Oxford University Press, 2011), 158; Melanie Jane Wright, *Moses in America: The Cultural Uses of Biblical Narrative* (American Academy of Religion Cultural Criticism Series; Oxford; New York: Oxford University Press, 2003), 90–92; Bruce Babington and Peter William Evans, *Biblical Epics: Sacred Narrative in the Hollywood Cinema* (Manchester: Manchester University Press; 1993), 54.

a peculiarly American story that both expresses and perpetuates a Puritan foundation narrative that persists, in an attenuated and often ambivalent way, to the present day.[2] Before proceeding to an analysis of the film, I begin with a very brief outline of this Puritan narrative.

Puritan Foundation Narrative

The role of the Bible in shaping America's foundation story has been demonstrated most persuasively by Sacvan Bercovitch, most succinctly in an essay entitled "The Biblical Basis of the American Myth."[3] Bercovitch sums up this biblical foundation as follows: "In the beginning was the word, and the word was with the New England way, and the word became 'America.'"[4] The Puritans were obsessed with Scripture. They saw their own history and mission in America as prophesied and grounded in Scripture; and, in turn, they believed that the Bible—and therefore God—supported, approved of, and even vindicated the social, political, and economic structures that they were creating. Indeed, in the Puritan view, the project of America was scripture brought to life.[5]

Historically, the Bible played a crucial role in unifying a diverse society that tended towards fragmentation; and it continues to play a unifying role today, especially in American politics.[6] In *The Puritan Origins of American Patriotism*, George McKenna notes that "when the chips are down, when the stakes are high, American political leaders go back to the narrative and even the language of the Puritans; they do it then, especially, because that is when Americans especially want to hear it."[7]

---

2. See also Jolyon Mitchell, "Ethics," in *The Routledge Companion to Religion and Film* (ed. John Lyden; New York: Routledge, 2009), 489.

3. Sacvan Bercovitch, "The Biblical Basis of the American Myth," in *Bible and American Arts and Letters* (Philadelphia: Fortress, 1983), 219–29.

4. Ibid., 219.

5. Ibid., 221.

6. See the essays by Jacques Berlinerblau ("The Bible in the Presidential Elections of 2012, 2008, 2004, and the Collapse of American Secularism") and Yaakov Ariel ("Biblical Imagery, the End Times, and Political Action: The Roots of Christian Support for Zionism and Israel") in this volume.

7. George McKenna, *The Puritan Origins of American Patriotism* (New Haven: Yale University Press, 2007), xiii.

McKenna describes the Puritans as the "founders of America's political culture and rhetoric"[8] and, above all, of American patriotism.[9] Fundamental to American patriotism, in all of its diverse forms, is "the belief that Americans are a people set apart, a people with a providential mission."[10] The American myth was articulated succinctly by Thomas Jefferson in his second inaugural address. Jefferson professed the need for "the favor of that Being in whose hands we are, who led our fathers, as Israel of old, from their native land and planted them in a country flowing with all the necessaries and comforts of life, who has covered our infancy with his providence and our riper years with his wisdom and power."[11] In the midst of all the changes in Puritanism, Protestantism more generally, and America writ large, this sense of biblical errand has remained constant, even if often unarticulated, even in "the most (seemingly) secular undertakings."[12]

The American myth has several elements relevant for our purposes. First, in this myth, America is identified with ancient Israel, not only as a metaphor or analogy, but in fact. America is God's covenant nation, prophesied in the Bible. Second, as God's chosen people, America is obliged to set an example for the world. Third, Americans, like the ancient Israelites, must remain faithful to God in order to prosper. Fourth, God's people—America—are in a cosmic battle against the devil and his servant, the antichrist, who aim to frustrate God's design for the world. Defeating the devil may require war and bloodshed.[13] But, finally, the devil's work is also internal. For that reason it is essential to engage in "anxious introspection" to excise "corruption, moral libertinism, hypocrisy, and, above all, pride." These ostensibly private sins are in fact communal; they undermine America as a nation in covenant with God.[14] Anyone tracking public discourse in the United States in the months leading up to the 2012 election will easily recognize these same elements in the campaign ads and public debates between the two candidates for president, especially on foreign policy.[15]

---

8. Ibid., 4.
9. Ibid., 5.
10. Ibid., 6.
11. Ibid., 46.
12. Ibid., 7.
13. Ibid., 49.
14. Ibid., 32.
15. See Berlinerblau, "The Bible in The Presidential Elections of 2012, 2008, 2004," in this volume.

With Bercovitch, then, we can sum up the American myth as follows: "In the beginning was the word 'America,' and the word was in the Bible, and the word was made flesh in the Americans, this new breed of humans, destined to build a shining city on a hill."[16] But, as Bercovitch has noted, there is a weakness inherent in the very structure of this narrative. Despite the profound biblical reinterpretation in which the Puritans engaged, they were still constrained by the Bible's own mythic patterns: the exodus paradigm of the Hebrew Bible or Old Testament, and the Christ-centred salvation paradigm of the New Testament.[17] The exodus is a story of communal liberation and redemption, and in that sense, it is a "story in process—communal, historical, prospective." The Christ story, by contrast, focuses on personal redemption, and "it is essentially spiritual, individual, and retrospective."[18]

The Ten Commandments: Analysis

If the Puritans forcefully and definitively inserted the Bible into the American public square, it is the Bible epic film of the 1950s and early 60s that kept it there. DeMille's 1956 film of the exodus account embodies and expresses both the Puritan myth of America as the new Israel and this tension between the exodus and Christ narratives. It does so by making the same moves with the exodus story that the Puritans did with the Bible as a whole. First, the movie elides the exodus and Christ myths by recasting the prophet Moses as a Jesus-like redeemer figure. Second, it identifies this redeemer figure as American. Third, it assigns to this Puritan American a divinely given mandate for striving for liberty—defined, of course, from an American perspective. Just as Moses led the Israelites to the Promised Land—a journey that involved hardship, even death—so too must those who now inhabit the promised land of America fight to preserve their liberty and the American way of life against any and all threats.

---

16. Bercovitch, "The Biblical Basis of the American Myth," 226, notes that the phrase "a city on a hill" stems from the Sermon on the Mount, in which Jesus tells his listeners, "You are the light of the world. A city built on a hill cannot be hid" (Matt 5:14). In his 1630 sermon, "A Model of Christian Charity," the Puritan John Winthrop described the future Massachusetts Bay colony as a "city upon a hill." This description was extended to the United States as a whole.
17. Ibid.
18. Ibid.

Moses as Jesus

DeMille's film portrays Moses as a Jesus figure by applying to Moses a number of passages, phrases, and concepts from the Hebrew Bible that in the New Testament and Christian thought are closely associated with Jesus. DeMille's film claims that Moses, like Jesus, was destined to be a redeemer from the time before he was born. Indeed, according to the film's unseen narrator, he was given by God to his parents for that very purpose: "So did the Egyptians cause the children of Israel to serve with rigor, and their lives were made bitter with hard bondage. And their cry came up unto God. And God heard them and cast into Egypt, into the lowly hut of Amram and Yochabel, the seed of a man upon whose mind and heart would be written God's law and God's commandments, one man to stand alone against an empire."[19] Moses, unlike Jesus, may have been born in the usual manner of human beings; but nevertheless it was God who cast his seed into this particular family as the instrument of God's salvific purpose.

The scene then shifts to the royal palace, where the pharaoh Sethi receives a prophecy of a redeemer who will lead the Israelites out of bondage.[20] "Divine one," his advisors tell him, "Last night, our astrologers saw an evil star enter into the House of Egypt.... The enemy to fear is in the heart of Egypt.... The Hebrew slaves in the land of Goshen.... Among these slaves, there is a prophecy of a deliverer who will lead them out of bondage. A star proclaims his birth." The Pharaoh orders the newborn boys to be killed. "So let it be written. So let it be done. So speaks Rameses I." For DeMille's film, Moses is a divinely-prophesied redeemer whom the Pharaoh is anxious to kill before he grows up. In the book of Exodus, Pharaoh does indeed order the death of all newborn Israelite males. This is not because he fears a prophesied redeemer, however, but because he fears that their rapidly growing numbers will embolden them to join Egypt's enemies, fight against Egypt, and escape from the land (Exod 1:10). The motif of a feared infant redeemer, rather, belongs to the Gospel of Matthew, in which the three wise men see a rising star and know that the redeemer has been born. Herod, alarmed, orders the wise

---

19. DeMille names Moses's Hebrew mother Yochabel instead of the biblical Yocheved (*yôkebed*; NRSV Jochebed), following Josephus, *A.J.* 2.217 (Ιωχαβέλη).

20. "Sethi" is the spelling that appears in the credits, rather than the more usual English spelling "Seti."

men to tell him where they find the child. When they do not, he orders all children under two to be killed (Matt 2:1–16).

Although Exodus does not describe Moses as a preordained redeemer, DeMille has not merely transposed a gospel story to this Israelite hero. In fact, he is drawing on Josephus, the first century Jewish historian. In *A.J.* 2.205–206, Josephus declares that the Egyptians' murderous intents towards the Israelites were spurred by a prophecy uttered by one of their own "sacred scribes" who "announced to the king that someone would be begotten at that time to the Israelites who would humble the rule of the Egyptians and would elevate the Israelites." According to Josephus, this is why the Pharaoh "ordered that every male fathered by the Israelites should be cast into the river and destroyed." Here Josephus's retelling of the exodus and Matthew's version of Jesus's childhood coincide to allow DeMille to describe Moses in a way that directly reminds us of Jesus.

Another point at which *The Ten Commandments* directly identifies Moses as a Jesus-like redeemer figure occurs when the prince of Egypt learns that he is born a Hebrew and not an Egyptian. In this scene, he must choose between two mothers—Yochabel the Hebrew slave and Bithia the Egyptian princess—both of whom love him. When he chooses his Hebrew mother, Bithia, deeply saddened, asks if he feels no shame. He responds: "What change is there in me? Egyptian or Hebrew, I am still Moses. These are the same hands, the same arms, the same face that were mine a moment ago." After Bithia leaves, Yochabel gives thanks: "God of our fathers, who has appointed an end to the bondage of Israel, blessed am I among all mothers in the land, for my eyes have beheld Thy deliverer."

Bithia's prayer has several explicit allusions to the infancy narrative of the Gospel of Luke. When the angel announces to Mary that she will have a son, he declares, "Blessed are you among women" (Luke 1:28), a formula that Mary's cousin Elizabeth, the mother of John the Baptist, repeats in Luke 1:42 and that Mary herself echoes in the hymn known as the Magnificat: "Surely, from now on all generations will call me blessed" (Luke 1:46–49).[21]

Moses's speech, however, alludes to a more recent text that while not biblical is also part of the canon of Western culture. In Shakespeare's *The Merchant of Venice* (act 3, scene 1, lines 49–61), the money-lender Shylock declares: "I am a Jew. Hath not a Jew eyes? Hath not a Jew hands, organs,

---

21. Unless otherwise noted, all biblical quotations follow that of the NRSV.

dimensions, senses, affections, passions; fed with the same food, hurt with the same weapons, subject to the same diseases, healed by the same means, warmed and cooled by the same winter and summer as a Christian is?" Shylock is here asserting his humanity, but also protesting the anti-Semitism of his enemies. DeMille's appropriation of this same language makes a similar statement: we are all human, whether Hebrew or Egyptian; the fact that Moses has thrown his lot in with the Hebrews does not change this fundamental identity, nor should it be an occasion for discrimination, oppression, and enslavement.

Moses as American

DeMille has reconstituted Moses as a redeemer like Jesus by a judicious, even inspired, choice of biblical and postbiblical allusions. But we know that this Jesus-like Moses is also an American by the same means that we can identify Americans on our foreign travels: by his accent. The redeemer's indisputably American accent is apparent in his pronunciation of the vowels as well as in the general rhythm and cadence of his speech. (This trait is even more obvious in the 1998 animated film, *Prince of Egypt*). Moses shares this accent with that quintessential redeemer, Jesus, who in Martin Scorsese's *The Last Temptation of* Christ (1988; Jesus played by Willem Dafoe) is identifiably American in speech, while his opponent, the Roman governor Pontius Pilate (played by David Bowie), is definitely a Brit. This web of aural allusions further identifies Moses and Jesus, at least in their popular-culture personas. The association also emphasizes that the global, even cosmic, conflict between good (exemplified by God and his biblical agents Moses and Jesus) and evil (exemplified by Egypt and Rome) is also at stake in the tension between America as the champion of liberty and democracy against foreign oppressive and totalitarian regimes.

A closer look at, or rather, listen to, DeMille's *Ten Commandments*, however, reveals a slightly more complex situation. The "old" Pharaoh Sethi (played by the well-known British actor Sir Cedric Hardwicke), a fair-minded pagan, has a British accent, whereas the true villain of the piece, his son Rameses (Yul Brynner), has an indeterminate but vaguely sinister European accent. Many film viewers do not consciously think about accents, perhaps assuming that actors deploy the accents of their native lands. But in fact, voice and accents are important markers of character, personality, and role; and movie actors are generally adept at speaking in whatever accent their roles require. Moses's American accent is therefore not incidental to his redemptive identity and role in the film, but essential to it. By depicting the "bad guy" not as British but simply as foreign, DeMille is in effect declaring that the enemies of America in the twentieth century were not the British, who are foreign but basically okay. Rather, America must beware of the Eastern Europeans among whom communism has taken root, lest these latter day Egyptians attempt to enslave the true Israel once more.

America and Liberty

All the themes come together in the final scene of the film, which celebrates, indeed, glorifies, America's role as the champion of liberty and justice for all. On the off chance that viewers missed the point in the previous three and a half hours of the film, Moses's aged wife Sepphora skilfully and succinctly coordinates Old Testament and New Testament allusions to drive the point home: "Look, Moses. The people have come to the River Jordan. In the ark, they carry the law you brought them. You taught them not to live by bread alone. You are God's torch that lights the way to freedom."

The idea that bread is not enough for humankind's survival stems from Deut 8:3: "One does not live by bread alone, but by every word that comes from the mouth of the Lord," an idea repeated by Jesus in Matt 4:4 as a response to Satan's taunt: "If you are the Son of God, command these stones to become loaves of bread" (Matt 4:3). Second, as God's torch, Moses is the instrument through which Israel—here, America—becomes a light unto the nations, as prophesied by the prophet Isaiah (42:6; 49:6). Especially relevant is Isa 60:3: "Nations shall come to your light, and kings to the brightness of your dawn."

The abundance of allusions continues in Moses's last words: "Go, proclaim liberty throughout all the lands, unto all the inhabitants thereof!" Moses's exhortation is a direct quotation of Lev 25:10, but it is taken completely out of context. In Lev 25:10 God, through Moses, instructs the Israelites as follows: "And you shall hallow the fiftieth year and you shall proclaim liberty throughout the land to all its inhabitants. It shall be a jubilee for you: you shall return, every one of you, to your property and every one of you to your family." In its original context, the point of this verse is not specifically freedom from slavery, or from foreign domination, but from reaping, sowing, and paying debts. In its cinematic context, however, these Old Testament words recall Jesus's proclamation at the end of the New Testament Gospel of Matthew: "Go ye therefore, and teach all nations, baptizing them in the name of the Father, and of the Son, and of the Holy Ghost," which concludes with the reassuring promise: "lo, I am with you always, *even* unto the end of the world. Amen" (Matt 28:19–20, KJV). But the Leviticus quotation also has an explicitly American resonance as the words written upon the Liberty Bell in Philadelphia. If all this is not enough, the elderly Moses models his final posture after the symbol of liberty par excellence, the Statue of Liberty, a fleeting but nevertheless striking image.[22]

Questioning the Puritan Bible

Despite his claims to be faithful both to the biblical texts and to history itself, DeMille has constructed a Moses who differs considerably from the biblical figure. To be sure, the Bible's Moses has a special prophetic status as the one who is commissioned by God as an instrument for divine liberation of God's covenant people from Egyptian bondage. Nevertheless, the point of the biblical story is not to raise Moses up as a redeemer figure but to focus on God as the one who saves Israel with mighty hand and outstretched arm (Deut 7:18–19; Ps 136:12; Jer 27:5). Whereas the New Testament posits Jesus as the prophet-like-Moses foretold in Deut 18:15–19), DeMille portrays Moses as a savior like Jesus whose activity in the world is closely aligned with America's divinely granted mission as God's covenant people.

Looking back on DeMille's *The Ten Commandments* from a vantage point almost sixty years after it was first released, it is sobering to realize that the end of the Cold War did not substantially affect the potency and global sweep of the Puritan myth of America as the true Israel. The enemy may have changed, but the idea of America as the God-given savior of the world and champion of freedom and democracy still seems powerfully present. *The Ten Commandments* is noteworthy not only because of the worldview that it projects, but also because of what it leaves out. DeMille's discourse around slavery and freedom has a resonance beyond America's global responsibility as God's light unto the nations, for it evokes the expe-

---

22. Michael Wood, *America in the Movies: Or, "Santa Maria, It Had Slipped My Mind"* (New York: Basic Books, 1975), 187.

rience of slavery in America's own history and the legacy of discrimination and oppression with which African Americans still live.

DeMille's movie, which came out right at the beginning of a decisive phase of the Civil Rights movement (1955–1968), indirectly acknowledges this fact of American history. When Moses declares his intention to stay with his Hebrew mother Yochabel, he declares: "Here I will stay ... to find the meaning of what I am ... why a Hebrew ... or any man must be a slave." Later, when the pagan priest Jethro offers to help the fugitive Moses, Moses asks if he is sure he wants to do that, for "it is death to give sanctuary to a runaway slave." In the biblical context, it is unlikely that Moses, who at this point in the biblical account is not a runaway slave but an escaped murderer, would have been pursued beyond the borders of Egypt; but in an American context his statement recalls the Fugitive Slave Act of 1793, which made it illegal to help runaway slaves. As with the theme of American triumphalism, cinema since DeMille has broadened to allow filmmakers to address issues of racism directly and explicitly in films such as *Monster Ball* (2001) and the controversial Blaxploitation genre.[23] In the current cultural moment, we might also wonder how the film, and the myth that it expresses, resonate with illegal immigrants and others who are refused refugee status and asylum in the United States.

Ours is an era that is more pessimistic, more openly diverse, and also less certain of leadership and political policies than America of the immediate postwar era. If Hollywood has not completely abandoned the worldview of DeMille and other filmmakers from the glory days of the epic film, American cinema since Vietnam and, more recently, the war in Iraq has often been highly critical of American wars fueled by the type of ideology that DeMille and others before and after him have embraced.

A recent example is a 2007 film *In the Valley of Elah*, directed, as it happens, by Canadian film director Paul Haggis. The film's protagonist, Hank Deerfield (Tommy Lee Jones), is a former military policeman who has just received word that his son Mike, a soldier who has just returned from a tour of duty in Iraq, has gone missing from his army base. Mike's body is found in a field, burned and dismembered. With the help of a policewoman, Emily Sanders (Charlize Theron), Hank sets out to discover the identity of his son's killer. The film firmly establishes Hank's commit-

---

23. Mia Mask, *Contemporary Black American Cinema: Race, Gender and Sexuality at the Movies* (New York: Routledge, 2012).

ment to the army, not only through his own service but through the strong positive value that he attached to the army. This allegiance he passed along to his sons, both of whom enlisted and died in the course of their service, though not in active combat (we learn early on that Hank's older son was killed in a helicopter accident at Fort Bragg). Hank is self-disciplined and organized; in fact, he still makes his bed military style, even when staying in a motel that presumably has a daily housekeeping service.

Hank's attempts to find out what happened to his son Mike, and why, are repeatedly and vigorously blocked by the military police. He is aided only by a female police detective, who herself has trouble getting the time of day not only from the military but also from her own colleagues in the police force. As he continues his investigation, Hank gradually loses his confidence in and respect for the army; as time goes on he comes to believe that the army leadership is less interested in finding out what happened than in covering it up and protecting their own. In the end, through persistence and strategic thinking, Hank and Emily succeed in learning the terrible truth.

The film does not address the basic question of whether the war in Iraq was a necessary or justified war. Rather, its focus is on the effect of war on the behavior and the emotional and psychological health of the soldiers who participate in active combat duty and on the nature of the army as an organization. Hank's increasingly critical attitude towards the army is signalled in a recurring scene involving the American flag. Near the beginning of the film, Hank enters the local high school to complain about the fact that the American flag is flying upside down. Hank seeks out Juan, the Salvadoran custodian, and teaches him to hang the flag correctly. Hank, the war veteran, explains to Juan, the new immigrant, that an upside down flag is an international distress signal. For Hank the army veteran, the idea that America could ever be in dire distress is unthinkable. Indeed, as the world's superpower, it is America's role to "save the asses" of weaker countries overseas, such as Iraq. By the end of the film, however, Hank's attitude has changed. After unravelling the mystery of his son's death, he returns home. There he finds a parcel sent by his son before his death. Inside is a tattered flag and a photo of his son, surrounded by friends, in front of that same flag. Hank brings the flag to the high school and runs it up the flagpole as the custodian Juan looks on. The last shot of the film is of the tattered flag, hanging upside down, flapping in the breeze. The message? America is a country in distress. But who will save her?

Conclusion

The films of Haggis, DeMille, and dozens of other directors help to put and keep the Bible in the public square and in the minds of their viewers. In doing so they also reflect the Puritan use of the Bible to describe and develop American identity. If films such as *The Ten Commandments* glorify America's role as the defender of global democracy in the face of the evil forces of fascism and communism, films such as *In the Valley of Elah* project an ambivalent perspective on the American role on the world stage. Both films illustrate Hollywood's use of the Bible to reflect the concerns, anxieties, and perspectives of America's public square in response to shifting events and changing attitudes. The global context in which we now live means that along with their consumption of American movies and television, audiences the world over are also absorbing the Puritan narrative of America as the promised land, and the Puritan use of the Bible as an allegory of American history and America's role in the world. In this way, old epics and newer, darker movies contribute to the way in which America is viewed in far corners of the globe. They also contribute both to an appreciation and a suspicion of America, to the desire to move here or to criticize those who do so.

History, Memory, and Forgetting in Psalm 137

David W. Stowe

Like few other psalms, Ps 137—"By the Rivers of Babylon"—shows up in unexpected places. Halfway through the first season of *Mad Men*, the Sterling Cooper ad agency has just secured an account with the Israeli Tourism Bureau. Judging from the obtuse, mildly anti-Semitic office banter, it would appear that this is the first time anyone in the WASP-laden agency has ever thought about Israel, or Jews. It's not clear they know the difference. But Leon Uris's *Exodus* is *au courant*, soon to be made into a movie starring Paul Newman; we see the show's dashing protagonist Don Draper reading it at bedtime to bone up for the new client.[1]

He has also been working closely with Rachel, a department store heiress, and appears to be heading toward an affair with her. They meet for coffee, ostensibly to discuss the new account with Israel. "I'm the only Jew you know in New York City?" she asks incredulously. Rachel explains that Jews have been living in exile for a very long time. "We've managed to make a go of it," she tells Draper. "It might have something to do with the fact that we thrive at doing business with people who hate us."

Meanwhile, Draper is cautiously sampling the bohemian world of his girlfriend, Midge. They make their way to the Gaslight, a subterranean nightclub on MacDougal Street in Greenwich Village. After a couple of cringe-inducing avant-garde poets, a folk trio comes onstage playing a haunting round in minor key. The banjo player wears a cap of the style made famous by the early Bob Dylan, who actually performed at the Gaslight. He sings:

---

1. Matthew Weiner, *Mad Men: Season One* (Santa Monica, Calif.: Lionsgate, 2008).

> By the waters, the waters, of Babylon
> We lay down and wept, and wept, for thee Zion.
> We remember, we remember, we remember thee Zion.

Mad Men viewers may vaguely remember this song from the iconic Don McLean album, *American Pie* (1971).[2] Some may have even sung it around campfires in youth groups. As the eerie music continues in the club, the camera cuts to vignettes suggesting Draper's stream of consciousness: scenes of Rachel, his wife and children, his boss.

Unique among the Hebrew psalms, Ps 137 transpires in a particular place and time. Along with the exodus, the Babylonian exile to which the psalm refers sits at the core of Judaism. The trauma it entailed served as a crucible, forcing the Israelites to rethink their relationship to Yahweh, revise their understanding of the covenant, reassess their standing as a chosen people, and rewrite their history. It inaugurated the Israelite sense of themselves as a nation of exile, a people who have somehow survived living in diaspora for more than 2500 years.

Psalm 137 has also been highly adaptable outside of Jewish communities. It has served as North America's longest running protest song, lending rhetorical support to anticolonial movements from the American Revolution to Jamaican Rastafari. In the United States, its most distinctive use has come in antiracist movements from abolitionism to civil rights.[3] Psalm 137 has also been used to articulate alienation and marginalization of a more private, existential variety. Its three distinct sections have distinct modes of address; they speak to different situations and have been deployed for different social uses.

The first four verses of the psalm, delivered in the first person plural, evoke communal memories of better times, remembered in moments of dislocation and humiliation, and ends with the question, "How could we sing the LORD's song in a foreign land?" The two middle verses take the form of an inward-looking oath by the psalmist, calling for corporal punishment—paralysis of tongue and hand—if he forgets Jerusalem. The lines have been of particular interest to political movements that invoke collective memory in order to mobilize social action. The final three verses are addressed to Yahweh. With their call for vengeance against Edom

---

2. Don McLean, "Babylon," *American Pie* (Capitol Records, 1988 [1971]).

3. David W. Stowe, "Babylon Revisited: Psalm 137 as American Protest Song," *Black Music Research Journal* 32 (2012): 95–112.

and Babylon, climaxing with the infamous celebration of dashing babies against rocks, they have usually been excised (and forgotten) in the North American context, even as vengeance has featured prominently in North American public life from the earliest conflicts with Native Americans through the triumphant take down of Osama bin Laden. While Psalm 137 has been widely adopted for Christian contexts, the American musician Matisyahu recently recorded a popular version reflecting his Jewish affiliations and Zionist leanings.

1. Psalm 137:1–4

> By the rivers of Babylon—there we sat down and there we wept, when we remembered Zion.
> On the willows there we hung up our harps.
> For there our captors asked us for songs; and our tormentors asked us for mirth, saying, "Sing us one of the songs of Zion!"
> How could we sing the LORD's song in a foreign land?[4]

These are the psalm's best-known verses, favored for innumerable musical settings over the centuries. The setting is Mesopotamia, the banks of the Euphrates River, or at least one of the irrigation canals connected with that river. The verbs indicate the time is past: we sat, we wept, we remembered, we hung; they asked. The psalm is unambiguous in its historicity; unlike other laments we do not have to guess which crisis is being invoked. It can be precisely dated to 587 B.C.E.

But to the psalmist, how distant is that past? The psalm's opening lines give the impression of an eyewitness account. Some traditions posit King David as the poet, implying that he had prophetic powers to foresee the future. Other traditions attribute the psalm to the prophet Jeremiah, who lived through the destruction of the Jerusalem temple and the exile to Babylon. But it could have been created by some other, unknown contemporary of Jeremiah. Or even someone living after the exile had ended, when many of the exiled Judeans had returned west of the Jordan River to Palestine.[5]

---

4. Unless otherwise noted, all biblical quotations follow the NRSV.
5. James L. Kugel, *In Potiphar's House: The Interpretive Life of Biblical Texts* (San Francisco: HarperSanFrancisco, 1990), 173–80.

We can picture this psalm in our mind's eye: bedraggled and forlorn human detritus, huddling on a riverbank. As water flows by, tears trickle down. Their salinity mixes with the river—muddy, brackish, clear, boggy, rapid—we're not told. Later translators would embellish this image of tears flowing into the river. There is shade provided by willows (the weeping tree), or in some translations, poplar trees. But these trees hold, as Billie Holiday sang in a different context, strange fruit: stringed instruments, harps, lyres, organs—again, the language varies among translations.[6] Why are captives transporting these musical instruments, and why go to the trouble of festooning trees with them?

David Noel Freedman alerts us to the verbal music of the psalm: "extensive use of alliteration, assonance, and similar sound effects to produce a mournful tone in keeping with the content of the psalm."[7] Repeated occurrence of the labials *b* and *m* simulate the sound of wind in the willows resonating over the waters; the keening note of ending *-nū* sounds repeatedly. Based on painstaking parsing of the Hebrew, Freedman emphasizes its elaborate symmetry: the psalm comprises an "envelope construction in which the outer sections fold around the inner ones producing a cohesive and integrated whole. Thus the opening and closing sections form an *inclusio* which is keyed on the word *Bābel*."[8] Even the inner core, verses 4–6, contains a nucleus, according to Freedman, "an artfully designed chiastic couplet which is at once the dramatic high point or apex of the poem and the axis linking the parts and exhibiting the essential structure of the whole."[9]

This formal symmetry reinforces the psalm's thematic symmetry, structured around a play of oppositions: Babylon and Jerusalem, river and rock, silence and singing, forgetting and remembering. It begins and ends with Babylon's physical topography: first watery, then dry rock. The psalm's opening and closing sections both feature passages of direct speech, the first from Babylonians, the last from Edomites.

---

6. Hannibal Hamlin, *Psalm Culture and Early Modern English Literature* (Cambridge: Cambridge University Press, 2004), 220–35.

7. David Noel Freedman, "The Structure of Psalm 137," in *Near Eastern Studies in Honor of William Foxwell Albright* (ed. Hans Goedicke; Baltimore: Johns Hopkins University Press, 1971), 191.

8. Freedman, "The Structure of Psalm 137," 203.

9. Ibid.

Psalm 137 as a whole is embedded in larger symmetries. The Bible itself is "pyramidal and symmetric," Freedman writes,

> like a domed building in which the apex is near or at the center, and the opening and closing form a ring or pair of interlocking parts that constitute the foundation. For the Hebrew Bible as a whole, the center comes at the end of the Primary History and at the beginning of the Latter Prophets—at which point the Bible tells of the captivity of the people of Judah, the loss of nationhood, and the destruction of the capital city of Jerusalem and the Temple.[10]

Freedman notes also that the Primary History begins and ends with the story of Babel: from the tower of Babel narrated early in Genesis to the end of 2 Kings: "They have come full circle: from Babylon to Babylon."[11] In that sense, then, the situation narrated by Ps 137 serves as a kind of axis for the entire Hebrew Bible.

Recent years have seen an outpouring of scholarship on the decades of exile. Much of the work emphasizes the split between the Golah (Diaspora) and Judah, between the "irrigation canals" of Babylon and "templeless Judah."[12] Scholars have forcefully countered the "myth of the empty land": that Judah was completely evacuated and barren, with all the people who mattered relocated to Babylon. Work over the past two decades challenges the notion of a dramatic rupture in the Judean experience, stressing the continuity experienced by the majority of the population who stayed in Palestine.[13] Also called into question: the conventional wisdom that the exile was relatively benign. Based on the most fragmentary textual evidence, scholars had concluded that after the initial trauma of conquest the hardships in Babylon were minimal. Drawing on methodologies from migration studies, refugee studies, diaspora studies, and trauma theory,

---

10. David Noel Freedman, *The Nine Commandments: Uncovering a Hidden Pattern of Crime and Punishment in the Hebrew Bible* (New York: Doubleday, 2000), xvii.

11. Freedman, *The Nine Commandments*, xii.

12. John J. Ahn and Jill Middlemas, eds., *By the Irrigation Canals of Babylon: Approaches to the Study of the Exile* (New York: T&T Clark, 2012).

13. Jill Anne Middlemas, *Troubles of Templeless Judah* (Oxford: Oxford University Press, 2005); Oded Lipschits, *The Fall and Rise of Jerusalem: Judah Under Babylonian Rule* (Winona Lake, Ind.: Eisenbrauns, 2005); Hans M. Barstad, *The Myth of the Empty Land: A Study in the History and Archaeology of Judah During the "Exilic" Period* (Oslo: Scandinavian University Press, 1996).

recent work has emphasized that even under the best circumstances exile is harrowing.[14] This work also has ventured theories about what the Judeans were likely doing in Babylon: supplying corvée labor, removing salt from irrigation canals. John Ahn suggests that careful attention to historical chronology, especially as it shaped differing generational perspectives between those who came to Babylon in 597, 587, and 582, can help clarify gaps and inconsistencies we find in biblical accounts.[15]

Fig. 1. Gypsum wall panel relief from showing an Assyrian soldier and three captives, possibly Judeans, carrying harps in wooded terrain. ca. 700 B.C.E. © Trustees of the British Museum.

---

14. Brad E. Kelle, Frank Ritchel Ames, and Jacob L. Wright, eds., *Interpreting Exile: Displacement and Deportation in Biblical and Modern Contexts* (Atlanta: Society of Biblical Literature, 2011); Daniel L. Smith-Christopher, *A Biblical Theology of Exile* (Minneapolis: Fortress, 2002). For a powerful critique of the romanticizing of exile, see Edward Said, "Reflections on Exile," in *Out There: Marginalization and Contemporary Cultures* (ed. Russell Ferguson; Cambridge: MIT Press, 1990), 357–66.

15. John J. Ahn, *Exile as Forced Migrations: A Sociological, Literary, and Theological Approach on the Displacement and Resettlement of the Southern Kingdom of Judah* (Berlin: de Gruyter, 2010), 27–28.

In short, throughout much of the West, conceptions of exile have long been subtly colored by the biblical account, while contemporary scholars extrapolate from recent findings on forced migration to better understand the plight of ancient Judeans. All of which sets up a tension between collective memory as sacred history narrated by the Hebrew Bible and rigorous historiography conducted by scholars using state-of-the-art social science methodologies. How is the meaning of the exile transformed when we historicize the period during which so much of the history of Israel was being compiled and redacted by Judeans who were themselves in or recently returned from exile?

In the less rigorous (but inversely more influential) domain of popular culture, the psalm's first four verses have generated by far the most musical settings and visual representations. The musical canon version that appears in *Mad Men* was included on McLean's best-selling album, but was not covered by other artists. Stephen Schwartz wrote a version of the psalm, "On the Willows," for *Godspell* (1971), the only part of the musical taken from the Hebrew Bible (the language is otherwise drawn from the Gospel of Matthew and the Book of Common Prayer).[16] But it was a slightly earlier version by the Jamaican group the Melodians that gave the psalm global exposure—and revivified a long American tradition of antiracist and anticolonialist adaptations of the psalm. First recorded in 1969 and featured in the groundbreaking Jimmy Cliff film *The Harder They Come* (1973),[17] "Rivers of Babylon" has since been covered by dozens of artists ranging from Linda Ronstadt and Sinead O'Connor to the Neville Brothers, Steve Earle, and Sublime. The chart-topping 1978 disco version by Boney M is probably the best-known of all versions; it appears as diegetic music in a number of international films, including the Chinese movie *Shanghai Dreams* (2005) and the Kazach film *Tulpan*, in both cases evoking the freedom of Western-style youth culture and social mobility in contrast to the stultifying confinement of the traditional family and village-centered life.[18]

---

16. Stephen Schwartz, "On the Willows," *Godspell* (Sony Music Entertainment, 2011 [1971]).

17. Perry Henzel, dir., *The Harder They Come* (International Films, 2000 [1973]).

18. Xiaoshuai Wang, dir., *Shanghai Dreams* (Stellar Megamedia Kingwood, 2005); Sergei Dvortsevoy, dir., *Tulpan* (Pallas Film, 2008).

2. Psalm 137:5–6

> If I forget you, O Jerusalem, let my right hand wither!
> Let my tongue cling to the roof of my mouth, if I do not remember you,
> if I do not set Jerusalem above my highest joy.

The two verses that make up the middle section of the psalm register a shift from collective voice to first-person singular, from declarative to conditional. They refer back to the psalm's best-known verse (v. 4)—"How could we sing the Lord's song in a foreign land?"—and suggest an answer. The penalties for unfaithfulness to Jerusalem and the covenant it symbolizes—loss of manual dexterity in the right hand, loss of the faculty of speech or song—imply that the speaker is a musician: possibly a Levite, one of the Jerusalem temple musicians.

So we can read this section as continuing the perspective of those musicians who hung up their harps in verse 2 and hesitated to sing in verse 4. And it shifts from evoking a memory through a vignette of exile to an exhortation to remember. As Yosef Yerushalmi observes,

> the Hebrew Bible seems to have no hesitations in commanding memory. Its injunctions to remember are unconditional, and even when not commanded, remembrance is always pivotal. Altogether the verb *zakar* appears in its various declensions in the Bible no less than one hundred and sixty-nine times, usually with either Israel or God as the subject, for memory is incumbent upon both. The verb is complemented by its obverse—forgetting.[19]

Verses 5–6 of the psalm invite questions about the dialectical relationship between history, memory, and forgetting—specifically, the notion of forcing memory under penalty of a curse.[20] How should the people "remember Jerusalem"? By singing its songs? But if collective memory requires this degree of self-coercion, is it really part of one's culture? Walter Benn Michaels articulates a familiar way of understanding the relationship

---

19. Yosef Hayim Yerushalmi, *Zakhor: Jewish History and Jewish Memory* (Seattle: University of Washington Press, 1996), 5.

20. Paul Ricouer's magisterial analysis of the dialectical interplay of memory, history, and forgetting has shaped my approach to the psalm. See Paul Ricouer, *Memory, History, Forgetting* (trans. Kathleen Blamey and David Pellauer; Chicago: University of Chicago Press, 2004).

between collective memory and social identity: "The fact ... that something belongs to our culture cannot count as a motive for our doing it since, if it does belong to our culture, we already do it and if we don't do it (if we've stopped or haven't yet started doing it), it doesn't belong to our culture."[21] Following this logic, the notion of coercing memory in the service of Jerusalem makes no sense.

Because of their interest in promoting change in the face of social inertia, champions of causes and movements have been especially drawn to the middle verses. Consider the chorus to a popular song by the contemporary American self-styled reggae-rapper Matisyahu: "Jerusalem, if I forget you/ Fire not gonna come from me tongue./Jerusalem, if I forget you/Let my right hand forget what it's supposed to do."[22] Though his religious commitments have shifted in recent years, at the time the song was recorded Matisyahu self-identified as Hasidic and a strong supporter of Israel.

Roughly two-and-a-half centuries earlier, the same lines drew the attention of William Billings, North America's first notable composer, who paraphrased Ps 137 in his anthem against British occupation of Boston:

> If I forget thee [Boston], yea if I do not remember thee,
> Then let my numbers cease to flow,
> Then be my Muse unkind.
> Then let my Tongue forget to move and ever be confin'd.
> Let horrid Jargon split the Air and rive my nerves asunder.
> Let hateful discord greet my ear as terrible as Thunder.
> Let Harmony be banish'd hence and Consonance depart.
> Let Dissonance erect her throne and reign within my Heart.[23]

For a composer and itinerant teacher of singing schools like Billings, these penalties could hardly be more formidable.

Three generations later, in his famous Fourth of July oration, Frederick Douglass became the first American to shift the role of Babylon to the United States themselves, which he viewed as complicit in the crime of slavery. He reminded his Rochester audience that by asking him to speak

---

21. Walter Benn Michaels, *Our America: Nativism, Modernism, and Pluralism* (Durham: Duke University Press, 1995), 128–29.

22. Matisyahu, *Youth* (Sony BMG, 2006). "Jerusalem" was written by Ivan Corraliza and Jimmy Douglass.

23. David P. McKay and Richard Crawford, *William Billings of Boston: Eighteenth-Century Composer* (Princeton: Princeton University Press, 1975), 64.

they risked replicating the example of Babylon, whose mockery of the Judeans presaged its own downfall:

> Fellow citizens, above your national, tumultuous joy, I hear the mournful wail of millions! whose chains, heavy and grievous yesterday, are, today, rendered more intolerable by the jubilee shouts that reach them. If I do forget, if I do not faithfully remember those bleeding children of sorrow this day, "may my right hand lose its cunning, may my tongue cleave to the roof of my mouth"! To forget them, to pass lightly over their wrongs, and to chime in with the popular theme would be treason most scandalous and shocking, and would make me a reproach before God and the world. My subject, then fellow-citizens, is American Slavery.[24]

Here Douglass formulated the reading of Ps 137 that has dominated its public meaning ever since, an interpretation that places the United States not in the favored role of Israel or Judah, but Babylon. This reading is echoed in several significant twentieth century renditions.

The singer Roland Hayes provides the crucial link. A kind of Jackie Robinson of the classical music world, Hayes had an extraordinary pathbreaking career as a concert singer in the 1920s. He toured widely across North America and Europe, performing before royalty and in some of the world's most prestigious concert halls. Hayes inspired Sterling Brown, a leading figure in the New Negro Movement of the 1920s, whose first published essay was inspired by an integrated recital in Washington, D.C. at which Hayes performed Antonin Dvořák's setting of Ps 137 as an encore. "The whites start at the wild summoning of beautiful distress," Brown wrote. "Why is there arranging of them in a cantor's song—sung by a Negro? What histrionic ability in this man to so feign passionate despair." For their part, he continued, "The Negroes brood; are stirred by something deep within, something as far away as all antiquity, as old as human wrong, as tragical as loss of worlds. What does he mean—and why are we so stirred—"[25]

Hayes also had a formative impact on Paul Robeson, the great singer/actor who was harassed and essentially broken by the United States government for his left-wing politics. Early in his career Robeson began work-

---

24. Frederick Douglass, *Speeches, Debates and Interviews: Vol. 2: 1847-54* (series 1 of *The Frederick Douglass Papers*; ed. John W. Blassingame; New Haven: Yale University Press, 1979), 368.

25. Sterling Brown, "Roland Hayes," *Opportunity: A Journal of Negro Life* 30 (1925): 173-74.

Fig. 2. Carl Van Vechten, *Portrait of Roland Hayes*, 1954. Courtesy of the Library of Congress Prints and Photographs Division.

ing with Lawrence Brown, Hayes's distinguished piano accompanist and arranger, and began singing a similar repertoire of European concert music and spirituals. Several decades later Robeson was asked to sing the same Dvořák setting that Hayes sang memorably for Brown. In an article for *Jewish Life* magazine, Robeson closed the circle between Douglass, the first American to draw attention to slave spirituals, and "the gifted Dvorak," who

> came to our country, studied the melodies and lyrics of Negro song, and drew upon its richness for his own creations—and so, in this way, the words of this very song must have traveled back across the ocean with him; and I am told the song was especially popular among the Czech people during their years of suffering under the terror of nazi [sic] occupation.[26]

"But history moves on," Robeson continued: "Hitler is gone; Prague lives and builds in a new people's democracy—and now I, an American Negro, sing for her this ancient Hebrew song in the language of the people of Huss and Dvořák, Fuchik and Gottwald."[27]

Finally, Hayes's example inspired Clarence L. Franklin, one of the century's great preachers, who used Ps 137 as the text for one of his best known sermons, which was recorded and distributed commercially by Chess records. The upshot of "Without a Song" is that the Judeans should

---

26. Paul Robeson, *Paul Robeson Speaks: Writings, Speeches, Interviews, 1918–1974* (ed. Philip S. Foner; Larchmont, N.Y.: Brunner/Mazel, 1978), 392.

27. Robeson, *Paul Robeson Speaks*, 393.

have sung. "Yes, they were in a strange land," Franklin intoned, "yes, they were among so-called heathens…. But even under adverse circumstances, you ought to sing sometimes. And not only sing, sing some of Zion's songs."[28] Franklin provided examples of enslaved African Americans who dared to sing under such circumstances, with historical consequences. And he included the example of Hayes coolly overcoming the objection of a German audience shortly after the end of World War I.

Though Franklin's sermon provides little detail, Hayes recounted the episode decades later for the *New York Times*. German newspapers were awash in what he called a flood of racist outbursts. "Well, I came out on stage," Hayes recalled, "and there was a burst of hissing that lasted about ten minutes. I just stood there, and then I decided to change my program. As soon as it was quiet, I began with Schubert's 'Du bist die Ruh.' I could see a change come over the hostile faces, and by the end of the song I knew I had won."[29]

Other prominent African American ministers preached and published sermons based on Ps 137, including Sandy Ray and Joseph Lowery, a close colleague of Martin Luther King, Jr., who helped found the Southern Christian Leadership Conference; he titled a recent book *Singing the Lord's Song in a Strange Land*.[30] Probably none had the impact of a sermon preached by Chicago minister Jeremiah Wright. He begins with the opening stanzas of the psalm, but chooses to read the exile through Dan 6, the chapter in which Daniel, who has distinguished himself as a Judean in the Babylonian court, is cast into a den of lions for praying to his god but emerges unharmed. Wright develops an analogy between the Judeans in Babylon and Africans in America. Like Daniel and his three fellow captives, Africans are stripped, first of their names, then of their history and culture. And in many cases this seems to work: "You will have African exiles who think that unless the Babylonians said it, it ain't true; unless Babylonians wrote it, it ain't right; unless the Baby-

---

28. Clarence L. Franklin, "Without a Song," in *Give Me This Mountain: Life History and Selected Sermons* (ed. Jeff Todd Titon; Urbana: University of Illinois Press, 1989), 90.

29. Alan Rich, "A Bouncy Seventy-Five: Roland Hayes, Despite His Age, Gives Concerts, Teaches and Reminisces," *New York Times*, June 3, 1962.

30. Joseph E. Lowery, *Singing the Lord's Song in a Strange Land* (Nashville: Abingdon, 2011).

lonians made it, it ain't gonna work."³¹ But the Babylonians ultimately overplayed their hand:

> You see, they had taken away his history and his name and had called him Belteshazzar. They had taken away his heritage and taught him Babylonian literature, language and philosophy. But when the tried the ultimate take-away—when they tried to take away his religion—they did what all oppressors do: they tried to take away his hope.³²

"But Daniel had"—and here Wright uses a phrase that would resonate in the writings of his best-known parishioner, Barack Obama—"But Daniel had the audacity to hope."³³

Wright's sermon reminds us of the complex interplay of history, memory, and forgetting that often run through interpretations of Ps 137. For Wright, whose frame of reference is the African American experience, or Michaels, whose focus is modern American literature, invoking culture as a reason for maintaining beliefs and practices requires an appeal to something that lies beyond culture. That determining reality, according to Michaels, can only be the category we call race. Exiled Judeans had neither culture nor race as categories of self-understanding, of course, and we have no reason to believe that they found grounds to distinguish between those categories. In other words, though coerced memory might be an anachronism in a contemporary pluralist culture, it would make perfect sense for the Hebrew psalmist, whose sense of self is defined wholly by a religious identity that is also a political affiliation.

3. Psalm 137:7–9

> Remember, O Lord, against the Edomites the day of Jerusalem's fall,
> how they said, "Tear it down! Tear it down! Down to its foundations!"
> O daughter Babylon, you devastator!
> Happy shall they be who pay you back what you have done to us!
> Happy shall they be who take your little ones
> and dash them against the rock!

---

31. Jeremiah A. Wright, "Faith in a Foreign Land," in *What Makes You So Strong? Sermons of Joy and Strength from Jeremiah A. Wright, Jr.* (ed. Jini Kilgore Ross; Valley Forge, Pa.: Judson, 1993), 138.

32. Wright, "Faith in a Foreign Land," 140.

33. Ibid.

Memory's imperative remains strong in the final verses of Ps 137: a series of commands to remember, addressed first to Yahweh and then to Babylon. The mode of address shifts from first person to second person imperative. Echoing the direct speech of the Babylonians recounted in verse 3, here it is the Edomites who are quoted. But these lines have virtually no presence in popular culture. The psalm's opening four lines are by far the most widely set by musicians writing in either sacred, art, or popular genres. The middle verses, as we have seen, have lent themselves to movements and causes. But the final section is almost never quoted or set to music.

It has posed challenges for interpreters for longer than one might expect. Whatever the provocation, few people who encounter the psalm in liturgy or devotional practice appreciate the celebration of violent revenge against children. Many commentators are quick to remind us that the indiscriminate slaughter of noncombatants was the norm in biblical times. The trope of killing babies by dashing them appears at several points in the Hebrew Bible. "Unyielding hatred of her foes was the correlate of intense love for Zion," writes Mitchell Dahood in the *Anchor Bible*. "To the psalmist the law of retaliation for cruelty seems only just, and the shocking form in which he expresses his desire for the extermination of his country's destroyer must be judged in the light of customs prevailing in his age."[34]

Of course, the final lines do not actually advocate committing violence. The sense of crushing injustice suffered by Judah has triggered a sense of violent rage, according to many contemporary Christian interpretations, which may be preferable to articulate than to suppress. The theological consensus seems to be to acknowledge anger in the face of overwhelming injustice but then to submit that anger to God rather than enact it. "In the imprecatory Psalms, torrents of rage have been allowed to flow freely, channeled only by the robust structure of a ritual prayer," observes Bosnian-born theologian Miroslav Volf, who has preached and written on Ps 137. "Strangely enough, they may point to a way out of slavery to revenge and into the freedom of forgiveness.... by placing unattended rage before God we place both our unjust enemy and our own vengeful self face to face with a God who loves and does justice."[35]

---

34. Mitchell Dahood, *Psalms III: 101–150* (AB 17A; Garden City, N.Y.: Doubleday, 1970), 269.

35. Miroslav Volf, *Exclusion and Embrace: A Theological Exploration of Identity, Otherness, and Reconciliation* (Nashville: Abingdon, 1996), 124. See also Nancy L. deClaissé-Walford, "The Theology of the Imprecatory Psalms," and Joel M. LeMon,

In view of the virtually taboo nature of the final three verses, which communities actually include them in song or liturgy? Augustine offers one way, interpreting the psalm as an allegory of Christian piety:

> What are the little ones of Babylon? Evil desires at their birth. For there are, who have to fight with inveterate lusts. When lust is born, before evil habit giveth it strength against thee, when lust is little, by no means let it gain the strength of evil habit; when it is little, dash it. But thou fearest, lest though dashed it die not; "Dash it against the Rock; and that Rock is Christ."[36]

Such an allegorical interpretation was not original to Augustine. Probably it originated with Origen; versions of it appear in writings by Hilary, Jerome, Ambrose, and Cassian. Such an interpretation was practically inevitable: "Since the desire that real Babylonian babies be smashed on real rocks was both historically no longer relevant and hardly consistent with the teaching of Jesus, it was obvious to the Patristic interpreter that the verse must have a 'spiritual' meaning."[37]

Nowhere did this interpretive strategy exercise more social impact than in the Rule of Saint Benedict. Compiled a century after the death of Augustine, the Rule of Benedict established a schedule for reciting the daily office; during eight daily prayers, the entire psalter would be recited in biblical sequence over the course of a week. Psalm 137 was to be chanted on Thursdays at Vespers. As a kind of common currency in the medieval religious world, then, any reference made to Ps 137 made would have had a far-reaching influence. The Rule of Benedict exhorts: "Hour by hour keep careful watch over all you do, aware that God's gaze is upon you, wherever you may be. As soon as wrongful thoughts come into your heart, dash them against Christ and disclose them to your spiritual father."[38]

Commentators and poets of the Reformation and Counter-Reformation, themselves often in exile to save their lives, were more likely to

---

"Saying Amen to Violent Psalms: Patterns of Prayer, Belief, and Action in the Psalter," in *Soundings in the Theology of Psalms: Perspectives and Methods in Contemporary Scholarship* (ed. Rolf A. Jacobson; Minneapolis: Fortress, 2011), 77–109.

36. St. Augustine, *Exposition on the Book of Psalms* (NPNF 1/8). Online: http://www.ccel.org/ccel/schaff/npnf108.ii.CXXXVII.html.

37. Benedict, *The Rule of Saint Benedict: In Latin and English With Notes* (ed. Timothy Fry; Collegeville, Minn: Liturgical Press, 1981), 475.

38. Ibid., 163, 185. Thanks to Andrew Irving for this reference.

embrace a literal reading of the psalm's final lines. "The French Civil Wars, like the English," speculates Hannibal Hamlin, "may have inured their participants and victims to a level of violence otherwise unacceptable to Christian readers of the Psalms."[39] John Calvin, for example, could write in a commentary on the psalm:

> It may seem to savor of cruelty, that he should wish the tender and innocent infants to be dashed and mangled upon the stones, but he does not speak under the impulse of personal feeling, and only employs words which God had himself authorized, so that this is but the declaration of a just judgment, as when our Lord says, "With what measure ye mete, it shall be measured to you again" (Matt 7:2).[40]

Writing centuries later from New England, Jonathan Edwards adopted a similarly dispassionate tone in his "Blank Bible": "The dashing the 'little ones' of Babylon 'against the stones' probably was fulfilled in some degrees when Cyrus took the city, but it had its greatest fulfillment afterwards, when that prophecy was fulfilled (Isa 47:9)."[41] Edwards continues:

> It was God's pleasure to show the event to be agreeable to his will by giving those that did it external prosperity. But the prophecy seems to look beyond the destruction of the literal Babylon to that of the spiritual Babylon. They indeed will do God's work, and will perform a good work, who shall be God's instruments of the utter overthrow of the Church of Rome with all her superstitions, and heathenish ceremonies, and other cursed fruits of her spiritual whoredoms, as it were without having any mercy upon them.[42]

Isaac Watts, though, who had a decisive impact on Protestant hymn singing, including Edwards, deliberately left the psalm out of his influential psalm collection of 1719, but included it in a book of occasional writings published late in life. His attitude toward the psalm remained ambivalent:

---

39. Hamlin, *Psalm Culture and Early Modern English Literature*, 250.

40. John Calvin, *Commentary on the Book of Psalms* (vol. 5; trans. James Anderson). Online: http://www.ccel.org/ccel/calvin/calcom12.xxi.ii.html.

41. Jonathan Edwards, "Blank Bible," *Works of Jonathan Edwards Online* (vol. 24; ed. Stephen J. Stein): 537. Online: http://edwards.yale.edu/archive?path=aHR0cDovL2Vkd2FyZHMueWFsZS5lZHUvY2dpLWJpbi9uZXdwaGlsby9qb250ZXh0LndFsaXplLnBsP3AuMjMud2plby4xNzYxNDI5LjE3NjE0MzY=.

42. Ibid.

This particular Psalm could not well be converted into Christianity, and accordingly it appears here in its Jewish Form: The Vengeance denounced against Babylon, in the Close of it, shall be executed (said a great Divine) upon Anti-christian [sic] Rome; but he was persuaded the Turks must do it, for Protestant Hearts, said he, have too much Compassion in them to embrue their Hands in such a bloody and terrible Execution.[43]

Watts offers this restrained paraphrase of the final verse:

As thou hast spar'd nor Sex nor Age,
Deaf to our Infants' dying Groans,
May some bless'd Hand, inspir'd with Rage,
Dash thy young Babes, and tinge the Stones.[44]

In contemporary Christian churches Ps 137 is often included in the lectionary but with the final verse omitted. Musical settings, modern or otherwise, that include the final verses are, to my knowledge, nonexistent.

The text poses obvious challenges for Jewish worshippers as well. While Christian readings of the psalm have tended to be personal and allegorical, Susan Gillingham shows, Jews have traditionally given it a more political and material interpretation.[45] In some Orthodox Ashkenazi communities, the entire psalm is recited in full on weekdays just before the Grace after Meals in remembrance of the destroyed temple; some Orthodox Sephardic communities recite it as part of Grace after Meals and also as part of the Tisha B'Av (Ninth of Ab) liturgy that commemorates the destruction of the first and second temples. However, as Athalya Brenner notes, over the past 150 years Conservative, Liberal, and Reform prayer books have taken a more ambivalent stance toward the text. Its use has become optional both for weekday liturgy and even for the Tisha B'Av, but in any event only the first six verses are used; the imprecatory verses are excised from prayers and services. In short, she concludes, these non-Orthodox communities reject the concluding sentiment of vengeance.[46]

---

43. Cited by Donald Davie, ed., *The Psalms in English* (New York: Penguin, 1996), 212.

44. Davie, *The Psalms in English*, 211.

45. Susan Gillingham, "The Reception of Psalm 137 in Jewish and Christian Traditions," in *Jewish and Christian Approaches to the Psalms: Conflict and Convergence* (ed. Susan Gillingham; Oxford: Oxford University Press, 2013), 64–82.

46. Athalya Brenner, "'On the Rivers of Babylon' (Psalm 137), or Between Victim

Moses and the exodus, Jeremiah (or Ezekiel) and the exile: these watershed characters and events in the formation of Judaism have provided guiding narratives for many communities around the globe. Bruce Feiler has documented the extraordinary resonance of Moses and the exodus on American history.[47] Without a dramatic hero and the rich narrative detail of the exodus, the exile story has had a more muted impact. Occasionally the two narratives appear fused in ritual, like this antiphonal lament for Tisha B'Av:

> A fire kindles within me as I recall—*when I left Egypt*,
> But I raise laments as I remember—*when I left Jerusalem*.
> Moses sang a song that would never be forgotten—*when I left Egypt*,
> Jeremiah mourned and cried out in grief—*when I left Jerusalem*.
> The sea-waves pounded but stood up like a wall—*when I left Egypt*,
> That waters overflowed and ran over my head—*when I left Jerusalem*.
> Moses led me and Aaron guided me—*when I left Egypt*,
> Nebuchadnezzar and the Emperor Hadrian—*when I left Jerusalem*.[48]

Yerushalmi emphasizes how the insistent antiphonal rhythm of the refrain, along with a lack of historical detail, reinforces and heightens the memory of both events. "That which is remembered here transcends the recollection of any particular episode in an ancient catastrophe," he writes. "It is rather the realization of a structural contrast in Jewish historical experience, built around the dramatic polarity of two great historical 'departures' (Egypt/Jerusalem—Exodus/Exile), each with its obvious though unstated clusters of meanings and implications."[49]

Any discussion of the modern Jewish relationship to Ps 137 must consider its resonance during the Holocaust, the most horrific in a series of traumas that began with the Babylonian conquest. Nazi concentration camps witnessed numerous examples of Jews being taunted and coerced to sing and dance. Typically they sponsored bands and orchestras to play for inmates on their way to work details or the gas chambers or for visit-

---

and Perpetrator," in *Sanctified Aggression: Legacies of Biblical and Post Biblical Vocabularies of Violence* (ed. Jonneke Bekkenkamp and Yvonne Sherwood; London: T&T Clark, 2003), 81, 85–86.

47. Bruce S. Feiler, *America's Prophet: Moses and the American Story* (New York: William Morrow, 2009).

48. Yerushalmi, *Zakhor*, 43.

49. Ibid., 44.

ing Nazi dignitaries. "In camps such as Auschwitz or Buchenwald," writes historian Michael Kater, "Jews were permitted and sometimes ordered to perform 'Jewish' music as a sport for the SS."[50]

Not all these horrors were organized directly by the Gestapo or SS. In summer 1941, to take one infamous episode chronicled by historian Jan Gross in the book *Neighbors*, the entire Jewish population of the Polish town of Jedwabne—some sixteen hundred men, women, and children—was rounded up, taunted, beaten, and incinerated in a barn by neighbors with whom they had coexisted for generations. This one horrific episode finds both verse three and verse nine of Ps 137 reenacted: Jews are both forced to sing and also to have their own children, in effect, dashed against the rocks: "the little children," Gross quotes an eyewitness, "they roped a few together by their legs and carried them on their backs, then put them on pitchforks and threw them onto smoldering coals."[51]

However, harsh conditions of forced migration and labor may have been under Nebuchadnezzar, the Babylonians and Edomites do not stand accused of such atrocities (though they may have occurred). To return to the original context of Ps 137 and the Hebrew Bible: Given the vengeance foreshadowed in the final verses, was any actually perpetrated? The Bible is silent on this point. Surprisingly little comment has been made regarding the one population that bears the brunt of a Judean reprisal: the Gentile wives and children of the exiles. They are divorced as part of renewing the covenant. The last chapter of Ezra documents the procedure by which the foreign wives were excised, ending with a long list of Judeans and the words: "All these had married foreign women, and they sent them away, together with their children" (Ezra 10:44). Nehemiah also castigates outmarrying Judeans:

> I contended with them and cursed them and beat some of them and pulled out their hair; and I made them take an oath in the name of God, saying: "You shall not give away your daughters to their sons, or take their daughters in for your sons or for yourselves. Did not King Solomon of Israel sin on account of such women?" (Neh 13:25–26).

---

50. Michael H. Kater, *Different Drummers: Jazz in the Culture of Nazi Germany* (New York: Oxford University Press, 1992), 181.

51. Jan T. Gross, *Neighbors: The Destruction of the Jewish Community in Jedwabne, Poland* (Princeton: Princeton University Press, 2001), 20. See also Brenner, "On the Rivers of Babylon," 78–81, 86–90.

Subtle gender overtones inflect the Hebrew of Ps 137. The imperative attributed to the Edomites as direct speech in verse 7—"Tear it down! Tear it down! Down to its foundations"—is sometimes rendered "strip her, strip her," or "lay bare" in other translations. The Hebrew ʿārû, repeated twice, shares a feminine suffix. It can be translated "make nakedness seen," when used in contexts of metaphorical nakedness, even as a euphemism for sexual intercourse. The direct speech of the Edomites, according to Dahood, is more properly translated, "Strip her, strip her to her foundation!" And the Hebrew word for "foundations" has a secondary meaning of "buttocks." In short, the connotations of Ps 137 in the original Hebrew suggest that Jerusalem under conquest is a woman being despoiled of her clothing, even subjected to sexual humiliation.[52] This is consistent with a number of biblical texts pertaining to the plight of Judah. Gendered and sexualized language abounds in Jeremiah, Lamentations, and Ezekiel, all books that recount the causes and conditions of conquest and exile.[53]

Which returns us in a roundabout way to the Manhattan milieu of *Mad Men*. The undercurrent of rampant misogyny and sexual harassment more than anything else may be what sets the world of that series apart from the professional world of our own time (not that misogyny and harassment have been eradicated, of course). As the folk musicians play "Waters of Babylon," we watch scenes out of Draper's internal flow of consciousness: Rachel at the end of a long work day, Betty Draper with their children. We see Draper's boss Roger and his mistress Joan dressing coolly, impersonally, in a Manhattan hotel room after a tryst. The song and scene invite us to feel we are watching Babylon, with its wealth, power, and sexual corruption, but with the knowledge that a cultural tsunami—what we remember as the sixties—is gathering force. The characters are unaware of the coming sea change; they are caught up in their own reveries of the particular time and place they occupy.

Walter Brueggemann advances a different analogy for the Babylonian conquest, comparing it to the trauma of 9/11. "I think 587 B.C.E. pierced the ideology of chosenness in which the elite thought they were immune from historical disruption," he writes. "In the same way I believe that 9/11 pierced the ideology of US exceptionalism and our privilege in the world. In both cases, the main issue is not political or economic, but the disrup-

---

52. Dahood, *Psalms III*, 273.
53. T. M. Lemos, "The Emasculation of Exile: Hypermasculinity and Feminization in the Book of Ezekiel," in Kelle, Ames, and Wright, *Interpreting Exile*, 377–93.

tion of an ideology grounded in a tribal notion of God."[54] As the destruction of Jerusalem is thought to have spurred a rethinking of Hebrew scripture and the meaning of the history it narrates, we might consider whether *Mad Men* offers a self-reflective backward glance—from the twenty-first century to an earlier, seemingly more innocent (though ingenuously decadent) era, the new frontier of the early sixties. In which case a popular song based on Ps 137 would represent an exceptionally fitting choice.

---

54. Walter Brueggemann, email to David Stowe, 20 August 2013; see also Walter Brueggemann, *The Message of the Psalms: A Theological Commentary* (Minneapolis: Fortress, 1984), 74–77.

Comic Book Bibles: Translation and the Politics of Interpretation

Rubén Dupertuis

In December 2013 several concerned consumers took to social media outlets to try to get Family Christian Stores, a major chain of Christian bookstores, to stop selling Brendan Powell Smith's books of Bible illustrations done in LEGO blocks. The complaint was that while the books available through the stores, *The Brick Bible* and *The Brick Bible for Kids* series, contained no objectionable materials themselves, readily available images on Smith's related website most certainly did.[1] A quick glance at the shelves of Christian book stores reveals a broad range of Bibles targeting "niche" markets. There are Bibles for hunters, for teens, for children, for fans of "manga" comics, and many, many other interests. The articulation of the objections noted above, as well as the fact that corporations are proving responsive, provides insights into the expectations associated with the genre of comic book and picture Bibles. While one can find a stunning variety of Bibles, for some there are apparently rules in place regarding what constitutes an appropriate adaptation or translation that can be broken.

Indeed, there is a striking range in the Bible illustration products Smith has available under the Brick Bible umbrella. There is a *Brick Bible*

---

1. The social media campaign was successful in getting Family Christian Stores to acknowledge the concern and to commit to review the issue (Sarah J. Flashing, "Family Christian Stores Acknowledges Problem with Brick Bible Books," SarahFlashing.com. Online: http://www.sarahflashing.com/family-christian-stores-brick-bible/). As of January 30, 2014, the products were still available on the Family Christian Stores website. Similar concerns appear to have led to the removal of the books from Sam's Club and Walmart stores in 2011 (The Brick Bible's Facebook page. Online: https://www.facebook.com/permalink.php?story_fbid=10150477413200928&id=30240090927).

for Kids series, "graphic novel" style books of the Old and New Testaments, and a website, which is how Smith's project started in 2001. The website, the Brick Testament, is described as "the world's largest, most comprehensive, illustrated Bible. A sprawling website for those with the maturity to read the entire Bible."[2] What Smith means by the required "maturity" is made clear in the Brick Testament's index page, which lists the biblical material illustrated, including Genesis, Exodus, the Law, David vs. Saul, Job, the Life and Teachings of Jesus, and Revelation, along with a content guide indicating which stories contain nudity, sexual content, violence, and cursing. Some scenes, such as Mary and Joseph walking to Bethlehem for the census (Luke 2:1, 3–5), make it in to all versions of the Brick Bible and are illustrated in an almost identical manner. But other images, such as Adam and Eve having sex in various positions (Gen 2:24; 4:25), various rapes (Judg 19:25; Deut 22:25), and beheadings (Mark 6:25; see fig. 1) are only on the Brick Testament website.

The existence of Bible illustration projects like Smith's may be shocking to the consumers who campaigned against his products, but given the cultural authority of the Bible and the diversity of meanings ascribed to it, it should not be too surprising to find more "adult" illustrated or comic book Bibles. Furthermore, as I will try to show in what follows, the Brick Testament and somewhat "adult" Bibles are inextricably linked to the "mainstream" illustrated or comic book Bibles against which they position themselves even as they raise questions about what it means to "faithfully"

Fig. 1. The Brick Testament (http://www.bricktestament.com/the_life_of_jesus/the_head_of_john_the_baptist/mk06_28a.html).

---

2. "The Brick Bible Presents," thebrickbible.com. Online: http://thebrickbible.com.

represent the Bible, the nature of reading, as well as the nature of the Bible itself.[3]

STRAIGHTFORWARD AND TRUE: COMIC BOOK BIBLES AND TRANSLATION

Although Bibles in comic book form have been around at least since the 1940s,[4] in the last decade or so there has been an explosion of comic book Bibles, largely from Christian publishers. These comic book Bibles are part of a larger movement that has seen an increase in the number of niche market and "value added" Bibles.[5] Through the 1950s, comic book versions of Bible stories were still being produced by major publishers within the comics industry, in part as a way to rescue a medium over which there was much concern and controversy.[6] Since then, however, comic book Bibles have developed along a separate track and in completely different markets. As Emily Alcock notes, most Bible comics have the goal of "making the Bible accessible to younger readers, encouraging children and teens to

---

3. I use the term "mainstream" to refer to what has become a largely Christian tradition of Bible illustration that has, for the last several decades, primarily produced and marketed comic book Bibles outside of the more general comics industry. I am aware of the irony of using "mainstream" for what is a subgenre controlled largely by Christian publication houses, especially when some of the comics that critique this tradition are clearly positioned within the larger industry. Nonetheless, I think it is useful given that the latter consist of a small handful of publications compared to the dozens of comic book Bibles produced for didactic and evangelistic purposes. I have also explored the Brick Testament elsewhere, arguing that it represents a sophisticated critique of a tradition of biblical illustration for children; see Rubén R. Dupertuis, "Translating the Bible into Pictures," in *Text, Image, and Otherness in Children's Bibles: What's in the Picture* (ed. Caroline Vander Stichele and Hugh Pyper; Semeia Studies 56; Atlanta: Society of Biblical Literature, 2012), 271–90.

4. The earliest example I have encountered is *Picture Stories of the Bible*, which was published serially by EC Comics beginning in 1942. The comics were later collected into book form and republished as M. C. Gaines, ed., *Picture Stories from the Bible: The Old Testament in Full-Color Comic-Strip Form* (New York: Scarf, 1979); and M. C. Gaines and Don Cameron, *Picture Stories from the Bible: The New Testament in Full-Color Comic-Strip Form* (New York: Scarf, 1980).

5. Timothy Beal, *The Rise and Fall of the Bible: The Unexpected History of an Accidental Book* (Boston: Houghton Mifflin Harcourt, 2011), 41–69.

6. Don Jolly, "Interpretive Treatments of Genesis in Comics: R. Crumb and Dave Sim," *Journal of Religion and Popular Culture* 25 (2013): 34–35.

become engaged in the stories and their morals."[7] While true for the large majority of comic book Bibles, projects like the Brick Testament highlight the fact that the comic book medium, like any medium, can be used to diverse ends, and not just for the purposes of making stories attractive to children. They also raise questions about the morals inherent in some of the Bible stories typically omitted from the children-friendly publications. This point came across very clearly to consumers who protested the availability of Brick Bible products at Family Christian Stores.

Smith, in fact, positions the Brick Testament precisely as a reaction to the "mainstream" of illustrated Bibles, most of which have clear didactic goals. Smith describes the purpose of the Brick Testament in the Frequently Asked Questions section of his site as follows:

> The goal of The Brick Testament is to give people an increased knowledge of the contents of the Bible in a way that is fun and compelling while remaining true to the text of the scriptures. To this end, all stories are retold using direct quotes from The Bible [sic] with chapters and verses provided. There are many other illustrated Bibles whose authors take a free hand in completely re-writing the Bible's stories, adding or subtracting from them as they see fit, often giving the stories re-interpretations that try to force them to fit a certain modern sense of morality or a particular post-Biblical theology. Although well-meaning, these authors do not let the Bible speak for itself, and do not provide an experience that is much like reading the actual Bible at all.... One of The Brick Testament's founding principles for its approach to illustrating the Bible has been to treat all of the Bible's types of content equally, so that the Bible's content is not filtered through the author's or anyone else's ideas about what sort of content is or isn't "appropriate." The goal has been to illustrate the content of the Bible as straightforwardly as the Bible tells it.[8]

---

7. Emily Alcock, "The Bible: Graphic Revelations of an Old Medium," in *Critical Survey of Graphic Novels: History, Theme and Technique* (ed. Stephen Weiner; Ipswick, Mass.: Salem, 2013), 62.

8. Smith gave a similar response in a 2003 interview, stating that the project presents him with "a chance to re-tell these stories in a way that's more faithful to the text than the other illustrated Bibles I've seen" (Meredith James, "Building a Colorful, Accessible Bible, Brick by Lego Brick," *Baltimore Sun*, November 30, 2003; online: http://articles.baltimoresun.com/2003-11-30/entertainment/0311290100_1_lego-brick-testament-bible).

Smith's claims are striking—at the very least bold. He presents the Brick Testament as more faithful than most in rendering the text of the Bible into a visual medium, as well as giving readers a truly authentic Bible-reading experience. The rhetoric is overdone, as Smith is often selective if not tendentious in the verses he chooses to illustrate and he often adds dialogue clearly not in the text of the Bible. What is important to highlight here, however, is Smith's claim to have captured the real Bible or what can be thought of as its true essence.

Smith is not alone in his claim to fidelity to the original and emphasis capturing the "real" Bible. In his critically acclaimed comic book version of Genesis published in 2009, R. Crumb uses similar strategies in positioning *The Book of Genesis Illustrated* relative to the original text and to other illustrations of the Bible.[9] In the same way that Smith alerts readers to the adult nature of some of the material he illustrates through a coding system in the index to his site, the cover of Crumb's *Genesis* provides a teaser claiming, "Nothing left out!" and announces, "Adult supervision recommended for minors." In an introduction to the book, Crumb tells the reader: "I, R. Crumb, the illustrator of this book, have, to the best of my ability, faithfully reproduced every word of the original text." Crumb goes on to apologize for the minimal amount of interpretation he was forced to do, noting that he typically "let [the biblical text] stand in its convoluted vagueness rather than monkey around with such a venerable text." Also like Smith, Crumb presents his version as a counter to the "mainstream" of biblical illustration, stating, "Every other comic version of the Bible that I've seen contains passages of completely made-up narrative and dialogue, in an attempt to streamline and 'modernize' the old scriptures." In contrast, he calls his version a "literal" interpretation that is basically a "straight illustration job."

The claim to straightforward illustration of the Bible appears also in two other comics that similarly place themselves against the "mainstream." *Outrageous Tales from the Old Testament* was published in 1987 by Knockabout Publications, a British publisher of underground comics, and contains a series of stories from the Hebrew Bible. With the exception of versions of the creation accounts in Gen 1–3, which get two treatments, the stories chosen typically do not make it into illustrated Bibles. They include, for example, the story of Sodom and Gomorrah (Gen 13), several stories from the book

---

9. R. Crumb, *The Book of Genesis Illustrated* (New York: W.W. Norton, 2009).

of Judges, the story of Job, and two episodes from 1 and 2 Kings. *Outrageous Tales* advertises its contents on the cover with images from its various stories along with a list of the book's subjects: "wrath of God, human sacrifice, murder, deadly tent pegs, enormous boils, and judges, kings and prophets." In the book itself, the artists graphically illustrate sex, dismemberment, beheading, and as much violence as possible. Neil Gaiman, the main creative force of the volume as he is involved in six of the fourteen stories, has claimed that the book almost landed a Swedish publisher in jail, but that the case was resolved when it became clear that the artists were simply retelling stories that are in the Bible.[10] As Smith and Crumb do, Gaiman claims that in his retelling of the rape of the Levite's concubine in Judg 19 he is simply retelling the biblical story "fairly straight."[11]

A final example of similar positioning can be found in *The Bible: Eden*, which contains the story of the garden of Eden (Gen 2–3) along with a handful of illustrations from other parts of the Bible, offered as a sort of appendix. Written by Dave Elliott and Keith Giffen, and illustrated by Scott Hampton, *Eden* was initially serialized in the pages of the adult magazine *Penthouse* where it ran for about a year. It was subsequently published as a graphic novel in 2003. Like Smith, Crumb, and the artists of *Outrageous Tales*, Hampton presents *Eden* in interviews as a project that first and foremost aims for fidelity to the text of the Bible: "The intention was to not take any liberties with it at all. We all feel that it is very faithful as to how we saw the word of God…. We didn't need to add to it or make anything up, just depict it exactly as it is in the Bible, because that hadn't been done before."[12] The authors also claim that they shied away from an adult spin on the story of Eden. In fact, serializing the story in an adult magazine allowed them to simply represent what was there: "The 'adult spin' was that we wanted to keep it faithful to the Bible."[13] For Hampton, Elliott, and Giffen, that meant a literal and graphic depiction of the first couple's pre-sin and pre-clothes state of innocence as well as multiple frames over six pages devoted to illustrating man and woman becoming one flesh (Gen

---

10. Neil Gaiman, "Why Defend Freedom of Icky Speech," NeilGaiman.com. Online: http://journal.neilgaiman.com/2008/12/why-defend-freedom-of-icky-speech.html.

11. Claire E. White, "A Conversation with Neil Gaiman," Writers Write: An Internet Writing Journal. Online: http://www.writerswrite.com/journal/mar99/gaiman.htm.

12. Jonah Weiland, "The Greatest Story of 'em All: Elliot Talks 'The Bible: Eden,'" ComicBookResources. Online: www.comicbookresources.com/?page=article&id=2797.

13. Ibid.

2:23). While the adult spin seems evident to me, in their view the creators of *Eden* were simply playing it straight and letting the Bible speak for itself without interpretive intervention.

The above claims to fidelity are overdone and in some ways simplistic, but what emerges is a rhetorical stance and positioning that assumes or implies the notion of translation. The appeal to accuracy is, I suggest, a function of the stance these authors and artists take vis-à-vis the "mainstream" of Bible illustration, which is itself steeped in claims to translational fidelity. M. C. Gaines's *Picture Stories from the Bible*, one of the earliest comic book Bibles I am aware of, has endorsements by church leaders on the back cover ratifying the fidelity of the "translation." *Picture Stories* is lauded for following the text of scripture closely and for rendering "the Bible stories into the modern comic form without sacrificing the accuracy of the biblical text, and with all due reverence," and for doing so truthfully.[14] Rob Suggs's *Comic Book Bible* from the late 1990s follows the trend of more recent Bible comics in not making claims to fidelity in representation quite so explicit, but it does assert that this Bible comic book is able to give children spiritual truths and can function as a kind of starter kit Bible that will lead to continued interest in reading the Bible.[15] Zondervan's more recent *Magna Bible: Names, Games, and Long Road Trip* announces the exciting and different look traditional Bible characters get in this Korean "manga" comic, but reassures readers that despite how much fun the comic book will be, it still allows discovery of the important truths of the Bible.[16] A similar claim appears on the back cover of *The Action Bible: God's Redemptive Story*: "The stories in *The Action Bible* communicate biblical truth clearly and forcefully to contemporary readers."[17] These comic book Bibles take pains to reassure young readers (or the parents buying them) that despite the medium, their versions are legitimate Bibles or at least contain the core Bible truths.

---

14. Gaines, *Pictures Stories*, back cover.

15. Rob Suggs, *The Comic Book Bible* (Uhrichsville, Ohio: Barbour, 1997), back cover.

16. Young Shin Lee, Brett Burner, and Jung Sun Hwang, *Names, Games and the Long Road Trip: Genesis–Exodus* (vol. 1 of the *Manga Bible*; ed. Bud Rogers; Grand Rapids: Zondervan, 2007), back cover. For discussion of the phenomenon of "manga" Bible comics, see Beal, *Rise and Fall*, 64–68.

17. Doug Mauss, ed., *The Action Bible: God's Redemptive Story* (Colorado Springs, Colo.: David C. Cook, 2010).

Claiming fidelity in translation is, in fact, a common feature of Bibles for children more generally, many of which include images even if they do not fall under the category of comic books. Jaqueline S. du Toit has pointed out the tendency in children's Bibles to invoke the rhetoric of translation, and specifically, what is known as dynamic equivalence, as part of a strategy of negotiating canonical status for what are typically very liberal adaptations of biblical materials.[18] They do so through explicit claims to fidelity, as seen in the above examples, as well as by intentionally trading upon the long tradition of the translator's invisibility to implicitly claim that the author is God.[19] Many comic book Bibles simply do not identify authors and/or artists on the front covers of the books.[20] The cover of *The Action Bible* goes further, placing the subtitle, "God's Redemptive Story" where one might expect the author's name.[21] In addition, the close association of children's Bibles and didactic translation has, as du Toit points out, "allowed their highly selective adaptation of the source text to be tolerated within religious traditions otherwise strongly regulated by strict adherence to the canon."[22]

Despite the fact that the concept of translation invoked both by "mainstream" comic book Bibles and those that position themselves against them is overly simplistic, translation is, in my judgment, a more useful lens through which to view comic book Bibles than retelling, reworking, or other ways of understanding the relationship of these texts.[23] Given the fact that images or pictures are central means through which the comic book medium conveys meaning, the medium is increasingly being understood as a language with a stable set of symbols.[24] As such, biblical stories rendered in the language of comics can effectively be understood as

---

18. Jaqueline S. du Toit, "Seeing Is Believing: Children's Bibles as Negotiated Translation," in *Ideology, Culture, and Translation* (ed. Scott S. Elliott and Roland Boer; Atlanta, Ga.: Society of Biblical Literature, 2012), 103–6.

19. Du Toit, "Seeing Is Believing," 106.

20. This is the case, for example, in Gaines, *Picture Stories of the Bible*; Suggs, *Comic Book Bible*; and Toni Matas, Picanyol, and Carlos Rojas, *The Comic Book Bible: The Old and New Testaments in Full Color!* (San Diego, Calif.: Silver Dolphin Books, 2013).

21. Mauss, *Action Bible*, front cover.

22. Du Toit, "Seeing is Believing," 103.

23. Dupertuis, "Translating," 274–76; see also du Toit, "Seeing Is Believing."

24. See Hillary Chute, "Comics as Literature? Reading Graphic Narrative," *Publications of the Modern Language Association* 123 (2008): 452–65. For a good introduc-

translations in their own right.²⁵ But here the claims to fidelity in translation, while expedient and perhaps rhetorically effective, are problematic; much of the recent work on translation theory has highlighted the fact that translations are always complex cultural transactions for which a simple understanding of "accuracy" in the transfer of meaning is inadequate.²⁶ As Lawrence Venuti puts it, there is some violence inherent in the activity of translation, since "translation is the forcible replacement of the linguistic and cultural difference of the foreign text with a text that will be intelligible to the target-language reader."²⁷ Venuti further argues that while some violence is unavoidable in the act of translation, translators have a choice between two tendencies. One option is what he calls a "domesticating" translation—one that privileges the values and cultural assumptions of the target-language reader. The other option is adopting a "foreignizing" translation that resists imposing target-language cultural values and foregrounds the cultural distance to and otherness of a source text.²⁸ English language translations have been dominated by "domesticating" translation practices. This applies to most contemporary English translations of the Bible,²⁹ especially Bibles aimed at niche markets, which, in addition to presenting the biblical texts in attractive, accessible, and understandable ways, work hard to highlight the relevance of these texts to modern readers.

TRANSLATING GENESIS 1–3 IN "MAINSTREAM" BIBLE COMIC BOOKS

What we find in the competing claims to accuracy in both "mainstream" Bible comic books and the handful of texts that position themselves against this tradition is a dialogue, of sorts, played out in the language of the medium, around questions concerning how much one can change a

---

tion to the conventions of the comic book medium, see Scott McCloud, *Understanding Comics: The Invisible Art* (New York: Harper Perrenniel, 1993).

25. Roman Jakobson, "On Linguistic Aspects of Translation," in *On Translation* (ed. Reuben A. Brower; Harvard Studies in Comparative Literature 23; Cambridge: Harvard University Press, 1959), 232–39.

26. See, for example, the discussion in Stanley E. Porter, "Some Issues in Modern Translation Theory and Study of the Greek New Testament," *Currents in Research: Biblical Studies* 9 (2001): 350–82.

27. Lawrence Venuti, *The Translator's Invisibility: A History of Translation* (Translation Studies; New York: Routledge, 1995), 18.

28. Ibid., 17–39, esp. 20.

29. Ibid., 21.

Bible story while still calling it a Bible and what parts of the Bible constitute its essence. To see this debate in action we can turn to a quick sampling of presentations of the creation accounts in Gen 1–3 in a handful of comic book Bibles. There are myriad interpretive issues we could focus on in looking at these texts, but I'll limit myself to two of them. The first is the way in which comic book Bibles handle the existence of two creation narratives in Gen 1–3, each with different theological emphases and different orders of creation.[30] The second is the presentation of Eve in the story.

Gaines's *Picture Stories of the Bible*, originally published in serialized form in the 1940s, is longer and contains more elements of Gen 1–3 than more recent publications, which tend to severely reduce to the biblical narratives to a few key elements. *Picture Stories* handles the difficulties caused by two creation stories by collapsing them. After presenting the first five days of creation according to Gen 1 on the first page, *Picture Stories* then provides a panel corresponding to the creation of humankind on the sixth day (Gen 1:26–27), but omits the reference to the creation of both male and female at this point and specifically brings forward elements of the second creation story by noting that "God placed him in the Garden of Eden." This is accompanied by an illustration containing only an image of Adam in dialogue with God (or rather, the voice of God). From there *Picture Stories* continues with elements from the second creation account, including the prohibition of the fruit of the tree of knowledge of good and evil (Gen 2:16–17), as well as Adam's naming of the animals (Gen 2:20). The first creation account is brought to a close rather awkwardly and out of sequence in a statement about God resting on the Sabbath (Gen 2:2–3), which stands alongside a frame depicting the creation of Eve from Adam's rib (Gen 2:21–22). The story then moves to Gen 3. *Picture Stories* is typical of Bible comics in devoting a panel to showing Adam explain the command not to eat from the forbidden tree to Eve, something that has to be assumed from a reading of Genesis (see fig. 2). And *Picture Stories* is again typical in using this as the beginning of an extended presentation of the weakness of Eve. Adam shows the tree to Eve and explains, "This is FORBIDDEN fruit." Eve's temptation has begun even before the encounter with the serpent, because she replies, "But it looks so good, Adam!" Eve is

---

30. I follow the majority opinion in taking Gen 1:1–2:4a and Gen 2:4b–3:24 as initially deriving from different sources. See, for example, Walter Brueggemann, *Genesis* (Interpretation; Atlanta: John Knox, 1982), 14–15.

Fig. 2. Gaines, *Picture Stories from the Bible*, 1978.

then shown rationalizing the act of eating from the tree, eating the fruit, then offering some to Adam.

The *Comic Book Bible* by Rob Suggs is a 1997 publication geared for children ages eight to twelve. As noted above, the stated goal of this comic book Bible is providing children with a kind of Bible starter kit by "plant[ing] the seeds of interest in reading and studying God's Word."[31] The *Comic Book Bible* is quite selective in what it presents. The first creation story is told with one frame devoted to each day of creation and simple illustrations depicting sky, clouds, trees, and animals. The story slows down, depicting the creation of humankind (Gen 1:26) with an image of a happy and very blonde first couple looking into each other's eyes, followed by a picture of Adam and a horse looking into each other's eyes. The latter is accompanied by text that explains, "They were to tend their beautiful garden, Eden, and to name and care for all the animals." Here Suggs simplifies the "dominion" over the creatures of the earth in Gen 1:26, part of which is printed at the top of the page, and collapses the two distinct creation stories by bringing the task of naming the animals (Gen 2:19) alongside the creation of humankind as articulated in Gen 1:26–28. Suggs avoids any repetition or contradiction between the two creation accounts by skipping most of the details of the second creation account and jumping to Eve's temptation by the serpent. As in *Picture Stories*, Eve's tendencies—her nature?—can already be seen before the encounter with the crafty serpent. A frame depicts Adam and Eve gushing over how much

---

31. Suggs, *Comic Book Bible*, back cover.

God loves them and their luck to have been given everything they could possibly need. As they talk, however, Eve is tenderly touching the trunk of a tree. In the next frame she asks, "Still—don't you wonder about this tree?" To which Adam responds, "Yes. But you know that's the only tree God warned us about. Its fruit is off limits." Here, too, we see the concern to have Adam relay God's command to Eve. In the next frame Adam walks away leaving Eve alone, prompting the serpent to say, "Hmm. We'll see about that?" With Adam out of the picture, the next few frames show Eve easily succumbing to the power of the serpent through the use of imagery that suggests mesmerism or hypnotism (see fig. 3). Suggs depicts the final scenes of Gen 3 quickly, showing the first couple being found by God, blaming each other, and being expelled from the garden.

Names, Games and the Long Road Trip is part of the *Manga Bible* series from Zondervan and contains stories from Genesis and Exodus. Published in 2007, it is striking in the extent to which the didactic purpose of the book drives a very liberal adaptation of the Bible. *Names* seems to equate humor with relevance for a younger audience. The fifth day of creation is illustrated with a small fish asking a large whale, "Excuse me! Have you seen my son Nemo?" In the same frame another fish states, "I am not trying to kiss you! My lips are always shaped like this!" Most of frames

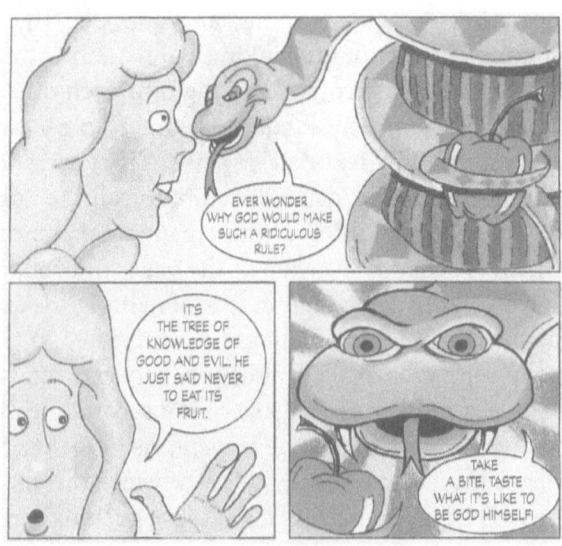

Fig. 3. Suggs, *The Comic Book Bible*, 1997.

throughout the comic turn on a joke of some sort. *Names* solves interpretive issues arising from the presence of two creation stories in Genesis by having only man created in the first story, reserving the creation of Eve for the second, where she becomes the primary focus. Eve's inherent sexuality is emphasized by drawing Adam as a young boy until he sees Eve, seductively leaning toward him; from that point on he is drawn as an adult who is clearly smitten (see fig. 4). *Names* makes a point of highlighting Adam's resistance to Eve's offer of fruit from the banned tree: Adam is shocked to see Eve eating from the forbidden fruit; he reminds her of God's command when she offers him a taste of the fruit and resists a second offer. Here Eve pours it on: she weeps and states, "Oh Adam … you've changed.… I'm telling you it's good, but all you can think about is getting in trouble with God." She continues to weep until he gives in, at which point her tears immediately stop; she winks at the reader and says, "Hee hee … girls can make guys do anything."

In all of the above, Eve is more gullible, more easily tempted, and expends some effort in getting Adam to taste the fruit, something that is not suggested by Gen 3:6, which simply notes that Eve "also gave some to her husband, who was with her, and he ate" (NRSV). In different ways each

Fig. 4. Lee and Hwang, *Names, Games and the Long Road Trip*, 2007.

of the comics reinforces "popular biblical stereotypes"[32] which are likely shaped by the history of Christian readings of the story of Eden.[33]

Concerns for contemporary relevance show up in other ways as well. A number of Bible comics introduce contemporary tensions between the Genesis creation accounts and modern scientific theories of origins, some explicitly. *Good and Evil*, for example, illustrates the fourth and fifth days of creation with images of sea and land creatures, accompanied by a narrator's statement, "It was not as many modern men suppose. The creator did not make use of evolution. He created all things by simply speaking them into existence. In six 24-hour days God made plants and animals to populate the earth."[34] A more subtle, yet far more common way of presenting Genesis as compatible with science is the practice of illustrating the creation of the bodies of light on the fourth day (1:14) with an image of planet earth as viewed from space, reflecting a cosmology that fits contemporary views, not the three-tiered cosmos assumed by the creation stories in Genesis.[35]

With regard to the presence of two creation narratives in Gen 1–3, all of the comic book Bibles highlighted above also solve any challenges two accounts might pose a reader by careful selection, omission, and rearrangement of the elements in the stories. That such liberal adaptations of the biblical stories can still be presented as Bibles is, as du Toit points out, a function of the somewhat ambiguous space these texts occupy as didactic translations mostly for children.[36] These comic book Bibles tend to land squarely on the "domesticating" end of the spectrum, clearly privileging the "relevance" to their contemporary audience and taking cover for the radical changes in the didactic nature of genre. But as projects such as Smith's Brick Testament and Crumb's *Genesis* show through their specific positioning against the tradition of Bible illustration and their counterclaims to accuracy, the selective practices of these "mainstream" Bibles have not gone unnoticed.

---

32. Beal says this of *Names*, but it applies to all of the comics referenced here (*Rise and Fall of the Bible*, 66).

33. For a brief discussion of Christian readings of the figure of Eve, see Brueggemann, *Genesis*, 42–44.

34. Michael Pearl, *Good and Evil* (Pleasantville, Tenn.: No Greater Joy Ministries, 2008), 3.

35. See, for example, Suggs, *Comic Book Bible*, 8; Pearl, *Good and Evil*, 3; Mauss, *Action Bible*, 19.

36. Du Toit, "Seeing Is Believing," 103–6.

Reading it Straight (with an Angle)

Presenting liberally adapted biblical stories as Bibles or even as products capable of presenting "biblical truths," as many of these Bible comics do, raises a number of questions about what gets left out and why, what constitutes the true core of a story, and who has the right to interpret or retell the Bible. These questions are played out in the small group of Bible comics critical of the "mainstream." *Outrageous Tales*, for example, highlights what is typically left out of comic book Bibles. But in its almost exclusive focus on scenes in the Hebrew Bible containing sex and violence, it is as selective as "mainstream" Christian comics Bibles. Despite Gaiman's claims to simply carrying out a "fairly straight" illustration what in the Bible, his contributions in *Outrageous Tales*, as well as the volume as a whole, can be understood as parodies of Bible stories that effect a "desacralization" of the Bible.[37]

Something similar is at work in R. Crumb's *Genesis*, although the critique is achieved through different means. Crumb's careful and methodical illustration of all of Genesis serves as a deliberate counter to the selective adaptation carried out in "mainstream" comic book and illustrated Bibles. Unlike *Outrageous Tales*, Crumb illustrates "adult" scenes but does not go out of his way to highlight nudity or violence. While Crumb positions his *Genesis* as a very literal presentation of the first book of the Bible, Crumb's version of Genesis represents a significant and in many ways sophisticated interpretation.[38] Viewed as a translation, it is "domesticating" by virtue of being an adaptation or translation into a modern medium and literary form. But it is also "foreignizing" in its attempt to explain the cultural context of the source text: Crumb's *Genesis* begins with a map and contains occasional footnotes giving the Hebrew meanings of place names and other relevant information. By virtue of committing to illustrating the entire text of Genesis, Crumb presents the two creation stories as discrete narratives. He leaves in place, for example, the creation of male and female

---

37. Cyril Camus, "The 'Outsider': Neil Gaiman and the Old Testament," *Shofar* 29 (2011): 82–90.

38. This is the argument of Jolly, "Interpretive Treatments of Genesis," 235–38. See also R. C. Harvey, "R. C. Harvey on R. Crumb's *The Book of Genesis*," The Comics Journal Blog. Online: http://classic.tcj.com/alternative/r-c-harvey-on-r-crumb%E2%80%99s-the-book-of-genesis/.

in Gen 1:27 before the creation of Eve from Adam's rib in Gen 2:21–22, an interpretive issue that is inevitably "solved" by most Bible comics.

But as with any translation, there are interpretive implications in the choices that are made in rendering the source text intelligible in the language of the receiving culture and context. In Crumb's case, we can highlight the choice to represent God at all (see fig. 5), something typically avoided in "mainstream" Bible comic books. Furthermore, Crumb's decision to represent God as an old man with a white beard drawn within the boundaries of traditional narrative panels of the comic book medium is, as Jolly notes, effectively an "exegetical move."[39] Crumb is respectful of the value and history of the Bible, but it is, in the end, just a story. Crumb's God is explicitly a character within this story, not a figure who transcends the world of the narrative and whose voice is heard and presence felt as is almost always the case in most mainstream Bible comic books.

Similar strategies carry out the critique of the Bible illustration tradition in the Brick Testament. While not technically a comic book, Smith plays with conventions of the genre on the website and describes his *Brick Bible* books as a "graphic novel set."[40] There are a number of striking similarities between Crumb's and Smith's treatments of Genesis that are the result of their goals of literal retellings of the Bible. The two

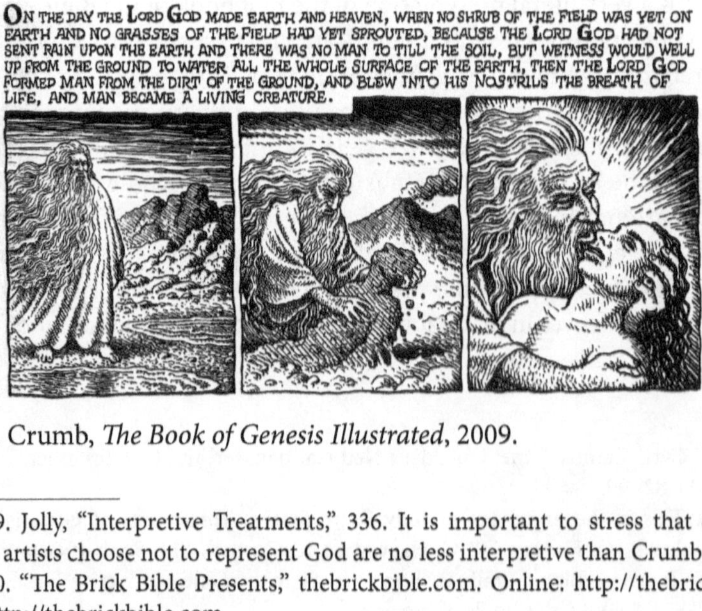

Fig. 5. Crumb, *The Book of Genesis Illustrated*, 2009.

---

39. Jolly, "Interpretive Treatments," 336. It is important to stress that comics whose artists choose not to represent God are no less interpretive than Crumb is.

40. "The Brick Bible Presents," thebrickbible.com. Online: http://thebrickbible.com http://thebrickbible.com

versions are the most extensive, detailed, and complete comic book versions of the Bible (at least of the sections they address.) Like Crumb, Smith presents the two accounts of creation as discrete stories—in fact, the reader has to click on different links to get to them. Also like Crumb, Smith represents God as an old, white-haired man with a beard—albeit made out of LEGOs (see fig. 6). While humorous, as is the case with Crumb's representation of God, this choice is not without interpretive implications in Smith's Brick Testament. Smith's God is a character in the narrative who is made of the same stuff as Adam and Eve and is of the same size. While this echoes Gen 1:26, there are clearly interpretive implications to portraying God in this way. A sense of God's transcendence, which I think is the effect of not representing God in many of the comics,[41] is harder to get from the Brick Testament.

But Smith goes further in some ways—or at least is less subtle—highlighting the cultural otherness, violence, and clearly "adult" themed content of much of the Bible. Smith uses several strategies, including the choice of medium. While illustrated Bibles, including those in the comics medium, have long been associated with children, the use of LEGO blocks—a children's toy—even more clearly evokes this association. This can lead to some humorous moments produced by the limits of the medium, such

Fig. 6. The Brick Testament (http://www.bricktestament.com/genesis/the_garden_of_eden/13_gn02_22-23.html).

---

41. This is, I think, the goal of most comics in choosing to represent God only through word bubbles rather than an anthropomorphic portrayal, as might be suggested from the second creation account. *Picture Stories* and *The Comic Book Bible* both distinguish God's speech from that of Adam and Eve by surrounding dialogue spoken by God with a yellow band, a halo of sorts.

as the representation of Jesus's baptism in Mark 1:10, wherein the top half of a LEGO Jesus figure sits on blue tiles representing water, while a white parrot sits on Jesus's head[42] (LEGO apparently has not made any doves), or the illustration of God resting on the seventh day (Gen 2:2), which is illustrated with image of God—depicted as an old man with a long, white beard—lying on a hammock.[43] But on the whole, Smith exploits LEGO's association with children to create a kind of visual dissonance. It is one thing to say, Adam and Eve had a son (Gen 4:1). It is quite another to offer a visual illustration of Eve giving birth to Cain.[44] The narratives in Genesis are notoriously sparse, leaving many questions unanswered and much to the imagination. Smith's tendency is to fill in the gaps and answer these questions with an emphasis on the violence implicit in the text. In his illustration of the flood, for example, Smith lingers over the statements in Gen 7:21–23 relating God's decision to kill all living creatures, illustrating this moment with five frames showing people and animals drowning, falling through the water, then landing at the bottom of the sea.[45] When Noah, his family, and the animals eventually emerge from the ark (Gen 8:18–19), Smith emphasizes the deaths of those who did not enter the ark by having those still living walk through a field littered with LEGO skeletons.[46]

In addition to the visual dissonance created by pairing a medium associated with children with material that is usually kept from children's Bibles, Smith adheres to a literalism that can look like reverence for the biblical text, but its effect is to highlight the oddity and cultural otherness of the Bible. Smith achieves this by having both captions containing the biblical text being illustrated and word balloons displaying any dialogue contained in the scripture in the caption. The effect is a rather stilted,

---

42. "Jesus is Baptised: Mark 1:10," The Brick Testament. Online: http://www.bricktestament.com/the_life_of_jesus/jesus_is_baptised/mk01_10.html.

43. "Creation: Genesis 2:1–3," The Brick Testament. Online: http://www.thebricktestament.com/genesis/creation/26_gn02_01-03.html.

44. "Cain and Abel: Genesis 4:1," The Brick Testament. http://www.thebricktestament.com/genesis/cain_kills_abel/01_gn04_01.html. Both Crumb and Smith illustrate this moment; "mainstream" Bible comics do not.

45. See, for example, "The Flood: Genesis 7:23, 22," The Brick Testament. Online: http://www.thebricktestament.com/genesis/god_drowns_everyone/20_gn07_22-23.html.

46. "The Flood: Genesis 8:18–19," The Brick Testament. Online: http://www.thebricktestament.com/genesis/god_drowns_everyone/24_gn08_18-19.html.

repetitive comic book narrative that can be read as a parody of a "literal" reading of the Bible.

Sometimes Smith's critique is carried by his choice of subject matter. There is no reason to illustrate some of the laws in Exodus through Deuteronomy, with headings such as "When to Stone your Children" and "Camp Defecation," other than to make the point that these materials are in the Bible too. Here Smith is as selective as the illustrated Bibles he critiques. At other times Smith does the opposite, slowing the pace of the adaptation down and illustrating every detail. This is the case with his presentation of Gen 1–3, which is marked by a detailed and methodical illustration of almost every verse in Gen 1–3. The first five days of creation (Gen 1:1–25) are typically covered in "mainstream" Bible comics in five or six frames over no more than three pages while Crumb uses twelve frames. Smith, in contrast, uses twenty frames to illustrate this material. And Smith devotes three frames to the illustration of the single verse describing God's creation of Adam from the ground (Gen 2:7). The effect is a Bible that is slow and plodding. This also allows Smith to present his very literal renditions as fidelity to scripture while at the same time highlighting "adult" moments in the Bible and passages that present interpretive difficulties. For example, he seizes on the plural in the Gen 1:26 statement, "Let us make humankind in our image, according to our likeness" (NRSV), to illustrate God standing in front of a number of winged figures. This could be understood as an illustration of the divine council, or perhaps it is simply the presentation of a polytheistic understanding of the deity.[47] In any case, Smith is alone in illustrating the plural in this passage in this way.

Crumb, Smith and others provide an interesting counterpoint to the assumptions supporting the production of most "mainstream" Bible comics. While some of their critique is explicit in the way in which they position themselves against the tradition of Bible illustration, more striking are the ways in which their critiques are carried out in the illustration projects themselves. Crumb and Smith highlight the at times extreme selectivity of most comic book Bibles by going in the opposite direction and illustrating every single verse. They achieve this also by illustrating parts of the Bible typically omitted in order to render the Bible appropriate for children. In so doing their works raise questions about what constitutes

---

47. "Creation: Genesis 1:26," The Brick Testament. Online: http://www.thebricktestament.com/genesis/creation/20_gn01_26.html.

a Bible story and how exactly one decides what the core or key biblical truth of a given story is. But Crumb and Smith are, despite their claims to "straightforward" retelling, no less interpretive, and in Smith's case especially, no less selective than the Bible comics they critique. Their vantage points just happen to be different.

Given the recent increase in Bibles marketed to children and Bible comics in particular, I suspect that Bible comics engaged in an adversarial way with the continuing practices of Bible illustration in "mainstream" comics will become more numerous. It will be interesting to watch the conversation develop.

Part 4
The Bible and Public Schools

Battling over the Bible in Public Schools: Is Common Ground Possible?

Charles C. Haynes

Before addressing battles over the Bible in schools, let me begin with a bold assertion about the current status of religion generally in public education. Contrary to rhetoric from the right about "godless public schools," there is actually more student religious expression and more study *about* religion in public schools today than at any time in the last one hundred years. And contrary to dire warnings from the left about evangelical Christian attempts to take over public schools, much, if not most, of the religion in public schools today comes in through the First Amendment door.

The (mostly) constitutional return of religion to public schools has taken place over the past twenty-five years—a relatively short time measured in school reform years—and has been nothing less than a quiet revolution. It is beyond the scope of this paper to discuss in detail the many cultural changes and legal developments that contributed to this revolution. Suffice it to say, court decisions over the past two decades have done much to clarify for school officials the difference between student religious expression, which in many circumstances is protected by the free exercise and free speech clauses of the First Amendment, and government endorsement of religion in public schools, which the establishment clause prohibits. Legislation has also played an important role, especially the federal Equal Access Act of 1984 that opened the door to student religious clubs in secondary schools.

Forging a New Consensus

Framed by litigation and legislation, a new consensus emerged in the late 1980s on the constitutional place of religion in public schools. Over the past two decades, religious, civil liberties, and education groups from across the political and religious spectrum have found common ground on many religion-in-schools issues that have long divided Americans. These agreements have given public schools a First Amendment safe harbor for teaching about religion, acknowledging religious holidays, protecting student religious expression, and cooperating with religious communities. The new consensus on these and other issues is now reflected in United States Department of Education guidelines as well as in many school district policies throughout the country.[1]

The Christian Legal Society, American Jewish Committee, National Schools Boards Association, Baptist Joint Committee for Religious Liberty, American Association of School Administrators, National Association of Evangelicals, People for the American Way, and many other organizations have joined together to demonstrate that it is possible to negotiate deep differences with civility and respect—and to reach agreement on how the First Amendment should be applied under current law. As an organizer and drafter of many of these guides, I can attest to the spirit of collaboration and trust that has moved opposing sides from battleground to common ground.

Not all public schools, of course, have adopted the new consensus. Some schools, especially in the rural South, continue to unconstitutionally promote religion (the majority faith in their communities). These are what might be called "sacred public schools," vestiges of the Protestant-dominated schools of the nineteenth and early twentieth centuries—places where school officials promote one faith (theirs) during the school day. On the other end of the spectrum, some schools still resemble "naked public schools"—places where school officials mistakenly believe that the Supreme Court's prayer decisions in the 1960s require public schools to be religion-free zones. Both sacred and naked public schools are unjust and, in many respects, unconstitutional.

Despite the remaining challenges in some districts, the good news is that a growing number of public schools are going beyond the failed models of our past by implementing the First Amendment framework agreed to in the common ground documents based on current law. Nei-

---

1. The consensus guidelines and the United States Department of Education guidance may be found in Charles C. Haynes and Oliver Thomas, *Finding Common Ground: A First Amendment Guide to Religion and Public Schools* (Nashville: First Amendment Center, 2007).

ther sacred nor naked, these are what might be best described as First Amendment schools—places that neither inculcate nor denigrate religion, but treat religion and religious conviction with fairness and respect.

In a First Amendment school, for example, students may pray alone or in groups as long as such prayers do not disrupt the school or interfere with the rights of others. Students may share their faith with classmates, including by distribution of religious literature subject to reasonable time, place, and manner restrictions. And, in the classroom, students may express their religious views during a class discussion or as part of a written assignment if it is relevant to the subject under consideration or meets the requirements of the assignment. On the secondary school level, students may form religious clubs if the school allows other extracurricular clubs.

Of course, agreement on key issues involving religion in schools does not mean agreement on all issues. Debate continues over some aspects of student religious expression, such as when school officials may draw the line on student religious speech in front of a captive audience. And, in spite of agreement on the need to include teaching about religion in the curriculum, conflicts continue to erupt over how to teach the Bible in a public school.

Teaching about the Bible

It is important to note that current disputes over the Bible in public schools are confined largely to the issue of Bible electives. Thanks in large part to the new consensus, many long-contested issues involving the Bible in public schools are no longer controversial. Most school leaders now understand that students may bring their scriptures to school to share with other students or to read during their free time. As already mentioned, students may form Bible clubs in secondary schools if the school allows other student clubs not related to the curriculum. A small number of administrators are still confused about what the law permits and continue to tell students to leave their Bibles at home. And a small number of administrators and teachers continue to use the Bible devotionally in the presence of students in defiance of the law. But most public schools are doing what the First Amendment requires by protecting the right of students to bring their Bibles to school and refraining from school promotion or denigration of the Bible.

Bible electives, however, continue to be a flash point for controversy and conflict. Of course, teaching *about* the Bible may be done in public schools—indeed, no world history or literature course would be adequate without some study of biblical texts. But *how* the Bible is taught remains controversial in large part because public schools have a long history of doing it in ways that are now understood to be unconstitutional. Some of the current Bible courses in Texas, North Carolina, and other states date back to the 1950s or earlier when local churches would often fund teachers—sometimes called the "Bible ladies"—to come in and offer what amounted to a Sunday school class. Many Bible electives of more recent vintage are a continuation of that history, reflecting the determination of the majority faith in the community to expose students to the word of God during the school day.

The growth in the number of Bible electives over the past few decades is part of a larger story about the increase in teaching about religion in the wake of the 1960s Supreme Court decisions striking down state-sponsored religious practices in public schools. In the mid-1960s and throughout the 1970s, some religious groups supported more study about religions to compensate for a loss of teacher-led prayers and devotional Bible reading. At the same time, some educators supported more study about religions, including the Bible, because the Supreme Court decisions striking down school-sponsored religious practices simultaneously encouraged the academic study of religion and the Bible in public schools. This unlikely coalition helped create the National Council on Religion in Public Education (NCRPE) and sparked a variety of initiatives at Wright State University, Indiana University, Harvard University's School of Education, and elsewhere to train teachers, develop curriculum materials, and, in other ways, increase study about religions.[2]

By the 1980s, however, support for study about religions and the Bible had waned. Many religious conservatives lost enthusiasm for the academic treatment of the Bible, and the public school establishment never adopted study about religions, much less the Bible, as a priority in education. Moreover, many administrators and teachers were afraid to tackle religion in the curriculum, either because they were confused about the Supreme Court's prayer decisions or because they feared controversy—or both. Many of the religious studies electives developed in the late 1960s

---

2. For a brief history of the NCRPE, see Charles R. Kniker, "National Council on Religion and Public Education," in *The Praeger Handbook of Religion and Education in the United States* (ed. James C. Carper and Thomas C. Hunt; 2 vols.; Westport, Conn.: Praeger, 2009), 2:326–28.

and early 1970s disappeared, and history curriculum frameworks and textbooks were once again largely silent about religion. NCRPE shut down for lack of interest.

In the mid-1980s, however, conflicts over the poor treatment of religion in the curriculum, including court cases in Tennessee and Alabama, sparked a renewed interest in teaching about religion. Several textbooks studies confirmed the obvious: The conventional wisdom in the curriculum was that students could learn everything they needed to know about all subjects without learning anything about religion.[3]

In 1987, the legal fights and textbook studies prompted a diverse coalition of educational and religious organizations to seek agreement on how public schools should address religion in the curriculum. This was the beginning of the common ground effort I have described as the "new consensus." After a year and a half of negotiations that I chaired with Oliver Thomas of the Baptist Joint Committee, seventeen national organizations—ranging from the National Association of Evangelicals to the National Education Association—agreed to the first consensus guidelines on teaching about religion. "Religion in the Public School Curriculum: Questions and Answers" was published and widely disseminated in 1988.[4]

These guidelines—together with the inclusion of religious studies in the California History/ Social Science Framework in 1989—helped bring about a sea change in how religion was treated in standards and textbooks, particularly in the social studies. Over the next twenty years, state standards in the social studies became increasingly generous to study of religion. Textbooks gradually added more information about religion. And new electives in religious studies were offered in various parts of the country.

---

3. A full discussion of how the public school curriculum ignored religion in the 1980s and, despite some progress toward inclusion of religious studies, still treats religion superficially today may be found in Warren A. Nord, *Does God Make a Difference?* (New York: Oxford University Press, 2011). See also Warren A. Nord and Charles C. Haynes, *Taking Religion Seriously Across the Curriculum* (Alexandria, Va.: Association for Supervision and Curriculum Development, 1998).

4. "Religion in the Public School Curriculum: Questions and Answers" is included in Haynes and Thomas, *Finding Common Ground*, 87–102 and can also be accessed at the Freedom Forum website (http://www.freedomforum.org/templates/document.asp?documentID=3979).

Finding Common Ground on Bible Courses

At the same time, however, some Christian conservatives took advantage of the new consensus on the importance of study about religion to advance a very different agenda. The biggest offender was—and still is—the National Council on Bible Curriculum in Public Schools (NCBCPS), headquartered in North Carolina. Quietly, but effectively, the NCBCPS pushed for Bible electives in many school districts, providing schools with a curriculum that critics charged promoted one religious view of the Bible. Although the council's materials claimed to be constitutional—and even quoted from the consensus guidelines—the curriculum was neither academically nor constitutionally sound.[5]

In response to the proliferation of problematic Bible courses, I met with Chuck Stetson, then on the board of the National Bible Association, to discuss the need for guidelines that explicitly address how to teach about the Bible in public schools under the First Amendment. In 1997 I reconvened the coalition of organizations that developed earlier guidelines to seek common ground on this issue. After almost two years of discussion and numerous drafts, we released *The Bible and Public Schools: A First Amendment Guide* in 1999.

As with earlier guidelines, we formed the broadest coalition possible. If guidelines are to be credible—and widely adopted in schools—they must have support from left to right on the religious and political spectrums. While it was not possible to get every advocacy group on board, it was possible to get enough agreement on both sides to insulate the document from attack. With the Christian Legal Society and the National Association of Evangelicals listed as sponsors, we knew that most conservatives Christians would take the guidelines seriously. With People for the American Way endorsing the document, we knew that most progressives and separationists would trust the agreement. And, of course, sign on from all of the leading education associations was needed to ensure that school districts would adopt the guidance. In the end, twenty-one national religious, civil liberties, and education groups, including the Society of Biblical Literature, agreed to endorse the guidelines.

---

5. The best analysis of the NCBCPS materials is found in Mark A. Chancey, "A Textbook Example of the Christian Right: The National Council on Bible Curriculum in Public Schools," *Journal of the American Academy of Religion* 75 (2007): 554–81.

The Bible and Public Schools describes our agreement on current law concerning student use of the Bible during the school day and then tackles the more difficult issue of how to teach *about* the Bible in the curriculum. Across our differences, we agree that biblical literacy is important. We also agree that any instruction about the Bible must be academic and not devotional and that "academic teaching about the Bible is not intended to either undermine or reinforce the beliefs of those who accept the Bible or of those who do not." We also agree that Bible electives—as well as units on the Bible in literature or history classes—should expose students to various versions and translations of the Bible, include a variety of interpretations of the Bible, and use academically sound secondary sources that discuss the various religious and secular approaches to the Bible. Equally important, we urge that teachers charged with teaching about the Bible be adequately prepared through in-service workshops or summer institutes. Electives in biblical studies, we argue, "should only be offered if there are teachers academically competent to teach them."[6]

The guidelines also make the case that schools should take care to avoid the appearance of privileging some religious tradition over others by including generous study of a variety of religions in the curriculum. If, for example, a school decides to offer a Bible elective, we recommend offering an elective in world religions as well.

Although the NCBCPS has ignored the guidelines, many school districts and state Departments of Education use the common ground statement to help determine when proposed Bible electives are unconstitutional. Soon after the guide was released, the South Carolina State Department of Education sent the guide to all teachers in the state. In 2005 the Alabama teacher's union distributed the Bible guide to all of its members. Contrary to the warnings from some critics on the separationist side that the guidelines would be misused to promote unconstitutional Bible courses, the publication has served to discourage adoption of materials that do not met the criteria outlined in the guidance.

---

6. The full text of *The Bible and Public Schools: A First Amendment Guide* (Nashville: First Amendment Center, 1999) may be found at www.religiousfreedomeducation.org and www.sbl-site.org/educational/thebibleinpublicschools.aspx.

Competing Approaches to Teaching the Bible

After the publication of *The Bible in Public Schools*, Chuck Stetson of the National Bible Association formed the Bible Literacy Project (BLP) in order to produce materials that would reflect the principles articulated in the guidelines.[7] In 2005, the BLP published *The Bible and Its Influence* edited by Stetson with Cullen Schippe. Like any textbook, this one has its critics, including some biblical scholars who would like to see a more rigorous and scholarly treatment of the material. As a First Amendment reviewer of the manuscript, however, I found it to be a good faith effort to provide an academically and constitutionally sound textbook for use in public schools. No textbook is perfect, and this one has been revised and improved in subsequent editions. But currently, *The Bible and Its Influence* is the only textbook available to public schools that provides a credible and constitutional alternative to the NCBCPS materials.[8]

Not surprisingly, leaders of the NCBCPS have not welcomed the completion. In fact, they have done everything possible to heap ridicule and scorn on *The Bible and Its Influence*, including making personal attacks on people who supported the BLP textbook. The aim has been to discredit the BLP in the eyes of evangelicals, the core constituency advocating for Bible electives around the country. This has been, in some respects, a family feud since both projects have strong support from different voices in the conservative Christian community. Unlike NCBCPS, however, the BLP also enjoys support from a variety of religious and civil liberties groups.

When *The Bible and Its Influence* was first published, the BLP attempted to avoid a fight, choosing not to respond in kind to attacks from the NCBCPS. But then in 2005 an evangelical leader in Alabama urged the state legislature to pass a "Bible bill" encouraging Bible electives—and he proposed that schools be required to use *The Bible and Its Influence* to ensure that the courses would be constitutional. NCBCPS reacted to being excluded by successfully lobbying the Republican minority in the legislature to block the bill when it was introduced in 2006. This unfortunate chain of events triggered a Bible war over the two approaches that continues to the present day.

---

7. The Bible Literacy Project. Online: www.bibleliteracy.org.

8. Cullen Schippe and Chuck Stetson, eds., *The Bible and Its Influence* (2nd ed.; Fairfax: Bible Literacy Project, 2006).

In March 2006 Georgia became the first state to pass a "Bible bill" encouraging local districts to adopt Bible electives and offering state support to make it happen. Thanks to support from the Republicans who controlled the legislature, NCBCPS was able to fight off proponents of the BLP textbook and build language into the bill that point to the adoption of NCBCPS material. For example, the bill requires that the textbook used in a Bible elective must be the Bible itself, a transparent attempt to prevent adoption of the BLP textbook. This strategy did not entirely work, however, when at least one large school district found a way to adopt *The Bible and Its Influence* by calling it "supplementary" to the primary text—the Bible.[9]

It should be noted that the NCBCPS material is not a textbook but rather a long curriculum outline or guide for teachers that explains how to teach the Bible (treating it as though it were a history book) and, in various ways, suggests that there is only one way to read and understand the text. Biblical scholarship is ignored, religious interpretations other than evangelical are excluded, and constitutionally suspect secondary materials are recommended for use in the classroom.

After the passage of the Georgia legislation, other states—Texas, Tennessee, Oklahoma, and Arizona—passed similar "Bible bills" encouraging Bible electives, and South Carolina passed a related released time law intended to promote off-campus Bible courses. Of course, schools in these states could already offer Bible electives without legislation; and, in fact, there have been Bible courses in all of these states for many years. But the Bible bills offer state-level support for Bible courses with the clear intention of encouraging more schools to offer Bible electives.

Thanks to the good work of the Texas Freedom Network and scholars like Mark Chancey, professor of religious studies at Southern Methodist University, the Texas legislation includes some safeguards such as requiring First Amendment training for teachers enlisted to teach Bible electives. Unfortunately, the state has done little to ensure such training and many of the current Bible electives in Texas do not pass constitutional muster.[10]

---

9. A full account of the adoption of the Bible bills in Alabama and Georgia may be found in Mark A. Chancey, "Bible Bills, Bible Curricula, and Controversies of Biblical Proportions: Legislative Efforts to Promote Bible Courses," *Religion and Education* 34 (2007): 28–47.

10. For Texas Freedom Network, see www.tfn.org. On Texas Bible courses, see two reports at that website: Mark A. Chancey, *Reading, Writing and Religion: Teach-*

A recent legislative resolution in South Dakota (HCR 1004, 2012) supporting the academic study of the Bible included notably strong language about the need for adhering to the First Amendment. In my view, it is the best of the recent state legislative proposals (it appears to have the BLP fingerprints all over it), because it also underscores the need for teacher preparation, scholarly materials, and First Amendment guidelines.

Meeting the Challenge

The efforts of the BLP and the NCBCPS to promote Bible courses through legislation and local advocacy have led to more Bible electives across the country. Just how many is very difficult to pin down since states do a poor job of tracking the number of electives taught in their schools. On its website, the NCBCPS claims to be in more than 2,441 high schools in thirty-nine states, numbers that cannot be verified (and are likely highly inflated) since the group does not reveal the names of schools where their material is being taught. The Bible Literacy Project's claim to be in more than 580 schools in forty-three states schools is more reliable. In addition, an unknown number of schools have created their own Bible curriculum.[11]

Whatever the exact numbers, the challenge, of course, is to ensure that all Bible electives in public schools are both academically and constitutionally sound. In my contact with schools and teachers over the past decade, I have found that too few Bible electives have been vetted for First Amendment problems. Some of the teachers I encounter teaching these courses have little or no background in religious studies, much less biblical studies. Most troubling of all, some local districts, especially in the Southeast, continue to adopt materials and pedagogy that turn public school classrooms into Sunday schools.

Nevertheless, there is good news about how public schools are handling Bible courses: Schools using *The Bible and Its Influence* receive teacher training and other support from the BLP. *The Bible and Public Schools: A First Amendment Guide* continues to be widely disseminated by education

---

ing the Bible in Texas Public Schools (Austin: Texas Freedom Network Education Fund, 2006), and Mark A. Chancey, *Reading, Writing and Religion II: Teaching the Bible in Texas Public Schools, 2011–2012* (Austin: Texas Freedom Network Education Fund, 2013).

11. These figures, drawn from the two organizations' websites, were current as of December 11, 2013.

groups, and it is frequently cited in school district policies. And the Society of Biblical Literature is now offering outstanding resources designed to provide the best scholarship to public school teachers assigned to teach about the Bible.[12]

Getting the Bible right in public schools matters, because biblical literacy is an essential part of what it means to be an educated person. Knowledge of biblical literature that has shaped Western civilization is essential if students are to have an adequate understanding of literature, history, law, art, and contemporary society.

But teaching about the Bible in public schools must be done in ways that are objective, scholarly, fair, and, most important, constitutional. Some critics of Bible electives on both the right and the left argue (for very different reasons) that public schools cannot be trusted with instruction about the Bible. Fortunately, there are enough examples of sound Bible courses currently offered in public schools to prove the critics wrong. Unfortunately, there are enough examples of poor Bible courses to provide opponents of such instruction with plenty of ammunition.

In my view, ignoring the Bible in the public school curriculum is not the answer, because it deprives students of a good education and violates the spirit of neutrality and fairness consistent with the First Amendment. But I fully acknowledge that getting the Bible right in the classroom will take work—and require vigilance by those who value religious freedom.

Ending conflicts over the Bible in the curriculum and strengthening study about the Bible in schools would be good for education—and good for the country. If we hope to live with our deepest differences in twenty-first century America, we must move from battleground to common ground on the role of religion in our public schools.

---

12. See especially *Bible Electives in Public Schools: A Guide* (Atlanta: Society of Biblical Literature, n.d.) and the ezine *Teaching the Bible*. Online at http://www.sbl-site.org/educational/teachingbible.aspx.

Public School Bible Courses in Historical Perspective: North Carolina as a Case Study*

Mark A. Chancey

In its controversial 1963 decision, *Abington Township School District v. Schempp*, the United States Supreme Court famously declared public school–sponsored devotional Bible reading unconstitutional as a government-led religious practice, a prohibition that included in its purview theologically oriented Bible courses. Yet the court explicitly affirmed the acceptability of another approach to the Bible:

> It might well be said that one's education is not complete without a study of comparative religion or the history of religion and its relationship to the advancement of civilization. It certainly may be said that the Bible is worthy of study for its literary and historic qualities. Nothing we have said here indicates that such study of the Bible or of religion, when presented objectively as part of a secular program of education, may not be affected consistently with the First Amendment.[1]

Thus, although the court's ruling signaled the beginning of the end of the practice of teachers, administrators, or students reading aloud Bible verses each day, it opened the door for what was de facto a new type of Bible course, an "objective" and "secular" one.

Today, Bible courses in public schools may be too few in number to be characterized as "flourishing," but it is true that they are experiencing a level of visibility not enjoyed in decades. Five states (Georgia, Texas, Tennessee, Oklahoma, and Arizona) have recently passed laws encouraging

---

* This article is adapted, with the permission of Taylor & Francis, from my article, with the same name, published in *Religion & Education* 40 (2013): 253–69.

1. *Abington Township School District v. Schempp*, 374 U.S. 203 (1963) at 225.

schools to offer courses, and another (South Dakota) has passed a supportive resolution.[2] School districts in states without such laws also offer Bible courses, insisting they are taught in the academic, nonsectarian spirit of *Abington v. Schempp*—although the extent to which they succeed in meeting that bar varies widely.[3]

The fiftieth anniversary of the court's decision affords us a good opportunity to examine public school Bible courses in their larger historical context. This article traces the development of such courses, considering their relation to the older practice of Bible reading; their own creation as a part of early twentieth-century religious education programs; the impact of *Abington v. Schempp* and other court cases; and efforts to define the characteristics of constitutionally permissible courses. Because unusually rich source materials exist for some historical aspects of North Carolina Bible courses, that state will serve as a case study to illuminate national trends.

Bible Reading in American Education

The Bible's place in the early American schoolhouse is well known. In the colonial period and early Republic, it often served as a textbook for reading and morals, and widely used primers contained ample biblical material.[4] When the Common Schools movement emerged, it emphasized religion alongside the other three R's, and reading from the Bible was daily practice. Because the Common Schools reflected the religious sensibilities of the nation's Protestant majority, the King James Version was the classroom standard. To maintain support from different denominations, a

---

2. Chet Browaw, "Law Urges South Dakota Schools to Expand Bible Instruction," *Tulsa World*, May 28, 2012; Mark A. Chancey, "Bible Bills, Bible Curricula, and Controversies of Biblical Proportions: Legislative Efforts to Promote Bible Courses," *Religion & Education* 34 (2007): 28–47.

3. Texas provides an example of the varying quality of courses. See Mark A. Chancey, "Sectarian Elements in Public School Bible Courses: Lessons from the Lone Star State," *Journal of Church and State* 49 (2007): 719–42; Chancey, *Reading, Writing and Religion: Teaching the Bible in Texas Public Schools* (Austin: Texas Freedom Network Education Fund, 2006); and Chancey, *Reading, Writing and Religion II: Teaching the Bible in Texas Public Schools, 2011–2012* (Austin: Texas Freedom Network Education Fund, 2013), both at www.tfn.org.

4. John H. Westerhoff, "The Struggle for a Common Culture: Biblical Images in Nineteenth-Century Schoolbooks," in *The Bible and American Education* (ed. David L. Barr and Nicholas Piediscalzi; Philadelphia: Fortress, 1982), 25–40.

system developed in which the Bible was read without comment, a practice intended to ensure that no group's theology was privileged. Common School proponents regarded this approach as nonsectarian, but the scope of its neutrality extended only to Protestants. Roman Catholics, Jews, agnostics, atheists, and freethinkers often regarded it as the promotion of Protestant beliefs over their own.[5]

As immigration brought more religious diversity to America, it was inevitable that this approach would generate conflict. The most famous of the ensuing controversies were the Philadelphia Bible Riots in 1844, in which whole city blocks were leveled, and the Cincinnati Bible War of 1869–1873, which occurred in the courts rather than the streets. The Philadelphia tragedy led to that city's affirmation of the King James Version as the only acceptable translation for Common School reading and its corresponding rejection of the Catholic Douai version, whereas the Cincinnati dispute resulted in the cessation of school-sponsored Bible reading altogether.[6]

Many Protestants were scandalized that anyone would question the appropriateness of Bible reading or the preeminence of the King James Version. In the late 1800s and early 1900s, some states passed laws requiring the Bible to be read in schools.[7] Bible reading practices—whether the Bible was read at all, and, if so, which version(s) could be read—varied from state to state, in some cases from community to community, and often from school to school.[8]

---

5. Stephen K. Green, *The Bible, the School, and the Constitution* (New York: Oxford University Press, 2012); James W. Fraser, *Between Church and State: Religion and Public Education in a Multicultural America* (New York: St. Martin's, 1999), 23–65; Robert Michaelsen, *Piety in the Public School* (London: MacMillan, 1970), 67–133.

6. Green, *The Bible, the School, and the Constitution*; Joan DelFattore, *The Fourth R: Conflicts over Religion in American Public Schools* (New Haven: Yale University Press, 2004), 32–46; Michaelsen, *Piety in the Public School*, 89–98; Tracy Fessenden, "The Nineteenth-Century Bible Wars and the Separation of Church and State," *Church History* 74 (2005): 1–28.

7. R. Laurence Moore, "Bible Reading and Nonsectarian Schooling: The Failure of Religious Instruction in Nineteenth-Century Public Education," *Journal of American History* 86 (2000): 1581–99.

8. Alvin W. Johnson, *The Legal Status of Church–State Relationships: With Special Reference to Public Schools* (Minneapolis: University of Minnesota Press, 1934).

Such variations are well documented in annual reports from the federal commissioner of education from the end of the nineteenth century.[9] North Carolina had no law on the matter, but the Commissioner's 1897–1898 report includes a summary of the state of affairs there from the state superintendent of public education:

> In our town and city graded schools, supported by local taxes ... the Bible is generally read, either in opening or at some other time, generally, however, at opening, the superintendent or principal in charge offering a short prayer or repeating the Lord's Prayer in concert with other teachers and pupils.... There is no rule about it, except as the custom of reading the book makes it a rule.

Although the superintendent believed that most Tar Heel schools read the Bible, he also noted a county in which "the Bible is read in about 50 percent of the schools."[10]

By 1923, the legal status of Bible reading across the country was dictated by a mishmash of state laws, court decisions, attorney general opinions, and state and local policies. A federal report on the subject found that six states required Bible reading; eleven explicitly allowed but did not mandate it; ten prohibited it; nineteen had no law or policy one way or the other; and in two the legal status was unclear.[11] The situation was so fluid that an updated report appeared only seven years later documenting that the number of states requiring it had increased to eleven, whereas that of states disallowing it had risen to twelve. Eleven additional states allowed but did not require it, and in the remainder of states, the law was silent, a status that many communities interpreted as permissive.[12] These types of variations would remain in place until 1963.[13]

---

9. Moore, "Bible Reading and Nonsectarian Schooling."

10. *Report of the Commissioner of Education* (Bureau of Education, 1899), 2: 1551.

11. William Ross Hood, *The Bible in the Public Schools: Legal Status and Current Practice* (Washington, D.C.: Department of the Interior, Bureau of Education, 1923), 1–4.

12. Ward W. Keesecker, *Legal Status of Bible Reading and Religious Instruction in Public Schools* (Washington, D.C.: United States Department of the Interior, Office of Education, 1930).

13. Donald E. Boles, *The Bible, Religion, and Public Schools* (3rd ed.; Ames: Iowa State University Press, 1965), 48–154.

North Carolina fell into the category of states with no law or court rulings on the matter. A 1913 attempt to insert a permissive provision into the state constitution ("The use of the Holy Bible shall not be prohibited in schools supported wholly or in part from public taxes") died in legislative committee in the face of opposition from Baptist leaders and rabbis.[14] Despite occasional objections, many Carolina communities—likely most, though it is hard to determine conclusively—incorporated Bible reading into their school day, whether in homeroom, opening assembly, or elsewhere.[15]

Weekday Religious Education and the Public School Bible Course

Debates over Bible reading both reflected and contributed to heightened interest in the Bible's place in public education. When this interest combined with growing support for more systematic religious education, the result was a new phenomenon: grade-school courses devoted to the Bible, as well as courses in theology and character formation. These classes were offered collaboratively by public schools and local faith communities in a program called Weekday (or Week-Day) Religious Education (often abbreviated WRE or WDRE). The traditionally cited pioneer in this area is Gary, Indiana, which instituted a program for Protestants and Jews in 1914.[16]

WRE took a variety of forms. In "released time" programs, public schools released students during regular school hours to attend religious classes taught by clergy or selected laypeople, sometimes at houses of worship or other nearby locations and sometimes on their own campuses. With "dismissed time," schools simply ended their own classes early on some days to facilitate participation in WRE. Some communities opted instead for "free time" programs in which students took religious classes outside of school hours. Most WRE programs were Protestant, but well-developed Jewish,

---

14. Commission on Constitutional Amendments, *Report of Commission on Constitutional Amendments to Governor Locke Craig* (Raleigh, 1913), 7; "Bible Amendment Lost," *Lumberton Semi-Weekly Robesonian*, Sept. 29, 1913.

15. For evidence of objections, see "'The Bible and the Public Schools' Again," *Biblical Recorder*, June 18, 1913.

16. Arlo A. Brown, "The Week-Day Church Schools of Gary, Indiana," *Religious Education* 11 (1916): 5–19.

Roman Catholic, and Mormon programs existed in parts of the country.[17] Some school systems awarded academic credit for these courses. This idea actually predates the Gary program, as North Dakota had launched a widely hailed plan in 1912 in which schools gave credit for Sunday school and similar off-campus religious education classes that covered material specified on an official state syllabus.[18]

When the first North Carolina Bible courses appeared is not clear, but by 1916–1917, the state had begun tracking the number of students taking them (twenty-nine in rural school systems, as opposed to 7,410 taking Latin, with no reported number for urban systems).[19] The number of courses and students increased modestly as communities devised policies allowing academic credit for Sunday school or similar classes and specifying requirements for instructional time, teacher certification, and administration of exams.[20] The North Carolina Teacher's Assembly declared in 1921: "We believe the time has come when schools should cooperate with the religious denominations in such a way that the Bible may be taught more effectively to the youth of our state." The assembly cited the value of the "historical and literary study of the Bible" and its importance as the "basis of good citizenship and community living."[21] The proposal prompted immediate controversy. The state Southern Baptist periodical, for example, cautiously raised concerns about separation of church and

---

17. Jonathan Zimmerman, *Whose America? Culture Wars in the Public Schools* (Cambridge: Harvard University Press, 2002), 135–50; Mary Dabney Davis, *Week-Day Religious Instruction: Classes for Public-School Pupils Conducted on Released School Time* (Washington, D.C.: United States Department of the Interior, Office of Education, 1933); Michaelsen, *Piety in the Public Schools*, 181–85; Johnson, *Legal Status of Church-State Relationships*, 129–47.

18. Vernon P. Squires, "The North Dakota Plan of High School Bible Study," *Religious Education* 8 (1913): 225–31.

19. N. W. Walker, *Tenth Annual Report: State Inspector of Public High Schools of North Carolina for the Scholastic Year Ending June 30, 1917* (Raleigh, 1917), 12. Online: https://archive.org/stream/reportofstatein191617nort#page/n5/mode/2up.

20. E. C. Brooks, "The Public School and the Churches," *North Carolina Education* 16 (1921): 14. For 1917 figures, see N. W. Walker, *Tenth Annual Report*. Numbers for other years are available in other annual reports of the state inspector of public high schools in the North Carolina Digital Collections. Online: http://digital.ncdcr.gov/cdm/search/searchterm/North%20Carolina.%20Department%20of%20Public%20Instruction./mode/exact.

21. "Thirty-Eighth Annual Session of the North Carolina Teachers' Assembly," *North Carolina Education* 16 (1921): 4.

state and the possibility of poorly taught or theologically suspect courses ("Suppose the principal is an infidel or German rationalist, what would he know about an examination on the Bible?").[22] One local paper countered such worries by affirming North Carolina's identity as "a Christian state, a part of a Christian nation" and hinting that newspapers criticizing the plan might be surreptitiously controlled by Roman Catholics.[23] Seemingly taken aback by the mixed public reaction, the Teacher's Assembly soon clarified that it had intended only to encourage academic credit for Sunday school, not the introduction of Bible courses in public schools themselves.[24] Although the proposal did not result in any sort of statewide Bible course program, the number of local Bible courses and students continued its slow rise.[25] Some programs created in this period lasted for decades, such as Charlotte's, which ran from 1925–1984. Its theological stance was representative: "The course was to be taught as the Word of God from the Christian viewpoint without denominational emphasis, elective to all students but compulsory for none." Despite this claim of denominational neutrality, however, the Charlotte program's bylaws specified further that the material be taught from "the conservative viewpoint."[26]

The early and mid-1940s were a heyday for WRE throughout much of the country.[27] The turning point for North Carolina Bible courses came when the Durham-based North Carolina Council of Churches (NCCC), a newly formed group comprised mostly of mainline Protestant churches, made such courses a top priority. By that time, the frequency of Bible courses had dwindled so far from the increases of the 1920s that the council's director could identify only six communities offering them.[28] In 1940 NCCC's Committee on Week-day Religious Education, which included

22. "Bible Study in Public Schools," *Biblical Recorder*, December 7, 1921.
23. "The Bible in the School," *Lumberton Robesonian*, December 8, 1921.
24. "Bible Study in Schools," *Statesville Landmark*, December 19, 1921.
25. See, for example, *Biennial Report of the Superintendent of Public Instruction of North Carolina for the Scholastic Years 1926–1927 and 1927–1928* (Raleigh: State Superintendent of Public Instruction, 1928), 10. North Carolina Digital Collections. Online: http://digital.ncdcr.gov/cdm/ref/collection/p249901coll22/id/499772.
26. *The Fifty-Nine Year Miracle: The History of Bible Teaching in the Public Schools of Charlotte (1925–1984)* (Charlotte: Friends of Bible Teaching in the Public Schools, 1984), 2, 22, quoting earlier documents.
27. Davis, *Week-Day Religious Instruction*.
28. Ruth LeValley, "Religious Education in the Public Schools of North Carolina," *High School Journal* 30 (1947): 77–84.

the state superintendent of public instruction, devised a Bible credit program to be collaboratively implemented by the NCCC, churches and other organizations, and state and local educational agencies. The council recommended that elective courses be offered "on school time and in the school building," although alternative locations were deemed acceptable, especially "if there is likely to be any protest against the use of public school property."[29] In each community local sponsors, whether churches, ministerial associations, YMCAs, women's groups, or other civic organizations, recommended a suitable teacher and raised sufficient funds to pay her (less often, him). The NCCC quickly became a job placement clearinghouse, connecting prospective instructors with searching schools.

"A veritable wave of enthusiasm for the teaching of the Bible in the public schools is sweeping the state of North Carolina," the council soon proclaimed.[30] Its newsletter carefully charted increases in the number of Bibles courses, claiming in late 1943 that courses in ninety to one hundred communities drew more than twenty thousand students ("both whites and Negroes").[31] Newsweek declared that year that North Carolina had the "fastest growing state program for religious education in the nation."[32]

The NCCC emphasized the importance of teacher qualification and professionalization. As early as spring 1941, Bible teachers were sufficiently organized to petition the North Carolina Education Association for official recognition as its Bible Department.[33] The state's Department

---

29. Price H. Gwynn Jr., *Teaching the Bible in The Public Schools of North Carolina* (Durham: North Carolina Council of Churches 1941), 5; "Minutes of Meeting of Interested Individuals Called Together to Discuss Possibilities of Mapping a Program of Biblical Instruction for the Public Schools of North Carolina," "1939–1940" Folder, Box 39 (2001-0100), North Carolina Council of Churches Records.

30. P. H. Gwynn Jr., "Elective Bible Courses are Offered in Many Schools," *Church Council Bulletin* 2 (1941): 1.

31. "Teaching the Bible in the Public Schools of North Carolina," *Church Council Bulletin* 4 (1943): 4. The North Carolina Council of Churches' enrollment figures were typically significantly higher than those reported by the state, presumably because of uneven reporting and different tallying methods. For example, the state reported only 3,952 Bible students for 1943–1944 (*North Carolina Public Schools Biennial Report, Part 1: 1942–1944* [Raleigh, 1944], 59. North Carolina Digital Collections. Online: http://digital.ncdcr.gov/cdm/compoundobject/collection/p249901coll22/id/259346/rec/8). As for African American students, the number participating appears to have been small, despite some efforts at inclusion by the council.

32. "N.C. Bible Classes," *Newsweek*, January 1943, 62.

33. "Bible Teachers Organize," *Church Council Bulletin* 2 (1941): 1–2. The group

of Public Instruction became the first in the country to issue formal certification for Bible teachers, requiring "15 hours of Bible in an accredited institution of higher learning," a number that later rose to twenty-one at the NCCC's urging.[34] Any courses taught by uncertified teachers would not count toward the credits required by the state for admission to college. In addition to having the pertinent educational credentials, each teacher was expected to be "a consecrated Christian," actively involved in a church, and "neat and attractive in appearance."[35] The NCCC occasionally succeeded in getting colleges and universities to provide training for Bible teachers. Duke University developed an undergraduate course for future teachers in 1941 or 1942,[36] it and other institutions provided summer training sessions in 1945,[37] and the University of North Carolina at Chapel offered a summer program in 1950.[38] Internal NCCC correspondence demonstrates that finding enough qualified teachers was an ongoing problem, and in some school systems ministers without teaching certification taught the courses.[39]

The sole textbook for students was the Bible, although teachers were free to draw upon supplemental resources. The course's focuses were life lessons and familiarity with biblical material, rather than critical analysis. Although local systems had tremendous freedom to craft their own

---

maintained its existence until at least 1968–1969, after which it disappeared from the North Carolina Education Directory.

34. Gwynn, *Teaching the Bible*, 2; "Report of Committee on Weekday Religious Education, September 1, 1941–August 31, 1945," Box 35 (2001-0100); and "Weekday Religious Education Report 1948–1949," "Reports of Weekday Committee of NC Council" Folder, Box 64 (2001-0100), both in North Carolina Council of Churches Records; Gwynn, Jr., "Elective Bible Courses"; "Week-day Religious Education in North Carolina: Growth," *Church Council Bulletin* 3 (1942): 1.

35. "Report of Committee on Weekday Religious Education."

36. Ernest J. Arnold to Rev. F. W. Wiegemann, Jan. 20, 1942, "1941–1942" Folder 2, Box 17 (2001-0100), North Carolina Council of Churches Records.

37. "Summer Opportunities for Teachers of Bible," *Church Council Bulletin* 6 (1945): 2–3; "Weekday Religious Education, Concern of Summer School," *Church Council Bulletin* 10 (1950): 3. The other institutions providing training in 1945 were Guilford College (Greensboro), Scarritt College for Christian Workers, and the Assembly's Training School for Lay Workers in Richmond.

38. "Weekday Religious Education, Concern of Summer School."

39. Ernest J. Arnold to Carrie Melvin, Aug. 25, 1942, "1941–1942" Folder 3, Box 17 (2001-0100), North Carolina Council of Churches Records; LeValley, "Religious Education."

courses, the council recognized the need for some degree of standardization.[40] Uncomfortable with existing materials, it worked with the Education Association to create its own curriculum, submitting a version to the state around 1946 or 1947 and receiving approval in 1951.[41] North Carolina thus became one of several states with an official Bible curriculum or syllabus.[42] The council's curriculum suggested course policies and best practices, which included regularly scheduled worship; specified which biblical books and stories should be read in particular grades; identified suitable memorization verses; recommended supplemental books, filmstrips, and other resources; proposed service projects; and provided advice for creating Bible clubs. Course objectives included moral training, spiritual growth, and cultural literacy. High school courses, for example, were to "teach the Bible as the Book among books, containing the supreme revelation of truth, the laws of God, the greatest of literature and the inspiration for the best in art and music" and to "help each student discover by experience a vital relationship with Jesus Christ as his personal Savior, Lord, and Friend."[43]

From the council's perspective, the program was perfectly compatible with the separation of church and state, a principle it vigorously affirmed.[44] Enrollment was voluntary, and public coffers were avoided, the latter step an extra precaution in light of the state attorney general office's opinion that

---

40. "Report from Committee on Weekday Religious Education," Sept. 22, 1942, "1940–1941" Folder, Box 39 (2001–0100), North Carolina Council of Churches Records; "Curriculum Studies," *Church Council Bulletin* 6 (1945): 5.

41. On an early version of this curriculum, see "Teacher's Workshop," *Church Council Bulletin* 5 (1944): 1, 3; on its submission to the state, see "President of Bible Department Reports Objectives," *Church Council Bulletin* 8 (1947): 3, 2 [sic]; on state approval, "Condensed Report of the Board of Christianity Activities for Year 1951," *Church Council Bulletin* 12 (1952): 3.

42. Davis, *Week-Day Religious Instruction*.

43. North Carolina Education Association, *Suggested Twelve-Year Program of Biblical Education for the Public Schools of North Carolina* (Raleigh: North Carolina Education Association, Bible Department, n.d.); for high school course goals, see 9. The sole copy of this book I have been able to locate contains no publication date, although the latest resource it cites dates to 1946. If it is not the 1951 version, it is largely equivalent to it, as indicated by its close similarities to a later revision, *North Carolina Education Association, Curriculum Guide for the Teaching of Bible in the Public Schools of North Carolina* (Raleigh: North Carolina Education Association, Department of Bible, 1965).

44. Gwynn, *Teaching the Bible*.

use of tax money was in fact acceptable.⁴⁵ The council promoted its courses as "non-sectarian in content and presentation,"⁴⁶ but its understanding of nonsectarianism extended only to avoiding preferential treatment of one traditional Protestant denomination over another. Other Christian groups were not excluded from the program—a 1947 study noted a smattering of courses sponsored by Roman Catholic, Greek Orthodox, Jehovah's Witness, and Christian Scientist churches.⁴⁷ In general, however, any concerns about how a widespread Protestant-dominated program might affect other Christians, Jews, adherents of other traditions, or the nonreligious are largely missing in the NCCC's materials.⁴⁸

The Schoolhouse and the Courthouse

Ironically, the major legal challenge to WRE was directed not at a solely Protestant program but rather at one designed to include Protestants, Catholics, and Jews. In 1945, Vashti McCollum filed suit against the WRE program in Champaign, Illinois, contending that religion classes taught by religious organizations on public school grounds during regular school hours violated the Constitution. As McCollum's case made its way up through the courts, WRE supporters nationwide worried that a far-reaching decision might prohibit all school-sponsored Bible reading and religion courses as well as in school prayers, devotionals, and hymns. Warning about a potential "staggering tragedy for Protestantism," the NCCC asked every local Bible committee to contribute five dollars for Champaign's legal defense fund.⁴⁹

---

45. Assistant Attorney General Harry McMullan to Statesville City Schools, July 10, 1941, "Loose Materials" Folder, Box 16 (2001-0100), North Carolina Council of Churches Records.

46. "Week-Day Religious Education in North Carolina: Constitutional Foundations," *Church Council Bulletin* 4 (1943): 1.

47. LeValley, "Religious Education;" see also "Greenville Initiates Course in Religion," *Church Council Bulletin* 3 (1942): 1 and "Report of the Weekday Religious Education Committee," "Memorandums to Bible Teachers 1946-1947" Folder, Box 35 (2001-0100), North Carolina Council of Churches Records.

48. Although other religious groups were free to create their own programs, their small numbers in North Carolina and correspondingly limited resources made such initiatives unlikely.

49. "Cooperative Action Imperative to Save Bible in Schools," *Church Council Bulletin* 8 (1947): 1-2.

The Supreme Court's 1948 ruling on the case was widely regarded as ambiguous. On the one hand, the court flatly declared the Champaign program unconstitutional, rejecting the use of "tax supported property for religious instruction and the close cooperation between the school authorities and the religious council in promoting religious education" and the "utilization of the tax-established and tax-supported public school system to aid religious groups to spread their faith."[50] Thus, on-campus courses taught on school grounds during class hours by religious groups were no longer acceptable. On the other hand, the decision was less clear about the legality of off-campus courses or, for that matter, on-campus courses taught by regularly certified teachers rather than religious representatives. It left Bible reading, prayer, and worship practices untouched.

The immediate reaction of many to the decision was confusion. One North Carolina headline proclaimed, "Religious Teaching Expected to End in All Public Schools," while another assured, "Local Schools to Continue Bible Studies Despite Court Rulings."[51] The NCCC ultimately determined that "the obscurity and ambiguity of the Supreme Court's decision entitle North Carolina to continue its present program of Biblical instruction in the public schools until such time as the implications of the decision have been authoritatively and explicitly clarified beyond any doubt as to their local application."[52] Charlotte's Bible committee decided that its thoroughly Protestant program was constitutional, because it was "entirely voluntary and wholly non-sectarian and non-denominational ... and without cost to the taxpayer."[53] Most North Carolina school systems with Bible courses decided likewise. Because state education officials demanded no changes,

---

50. *McCollum v. Board of Education*, 333 U.S. 203 (1948), quotes from 209, 210.

51. "Religious Teaching Expected to End in All Public Schools," *Lumberton Robesonian*, March 10, 1948; Lyle Edwards, "Local Schools to Continue Bible Studies Despite Court Rulings," *Gastonia Gazette*, March 13, 1948. On a national level, see Erwin L. Shaver, "Three Years After the Champaign Case," *Religious Education* 46 (1951): 33–38; Zimmerman, *Whose America?* 150–59.

52. "Weekday Religious Education in N. C.," *Church Council Bulletin* 10 (1950): 2; see also "Supreme Court Decision on McCollum Champaign Case," *Memorandum #12 to Teachers of Bible in the Public Schools of North Carolina*, April 1, 1948, in "Memorandums to Bible Teachers 1946–1947" Folder, Box 35 (2001–0100), North Carolina Council of Churches Records.

53. *Fifty-Nine Year Miracle*, 15.

many Bible programs continued pretty much as they had before the case, though not without occasional complaints.[54]

The NCCC's decision to continue its program without alteration set it apart from the chief national proponent of religion courses, the International Council of Religious Education. The International Council of Religious Education emphasized after *McCollum v. Board of Education* that it favored only ungraded off-campus released time classes not administered by public schools.[55] Throughout the country, although some released time programs ceased and others underwent modification, some continued, whether taught on campus or off—even after the court implied in 1952 that only released time done off campus was acceptable.[56]

McCollum v. Board of Education's neutrality on Bible reading came in the midst of an overall decline for the custom. In the late 1950s, a national survey of four thousand communities showed that only a minority of schools still mandated daily reading, with tremendous variations between regions. In the West and Midwest, very few schools maintained the practice, whereas in the South, three-quarters did. The survey found that the King James Version was most often read, followed by the American Revised Standard Version and, in much fewer schools, a Roman Catholic Bible. In many cases, Bible readings were accompanied by prayer, often the Lord's Prayer.[57]

The Supreme Court decisions of 1962 and 1963 addressed these practices. The first, *Engel v. Vitale*, prohibited school-sponsored prayer, whereas the second, *Abington v. Schempp*, barred school-sponsored Bible reading.[58] Like *McCollum v. Board of Education*, these decisions met with confusion, with some thinking that they applied only to laws and policies mandating the practices. "We do not require the Bible and praying but we do these things because we want to," North Carolina Governor Terry Sanford reasoned. "We will go on having Bible readings and prayers in the schools of

---

54. Bill Lamkin, "Bible Classes in School Violate Constitution, Baptists are Told," *Charlotte Observer*, Nov. 12, 1959.

55. International Council of Religious Education, *Statement of Policy Regarding Weekday Religious Education* (Chicago: International Council of Religious Education, 1949).

56. *Zorach v. Clauson*, 343 U.S. 306 (1952); Richard B. Dierenfield, *Religion in American Public Schools* (Washington, D.C.: Public Affairs, 1962), 78–81.

57. Dierenfield, *Religion in American Public Schools*, 49–51.

58. *Engel v. Vitale*, 370 U.S. 421 (1962); DelFattore, *Fourth R*, 67–105.

this state just as we always have. As I read the decision, this kind of thing is not forbidden by the Constitution, and indeed, it should not be."[59] Sanford's interpretation of the decision proved to be wrong, but both prayer and Bible readings continued in some communities.[60] Twenty years later, an investigation by People for the American Way (PFAW) found North Carolina schools continuing these practices.[61]

Abington v. Schempp made clear that Bible courses taught for religious purposes were no longer acceptable, a point that had direct implications for North Carolina's Bible program. The decision's immediate impact on North Carolina is difficult to determine. Although NCCC enrollment figures are not available for this period, the state's own statistics show decreasing Bible enrollments—but how much of this decline was due to legal concerns is unclear.[62] Student interest in religion courses had already been fading in some communities; only days before the court's decision, one newspaper announced the cessation of local courses because of low enrollments.[63]

Of the North Carolina courses that continued, although some may have met the court's goals of objectivity, others maintained their overtly Protestant nature. The very detailed insider history of the Charlotte course notes no changes in curriculum, for example.[64] More significantly, when the Education Association revised its Bible curriculum guide in 1965, it deleted little of the earlier version's explicitly religious content, retaining goals such as "cultivating a personal relationship with Jesus" and advice on planning devotionals and creating Bible clubs. Its introduction directed, "When questions arise on which our Christian groups differ, either an

---

59. "Some Schools Will Keep Religious Note," *Burlington Daily Times News*, Aug. 7, 1963.

60. "Ruling Has No Effect in K. M. [Kings Mountain]," *Gastonia Gazette*, June 20, 1963. On the continuation of the course, see Bo Peterson, "Religion in Schools: Districts Offering Courses on Bible," *Gastonia Gazette*, March 15, 1995. For elsewhere nationally, see Boles, *Bible, Religion*, 288–92.

61. People for the American Way, *Religion in North Carolina's Schools: The Hidden Reality* (Washington, D.C.: People for the American Way, 1983).

62. See the various issues of the *Biennial Report of the Superintendent of Public Instruction of North Carolina for the Scholastic Years* (Raleigh: State Superintendent of Public Instruction). North Carolina Digital Collections. Online: http://digital.ncdcr.gov/cdm/compoundobject/collection/p249901coll22/id/259346/rec/8.

63. "Two Schools Drop Bible," *Gastonia Gazette*, June 13, 1963.

64. *Fifty-Nine Year Miracle*.

unbiased explanation of the attitude of each group is given or the students are referred to the ministers of their own denominations."[65] The guide's understanding of "nonsectarianism" was still merely intra-Protestant non-denominationalism. In its ongoing affirmation of Christianity, the state's official Bible curriculum thus displayed no hint that *Abington v. Schempp* had ever occurred. As for the NCCC, it retreated entirely from on-campus religious education, although it affirmed *Abington*-style neutral courses and off campus released time and dismissed time programs.[66]

Some academics and educators devoted themselves to the creation of appropriate resources and preservice and inservice teacher training.[67] One resulting resource was *The Bible Reader: An Interfaith Interpretation*, which presented biblical excerpts and commentary written by a rabbi, a Catholic priest, and a Protestant minister. *The Bible As/ In Literature*, by a religious studies professor and a high school English teacher, adopted an entirely different approach that focused on biblical themes and allusions in Western literature.[68]

While some schools put such resources to effective use in creating *Abington*-style courses, others continued to offer courses with religious content. This circumstance is at least partly due to the Supreme Court's failure to provide sufficient instruction on what "objective" courses taught "as part of a secular program of education" might look like. In the 1970s, lower federal courts began identifying constitutional parameters, a process that is still ongoing.[69] Courts have considered courses from several Bible Belt states (Virginia, Tennessee, Alabama, Mississippi, Arkansas, and Florida).[70] Issues that have figured prominently include the incorporation

---

65. North Carolina Education Association, *Curriculum Guide*, quotes from 3, 2.

66. "Statement of Legislative Principles of the Commission on Christian Social Action of the North Carolina Council of Churches," *Church Council Bulletin* 27 (1968): 6.

67. Arthur Gilbert, "Reactions and Resources," in *Religion and Public Education* (ed. Theodore R. Sizer; New York: Houghton Mifflin, 1967), 37–83; Peter S. Bracher and David L. Barr, "The Bible is Worthy of Secular Study: The Bible in Public Education Today," in Barr and Piediscalzi, *Bible and American Education*, 165–97.

68. Walter M. Abbott et al., *The Bible Reader: An Interfaith Interpretation* (London: Geoffrey Chapman, 1969); James S. Ackerman and Thayer S. Warshaw, *The Bible As/ In Literature* (Palo Alto: ScottForesman, 1971; repr. 2nd ed.; Glennview: ScottForesman, 1995).

69. On recent cases, see DelFattore, *Fourth R*, 236–54.

70. Virginia: *Vaughn v. Reed*, 313 F. Supp. 431 (W.D. Va., 1970); *Crockett v. Soren-*

of worship or devotional practices in class; the teacher selection process; the role of outside groups in organizing and financially supporting the course; the presence or absence of pressure to attend purportedly "elective" courses; and course content, with judges noting elements such as the following as problematic:

- proselytizing and the advocacy of theological claims;
- overreliance on the King James Version, because of its specifically Protestant nature;
- definitions of the Bible that exclude Roman Catholic and Jewish canons;
- the portrayal of biblical stories (especially those depicting the miraculous or supernatural) as literal, straightforward history;
- the presentation of the interpretive traditions of particular religious traditions as normative;
- and the use of curricular materials designed for religious settings.[71]

Some of the courses that prompted these rulings were WRE-style programs that had continued long after *Abington v. Schempp*, as seen in *Crockett v. Sorenson*. This 1983 case revolved around a fourth- and fifth-grade Bible course in Bristol, Virginia that had been taught since 1941. Interdenominational Protestant groups had long funded the course, chosen its curriculum, and selected its teacher, with theological viewpoint a primary criterion. The course included hymns and prayers and typically used only the King James Version. Determining that the course was designed "to inculcate religious

---

son, 568 F. Supp. 1422 (W.D. Va., 1983); Tennessee: *Wiley v. Franklin*, 468 F. Supp. 133 (E.D. Tenn., 1979); *Wiley v. Franklin*, 474 F. Supp. 525 (E.D. Tenn., 1979); *Wiley v. Franklin*, 497 F. Supp. 390 (E.D. Tenn., 1980); *Doe v. Porter*, 188 F. Supp. 2d 904 (E.D. Tenn., 2002); Alabama: *Hall. v. Board of School Commissioners of Conecuh County*, 656 F.2d 999 (5th Cir. 1981); Mississippi: *Herdahl v. Pontotoc County School District*, 933 F. Supp. 582 (N.D. Miss., 1996); Arkansas: *Doe v. Human*, 725 F. Supp. 1499 (W.D. Ark., 1989); *Doe v. Human*, 725 F. Supp. 1503 (W.D. Ark., 1989); Florida: *Gibson v. Lee County School Board*, 1 F. Supp. 2d 1426 (M.D. Fla., 1998).

71. *Bible Electives in Public Schools: A Guide* (Atlanta: Society of Biblical Literature, n.d.) and *The Bible and Public Schools: A First Amendment Guide* (New York: Bible Literacy Project, 1999), both online: http://www.sbl-site.org/educational/thebibleinpublicschools.aspx; and Chancey, "Sectarian Elements."

beliefs in the students," the court mandated significant changes. Henceforth, the school board was to prescribe the curriculum and appoint a properly certified teacher without regard to his or her religious perspective, and any money raised by private groups to support the course had to be given with "no strings attached." Furthermore, the court specified, "the course should be taught in an objective manner with no attempt made to indoctrinate the children as to either the truth or falsity of the biblical materials."[72]

North Carolina Bible courses may not have generated a federal court case, but the state did experience occasional controversies in the decades after *Abington v. Schempp*. In 1977, Haywood County Schools stopped allowing visits to its elementary grades by so-called "Bible story ladies" equipped with flannel boards, but only after a query from the American Civil Liberties Union (ACLU).[73] In 1983, a report by PFAW raised concerns about Bible courses, which at the time were offered in roughly 6 percent of the state's schools. It complained about the widespread use of ministers as instructors and the teaching of courses from a religious perspective. Many courses, it noted, were taught as "Bible History," a name that seemed to suggest conservative theological views about the Bible's historical accuracy. As a particularly egregious example, the report cited the religious language on a Rowan County syllabus, which noted that the Bible would be taught "as the word of God, containing the basic moral principles on which good character and a Christian society are to be built"— phraseology in fact adapted from the old 1965 North Carolina Education Association guide.[74] The PFAW also questioned widespread financial support of courses by religious groups, one of the issues ultimately clarified by *Crockett v. Sorenson*. The following year, Charlotte ended its Bible course program, probably the oldest in the state, in response to PFAW and ACLU queries about its religious orientation and the administrative and instructional role of outside religious groups.[75] In the city of Dunn, a 1985

---

72. *Crockett v. Sorenson*, 568 F. Supp. at 1430–1431.

73. "Haywood Co. Public Schools Bible Teaching" Folder, Box 158, American Civil Liberties Union of North Carolina Records; "Schools Abandon Bible Story Time," *Waynesville Mountaineer*, Aug. 3, 1977.

74. People for the American Way, *Religion in North Carolina Schools*, 7; North Carolina Education Association, *Curriculum Guide*, 2.

75. "Charlotte Mecklenburg Public School (Religious Courses)" Folder, Box 181, American Civil Liberties Union of North Carolina Records; *Fifty-Nine Year Miracle*, 42–44.

parental complaint and ACLU letter charging that its forty-four-year-old local course was taught "for the purposes of religious inculcation, and not merely educational purposes," led to its immediate cessation—and the departure from town of the complaining family in response to harassment and threats.[76]

The Contemporary Situation

Over three thousand North Carolina students have signed up for Bible classes most years since 1995, mostly at the high school level but also in lower grades. In 2010–2011, the last year for which figures are available, 236 Bible courses drew 3,896 students—a small percentage of the state's total student population but still higher than many observers might expect.[77] Some of North Carolina's major cities have offered Bible courses, such as Raleigh, Charlotte, and Winston-Salem.[78] The state's internal working name for its courses is "Bible History."[79]

How do recent and contemporary Bible courses compare to those offered pre-*Abington*? Lack of detailed information about individual courses precludes in-depth analysis, but several general observations seem clear enough. The single biggest difference between recent courses and

---

76. "Wyble, Laurey: Harnett Primary School in Dunn (Bible Study)" Folder, Box 177, American Civil Liberties Union of North Carolina Records; Joan Oleck, "Bible Study Dispute Not Over in Dunn," *Raleigh News and Observer*, Sept. 22, 1985. Online: http://statelibrarync.org/noi/cards/264030; Nash Herndon, "Family Leaves Dunn after Harassment Tied to Bible Class," *Raleigh News and Observer*, Oct. 6, 1985. Online: http://statelibrarync.org/noi/cards/264030.

77. Each year's figures include a small number of students taking community college courses; otherwise, the statistics refer to courses taught at public high schools. Released time programs do not play a significant role in the state, although they exist in neighboring South Carolina and Virginia. Enrollment statistics back to 2003–2004 are available at the "Course Membership Summary" link on the Department of Public Instruction's Statistical Profile page (http://apps.schools.nc.gov/pls/apex/f?p=1:1:0); for earlier figures, see North Carolina Public Schools Statistical Profile, North Carolina Digital Collections. Online: http://digital.ncdcr.gov/cdm/compoundobject/collection/p249901coll22/id/17208/rec/3.

78. Associated Press, "More High Schools Getting Back to Teaching the Bible," Tyrone, PA, *Daily Herald*, Oct. 25, 1997.

79. Compare the statistical information available at the North Carolina Department of Public Instruction's Data and Reports web page (http://www.ncpublicschools.org/fbs/resources/data/).

those offered before *Abington v. Schempp* are that courses no longer bear the trappings of worship in the form of prayers, hymns, and devotions. Any such practices that do occur under the radar are anomalies rather than the norm. Similarly, courses are (theoretically, at least) no longer offered for the primary purpose of faith formation, and they no longer explicitly function as extensions of church-related religious education programs.

There is also no longer a central religious organization coordinating Bible courses on a statewide level the way the NCCC once did. But churches and religious organizations continue to raise funds for courses in some communities, just as they did fifty years ago.[80] In 2012, for example, Concord's Bible Teaching Association sold Vidalia onions (ten pounds for ten dollars) to raise money. In Mooresville, a Bible teachers association recently sponsored golf tournaments and barbecue sales to support its course. As long as no expectations accompany these groups' donations, this practice is legally acceptable.[81]

On occasion, however, relationships between schools and outside organizations enter into questionable territory, as happened in 2006 and 2007 in Wilmington and nearby Pender County.[82] In Wilmington, a church had been providing not only funds but also instructors, sending ministers, youth directors, or lay members to teach. In Pender County, the teachers were ministers associated with local ministerial alliances. These arrangements were problematic in light of court cases considering similar plans, such as *Crockett v. Sorenson* and *Wiley v. Franklin*. Furthermore, these teachers typically held no teaching licenses and were thus unqualified. Both school systems had to make adjustments in how their courses were taught and administered.

One might question whether a teaching license and the training it represents are by themselves sufficient background for Bible classes, where

---

80. *Crockett v. Sorenson*, 568 F. Supp. at 1431.

81. "Vidalia Onions Fund Raiser" flyer posted on Cabarrus County Schools website (http://www.ccsweb.cabarrus.k12.nc.us/education/components/scrapbook/default.php?sectionid=1), retrieved Sept. 4, 2012; Melinda Skutnick, "High School's Bible Classes Face Funding Shortfall," *Mooresville Tribune*, May 22, 2011; Jessica Osborne, "Despite Shortfall, Bible Classes Back for 18th Year," *Mooresville Tribune*, Aug. 24, 2011.

82. Sam Scott, "Schools Shifting Bible Classes," *Wilmington StarNews*, Aug. 22, 2006; Amanda Greene, "Bible a Class Act in Pender: Board of Education Hopes to Keep Subject Available at High Schools," *Wilmington StarNews*, June 4, 2007. Online: http://www.starnewsonline.com/article/20060822/NEWS/608220392.

the need not to privilege a particular religious viewpoint poses special demands. The NCCC emphasized the importance of preservice training for Bible teachers, successfully urging the state to require multiple college or graduate courses in biblical studies and related fields for certification. Its desire for teachers to have academic background in the subject matter set North Carolina apart from many states. Today, however, North Carolina requires only that Bible instructors meet its general requirements for all teachers: a college degree and certification in a broad field such as elementary education or secondary history and social science.[83] Although teachers in other subjects must pass ETS Praxis tests,[84] there is no comparable requirement for Bible. The result is that many Bible teachers have likely never had any coursework in biblical studies or had their expertise in the area assessed. North Carolina is typical of the states in this regard.

In both the pre- and post-*Abington* periods, individual teachers and school systems have had wide latitude over their choice of Bible curriculum. In the past, however, they at least had the benefit of the general guidelines, outlines of study, and recommended bibliography prepared by the NCCC and state Education Association. Currently, Bible courses have no state guidelines of any type—no learning objectives, course standards, or recommended resources. In this respect, too, North Carolina is typical.[85]

Today's Bible courses likely exhibit considerable variety in content. Many may be completely locally produced, based on whatever resources (sometimes nonsectarian, sometimes religious) available to their teachers. Others may still use older works like *The Bible As/ In Literature*.[86] Most, however, probably utilize materials from two national organizations, the National Council on Bible Curriculum in Public Schools (NCBCPS) and the Bible Literacy Project (BLP).

---

83. Details available at the Public Schools of North Carolina State Board of Education website: http://www.ncpublicschools.org/licensure/.

84. http://www.ets.org/praxis.

85. Only a few states have created Bible standards. See examples from Florida, Georgia, and Tennessee at the Society of Biblical Literature's The Bible in Secondary Schools webpage (http://www.sbl-site.org/educational/thebibleinpublicschools.aspx).

86. Use of the textbook is implied in the title of Brunswick's 2005 course ("The Bible As/In Literature") (Paul R. Jefferson, "Bible Class Introduced in Area High Schools," *Wilmington StarNews*, Aug. 28, 2005. Online: http://www.starnewsonline.com/article/20050828/NEWS/50827009?Title=Bible-class-introduced-in-area-high-schools.)

The NCBCPS is a Greensboro, North Carolina-based group comprised primarily of individuals associated with Christian Right organizations, current and former legislators (including several from North Carolina), and celebrities such as Chuck Norris.[87] The council claims that its curriculum has been "voted into 687 school districts (2262 high schools) in 38 states," although these numbers appear to be exaggerated.[88] Because of the group's local roots, its course is likely used across the state. The NCBCPS insists that its curriculum is completely nonsectarian, but its various editions have reflected conservative Protestant presuppositions, recommending the King James Version as the course textbook; suggesting the complete accuracy of the Bible, including miracle stories; and simplistically claiming that biblical manuscripts were copied largely without errors. Some have advocated creation science, even going so far as to embrace the urban legend that NASA found a missing day in time corresponding to the biblical story of the sun standing still (Josh 10). A federal court found an NCBCPS course to be flawed in the 1998 Florida case *Gibson v. Lee County*.[89]

The BLP also appears to be well represented in North Carolina. According to its website, thirty to thirty-nine North Carolina high schools have used its curriculum, or 5.8% of the state's total.[90] The group offers a student textbook, teacher's guide, teacher workshops, and online training. Written specifically to address First Amendment concerns, its textbook is often quite strong in examining how interpretations of particular biblical passages vary between different religious groups. It is also adept in employing a "Bible as literature" approach and exploring the Bible's reception in art, music, literature, and other media. In my opinion, its treatment

---

87. See the NCBCPS's website: www.bibleinschools.net.

88. Chancey, "'Complete Victory is Our Objective': The National Council on Bible Curriculum in Public Schools," *Religion & Education* 35 (2008): 1–21. For the council's claims regarding usage, see "Where This Has Been Implemented," NCBCPS website. Online: http://www.bibleinschools.net/Where-This-Has-Been-Implemented.

89. On the NCBCPS's *The Bible in History and Literature* (Ablu Publishing, various dates), see Chancey, "A Textbook Example of the Christian Right: The National Council on Bible Curriculum in Public Schools," *Journal of the American Academy of Religion* 75 (2007): 554–81; Brennan Breed and Kent Harold Richards, "Review of The Bible in History and Literature," *Religion & Education* 34 (2007): 94–102; and Frances R. A. Paterson, "Anatomy of a Bible Course Curriculum," *Journal of Law and Education* 32 (2003): 41–65.

90. See the BLP's website: http://www.bibleliteracy.org/site/.

of historical-critical issues is less even and sometimes reflects a theologically conservative bias. For example, it often simply asserts without question traditional authorship claims of biblical books and sometimes adopts a tone that unproblematically assumes the Bible's historical accuracy. The BLP has not yet been challenged in court.[91]

The comparisons above between Bible courses prior and subsequent to *Abington v. Schempp* make clear enough the decision's impact on how, why, and by whom such classes are taught, both in North Carolina and elsewhere. At the same time, these comparisons also demonstrate that the transition from courses taught to promote religious views to those taught "objectively as part of a secular program of education" did not happen quickly. In fact, that transition appears to be incomplete, even fifty years later. Although a district-by-district review of current course materials would no doubt discover notable successes that exemplify the hopes of the Warren Court, it would almost certainly also find courses that promoted sectarian viewpoints. Ultimately, if North Carolina and the country as a whole are going to ensure progress toward the court's goal of genuinely academic, nonsectarian Bible courses, educational authorities will have to create expectations for those courses, their teachers, and their curricula that go beyond laissez-faire.

---

91. Cullen Schippe and Chuck Stetson, eds., *The Bible and Its Influence* (2nd ed.; Fairfax: BLP, 2006).

Contributors

Yaakov Ariel teaches in the Department of Religious Studies at the University of North Carolina at Chapel Hill. His research interests include Protestant-Jewish relations, Jewish conversions to Christianity, and Christian attitudes towards Zionism and Israel. His book *Evangelizing the Chosen People* (Chapel Hill: University of North Carolina Press, 2000) received an award from the American Society of Church History. Another book, *An Unusual Relationship: Evangelical Christians and Jews*, has just been published by New York University Press.

Jacques Berlinerblau is Professor and director of Jewish Civilization in the Edmund A. Walsh School of Foreign Service at Georgetown University. He specializes in secularism, secular Judaism, politics and religion, and Jewish-American literature. He has published five books, his two most recent being *How to Be Secular: A Call to Arms for Religious Freedom* (Boston: Houghton-Mifflin Harcourt, 2012) and *Thumpin' It: The Use and Abuse of the Bible in Today's Presidential Politics* (Louisville: Westminster John Knox) released in 2008.

Mark A. Chancey is Professor of Religious Studies in Dedman College of Humanities and Sciences, Southern Methodist University, Dallas. His most recent book, with Eric M. Meyers, is *Alexander to Constantine: Archaeology of the Land of the Bible* (New Haven: Yale University Press, 2012). In addition to his work on the archaeology of Palestine, New Testament studies, and early Judaism, he has written extensively on religion and public education.

Rubén Dupertuis is Associate Professor in the Department of Religion at Trinity University in San Antonio. His research interests include Acts of the Apostles and early Christian narrative more generally, education in the ancient world, and the role of the Bible in American popular culture. He is the author of "Translating the Bible into Pictures," an essay in Caroline Vander Stichele and Hugh Pyper, eds., *Text, Image, and Otherness in Children's Bibles: What Is in the Picture?* (Semeia Studies 56; Atlanta: Society of Biblical Literature, 2012).

John Fea is Professor of American History and chair of the Department of History at Messiah College in Grantham, Pa. His research focuses on the intersection between religion and early American life. He is the author of *Was America Founded as a Christian Nation? A Historical Introduction* (Louisville: Westminster John Knox, 2011).

Shalom Goldman is Professor of Religion and Middle Eastern Studies at Duke University. His most recent book is *Zeal for Zion: Christians, Jews, and the Idea of the Promised Land* (Chapel Hill: University of North Carolina Press, 2009).

Charles C. Haynes is director of the Religious Freedom Center of the Newseum Institute in Washington, D.C. He is the author of *Finding Common Ground: A First Amendment Guide to Religion and Public Schools* (Nashville: First Amendment Center, 2007). Over the past two decades, he has been the principal organizer and drafter of a series of consensus guides on the role of religion in public schools, including "The Bible and Public Schools," endorsed by a broad spectrum of religious, civil liberties and education groups.

Carol Meyers is the Mary Grace Wilson Professor of Religion at Duke University, where she is a specialist in Hebrew Bible, archaeology of Syria-Palestine, and women in the biblical world. Many of her publications strive to make biblical scholarship accessible to a general audience. A recent example is *Rediscovering Eve: Ancient Israelite Women in Context* (New York: Oxford University Press, 2013), which dispels common misconceptions about Eve and provides information about the reality of women's lives in biblical antiquity.

Eric M. Meyers is the Bernice and Morton Lerner Professor of Jewish Studies at Duke University and also Director of the Center for Jewish Studies. His specialties include Hebrew Bible, biblical archaeology, Second Temple Judaism, and Jewish thought. Among his recent publications is

Alexander to Constantine: Archaeology of the Land of the Bible, with Mark A. Chancey (New Haven: Yale University Press, 2012).

David Morgan is Professor of Religion and chair of the Department of Religion at Duke University with an additional appointment in the Department of Art, Art History, and Visual Studies at Duke. Author of several books, including *Visual Piety: A History and Theory of Popular Religious Images* (Berkeley: University of California Press, 1998), *Protestants and Pictures: Religion, Visual Culture, and the Age of American Mass Production* (New York: Oxford University Press, 1999), *The Lure of Images: A History of Religion and Visual Media in America* (New York: Routledge, 2007), and *The Embodied Eye: Religious Visual Culture and the Social Life of Feeling* (Berkeley: University of California Press, 2012), Morgan specializes in the visual culture of American religious history and in visual theory. He is a founding editor of the journal, *Material Religion*, and is coeditor of the book series "Media, Religion, and Culture" published by Routledge.

Adele Reinhartz is Professor in the Department of Classics and Religious Studies at the University of Ottawa, in Canada. Her main areas of research are New Testament, early Jewish-Christian relations, the Bible and Film, and feminist biblical criticism. She is the author of numerous articles and books, including *Scripture on the Silver Screen* (Louisville: Westminster John Knox, 2003), *Jesus of Hollywood* (New York: Oxford University Press, 2007), and *Bible and Cinema: An Introduction* (New York: Routledge, 2013).

David W. Stowe is Professor of English and Religious Studies at Michigan State University, where he directed the program in American Studies. He is the author of several books, most recently *No Sympathy for the Devil: Christian Pop Music and the Transformation of American Evangelicalism* (Chapel Hill: University of North Carolina Press, 2011). During 2012–2013, he was a Research Fellow in the Institute of Sacred Music at Yale University, working on a book on the reception history of Ps 137.

Subject Index

Abington v. Schempp, 4, 10, 193–94, 205–14
Action Bible: God's Redemptive Story, 165–65
Adams, John, 68, 76, 77 n. 28
African Americans, 31, 49, 84–85, 88, 133, 148–49, 200 n. 31
Akin, Todd, 32
abortion, 22, 25–26, 31–32, 34 n. 67
Alabama, 118–19, 185, 187–89, 207, 208 n. 70
Allen, John, 70
American Colony, Jerusalem, 87–88
American flag, 7, 93, 111–18, 134
American Vision, 66–67
Arizona, 3, 189, 193
Arkansas, 16, 48–49, 207, 208 n. 70
atheist, 1, 195
attack ads, 18
Babylon, America as, 145–46, 148–49, 152
Balfour Declaration, 44, 90
Barton, David, 66
Beck, Glenn, 66
Bible
    American Revolution, 6–7, 67–69, 72, 74–75, 79
    as marker of social status, 94, 96
    Belt, 49, 51, 207
    devotional tool, 94, 96
    in schools, 4, 105–6, 93, 106, 111, 181–214
    symbol of power and authority, 98–99
    Week, 3
    Year of, 1–4, 65
Bible and Its Influence, The, 188, 190, 214 n. 91
Bible and Public Schools: A First Amendment Guide, The, 186–88, 190
Bible: Eden, The, 164–65
biblical scholars, roles and contributions of, 15–16, 19–20, 23–25, 27, 86, 108, 188–89
Blackstone Memorial, 88–90
Blackstone, William, 37, 42–44
Book of Genesis Illustrated, The, 163, 172–75, 177–78
Brandeis, Louis, 44, 90
Brick Bible, The, 159–60
Brick Testament, 160–63, 172, 174–78
Bush, George H. W., 48–49, 81
Bush, George W., 5, 21, 28, 31, 33, 35
Cain, Herman, 18, 22
California, 51 n. 37, 185
Calvin, John, 78–79, 152
canon, 3, 166, 208
Carter, Jimmy, 34, 48
Castle-DeGette Bill, 22
Catholic, 3, 24, 30–31, 102, 104–6, 111, 195, 199, 203
Catholics United, 18, 19
Chanukah. *See* Hanukkah
Christians
    Arab, 47
    liberal, 40
    pro-Arab, 52
Christian flag, 115–16
Christian Right, 22 n. 26, 26, 31, 34, 47 n. 29, 67, 186 n. 5, 213
church fathers, 24

Church of Jesus Christ of Latter-day Saints. *See* Mormons
Cincinnati Bible War of 1869–1873, 195
civil rights, 68, 133, 138
Clinton, Bill, 33, 48–49
Colorado, 25, 28
Comic Book Bible, 165, 169–70, 175 n. 41
Common School movement, 106 n. 20, 194–95
Constitution of the United States, 16, 26, 65–66, 100, 115, 203, 205 n. 54, 206
Cooper, Lord Ashley, 37
Crockett v. Sorenson, 207–209, 211
Declaration of Independence, 65
Deism, 108
Deutero-Isaiah, 18
dispensationalism, 21, 40–42, 49, 110, 116
Doe v. Human, 208 n. 70
Doe v. Porter, 208 n. 70
Eastern Orthodox, 3
Edwards, John, 17
Edwards, Jonathan, 101, 152
Engel v. Vitale, 4 n. 13, 205
Equal Access Act of 1984, 181
evangelicalism, 5–6, 22, 24, 28, 31, 34–35, 38–40, 43,48, 66, 75, 93–100, 118, 181, 186, 188–89
Falwell, Jerry, 34
First Amendment. 2 n. 8, 3, 9, 10, 100, 105, 115, 181–83, 186, 187 n. 6, 188–91, 193, 208 n. 71, 213,
Florida, 28, 51 n. 37, 90, 119 n. 45, 207–208, 212 n. 85, 213
Flower Mound, Texas, 1–2
gay. *See* homosexuality
Georgia, 2, 51 n. 37, 189, 193, 212 n. 85,
Gibson v. Lee County School Board, 208 n. 70, 213
Gingrich, Newt, 28
Greek Orthodox, 203
Green, Enoch, 70–71
Hagee, John, 33
Hall. v. Board of School Commissioners of Conecuh County, 208 n. 70
Hanukkah, 17

Hechler, William, 43
Herdahl v. Pontotoc County School District, 208 n.70
Herzl, Theodore, 43
Hayden, Tom, 1–2
Helms, Jesse, 49
Hindu, 1
Hirsch, Rabbi Emil, 89
Holy Land, 38–40, 49, 51, 83, 85–87, 90,
homosexuality, 25, 31–32
Huckabee, Mike, 16, 19 n. 14
Illinois, 203
Indiana, 197
Inglis, Charles, 75–76
Israel, 5–6, 37–62, 94–95, 100, 102, 143, 145
    America as, 69–70, 81–92, 123–135
    Arab opposition to, 5–6, 37, 45–48, 51–52, 58
International Christian Embassy in Jerusalem, 50–52, 55, 60 n. 71
Jefferson, Thomas, 66, 68, 100, 106–108, 110, 112, 126,
Jehovah's Witness, 110, 117, 203
Jews, 3, 6, 24, 83, 88, 137, 195, 203
Joseph Smith translation, 19
Kennedy, John F., 35
Kerry, John, 31
Keteltas, Abraham, 71–72
Latter-day Saints. *See* Mormons
Left Behind, 40 n. 13, 59–60
liberal Christians. *See* Christians, liberal
Lincoln, Abraham, 67, 103
Lindsey, Hal, 41 n. 14, 57, 60,
Locke, John, 77–79
Louisiana, 25
Lowenthal, David, 67
Luther, Martin, 78
Madison, James, 68, 100
Magna Bible: Names, Games, and Long Road Trip, 165, 170–72
Marty, Martin, 20
Maryland, 51 n. 37
Massachusetts Bay Colony, 67, 84, 100, 114, 127 n. 16

Mather, Richard, 94–95
Matthew 25 Network, 17
Mayhew, Jonathan, 76–78
McCain, John, 33
McCaskill, Claire, 32
McCollum, Vashti, 203
McCollum v. Board of Education, 204 n. 50, 205
messianism, 37–49, 52–55, 57–58, 60–62
Middle East, 21
Miller, William, 108–11
Minnesota, 114
Mississippi, 25, 51 n. 37, 59 n. 66, 207–208
Moses, 18, 82, 123–24, 131–33, 154
   as American, 130–31
   as Jesus, 127–29
Mormons, 19, 30–31, 85
Mourdock, Richard, 32
Muslim, 1
National Council on Bible Curriculum in Public Schools, 186–90, 212–13,
National Council on Religion in Public Education, 184–85
Native Americans, 68, 88, 98–99, 104, 139
New Mexico, 2
North Carolina, 9–10, 184, 186, 193–94, 196–207, 209–10, 212–14
North Dakota, 198
Obama, Barack, 2, 10, 16, 17, 22–23, 30, 32 n 59, 33, 35, 49, 81, 149,
Oklahoma, 189, 193
Office of Faith-based and Community Initiatives, 35
Ohio, 2, 18, 31
Outrageous Tales from the Old Testament, 163–64, 173
Paine, Thomas, 68, 108
Palestine, 6, 38–40, 42, 44–46, 61–62, 85–90, 129, 141
Parsley, Rod, 33
Pennsylvania, 2, 3165, 105, 117
Perry, Rick, 18, 29–30, 36
Philadelphia Bible Riots, 195
Phillips, Kevin, 21

Picture Stories from the Bible, 165, 168–69, 175 n. 41
Pilgrim's Going to Church, 102–104
Pilgrim's Progress, 95–97
Pledge of Allegiance, 112–13, 115, 117
poor, care for the, 17, 19
prayer in schools, 4, 106, 182–84, 196, 203–6, 208, 211
premillennialism, 6, 21, 38–40, 42–46, 48–49, 52–54, 57–61
pro-choice. *See* abortion
pro-life. *See* abortion
Protestant, 1, 3, 5–7, 27 n. 45, 30–31, 35, 37–38, 42–44, 51, 55, 68, 73, 78, 83, 86–87, 89–90, 92–94, 97, 99–104, 106, 108, 110–111, 115, 118–19, 126, 152–53, 182, 194–95, 197, 199, 203–204, 206–208, 213
Protestantism. *See* Protestant
Puritans, 8, 67, 70, 79, 83, 90, 94–95, 100–104, 119, 12527, 132, 135
Qur'an burning, 119
Rand, Ayn, 18
Rape, 32
Reagan, Ronald, 2, 34, 48
Rehnquist, William, 35
Robertson, Pat, 60, 118 n. 41
Roe v. Wade, 22
Rohan, Dennis Michael, 58
Romney, Mitt, 18, 19, 28, 29, 30 f 53
Roosevelt, Franklin Delano, 34
Rubio, Marco, 28
Ryan, Paul, 18, 26
Sanford, Terry, 205–206
Santorum, Rick, 17, 31
Scofield Reference Bible, 21, 110
Seabury, Samuel, 75–76
secularism, 20, 28, 31–33
Seventh-day Adventists, 86, 108–10
Shaftsbury, Earl of. *See* Cooper, Lord Ashley
Sherwood, Samuel, 72–74
slavery
   as metaphor for America's relation to Great Britain, 71, 79, 83

slavery (cont.)
  biblical narrative, 84
  of Africans, 67, 84, 104, 131–33, 145–48
South Carolina, 28 n. 4751 n. 37, 187, 189, 210 n. 77
South Dakota, 190, 194
stem-cell research, 22
Stiles, Ezra, 81–84, 88
Strickland, Ted, 18
Supreme Court, 4, 35, 117
Talmud, 24
Tanak, 24
taxes, 26–27
teavangelicals, 27
temple, reestablishment, 57–61
Ten Commandments
  monument 118–19
  movie, 8, 123–135
Tennessee, 185, 189, 193, 207, 208 n. 70, 212
Texas, 1–2, 18–19, 40 n. 11, 30, 51 n. 37, 104, 184, 189–90, 193, 194 n. 3

Truman, Harry, 90–91
Unitarian, 76
"values voters," 22
Vaughn v. Reed, 207 n. 70
Virginia, 25, 207–208, 210 n. 77,
Wallace v Jaffree, 35
Warren, Elizabeth, 17
Warren, Rick, 16
Washington, George, 68
West Virginia, 117
Wiley v. Franklin, 208 n. 70, 211
Wilson, Woodrow, 43 n. 1744, 90
Winthrop, John, 67, 84, 100, 102, 112, 114, 127 n. 16
Wright, Jeremiah, 33
Wyoming, 51 n. 37
Zionism
  Christian, 7, 38, 44–62, 83, 85–87, 90–91
  Jewish, 43–44, 85–91
Zorach v. Clauson, 205 n. 56
Zoroastrian, 1

www.ingramcontent.com/pod-product-compliance
Lightning Source LLC
Chambersburg PA
CBHW021809220426
43662CB00006B/239